TIME *and* NAVIGATION

The Untold Story of Getting from Here to There

TIME *and* NAVIGATION

The Untold Story of Getting from Here to There

Andrew K. Johnston
Roger D. Connor
Carlene E. Stephens
Paul E. Ceruzzi

Smithsonian Books
Washington, D.C.

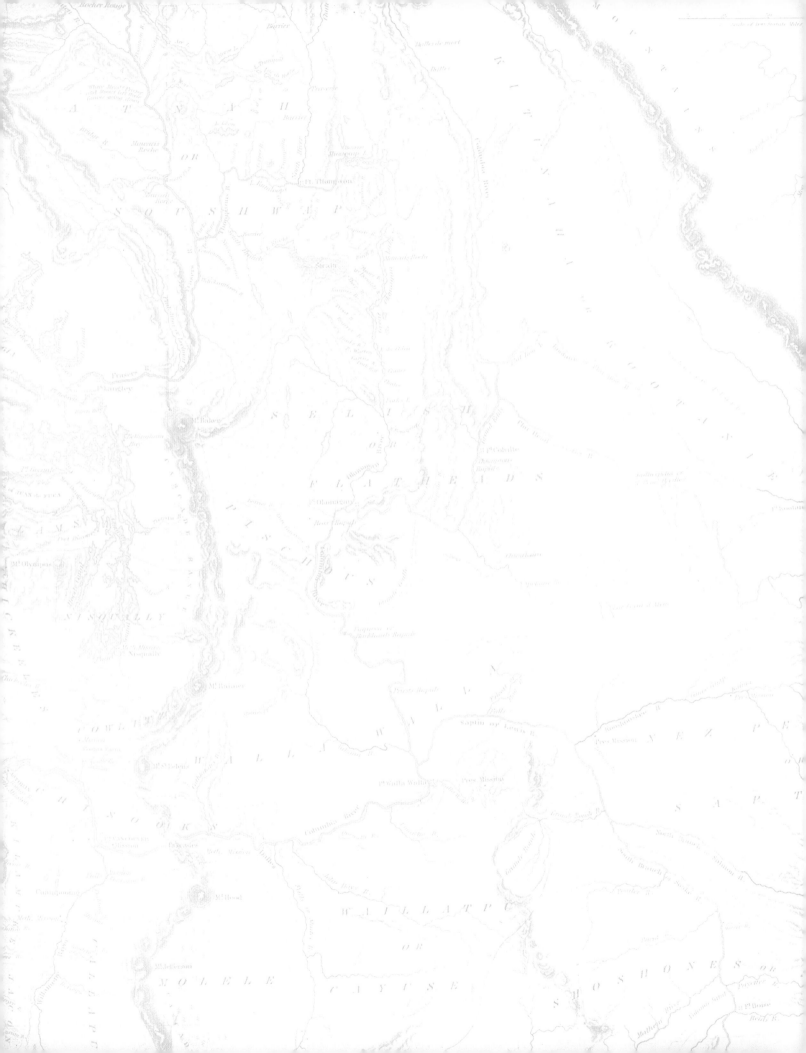

CONTENTS

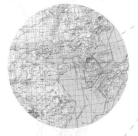

TIME *and* PLACE *Connection*

ABOVE: Time display at the U.S. Naval Observatory in Washington, D.C.

OPPOSITE: Prime Meridian line at Royal Greenwich Observatory near London.

We are all navigators. To find our way from here to there, we often look for landmarks or use maps. Today, we use smartphones and GPS to get around. But navigating has not always been effortless. Across the centuries, as people crafted new methods by which to navigate, they faced technical complexities, harsh environments, and personal peril. Voyagers often became lost, never to be found. Having a reliable way to navigate could mean the difference between life and death. The human need to travel and make connections across the world has inspired, among many other things, the art and science of navigation.

Getting from one place to another involves more than just knowing *where*. We also need to know *when*. If we want to know where we are, we need a reliable clock.

This surprising connection between time and place has been crucial for centuries. About 250 years ago, mariners first used mechanical clocks to navigate the oceans. Today we locate ourselves on the globe with synchronized atomic clocks in orbiting satellites. Among the many challenges facing navigation from then to now, one stands out: keeping accurate time. Time and place are connected in ways that most people do not realize in their daily lives, and this connection has been an essential element in the development of global commerce and modern society.

There is no better place on Earth for understanding the connections between time and place than the courtyard of the Royal Observatory in Greenwich, England. On this spot overlooking the city of London, those connections, first established generations ago, endure to this day on a

Sundial in the Smithsonian's Enid Haupt Garden made by William David Todd for the latitude of Washington, D.C.

global scale. Visitors can straddle a brass line in the courtyard corresponding to zero degrees longitude. This is the line from which all the other lines of longitude are based, reaching all the way around the globe. Greenwich reminds us that the oldest clock is Earth itself, and the oldest means of keeping time came from observing changes in the sky. Some of the earliest forms of navigation were based on the same principles. Prominent clocks at Greenwich and other observatories count the hours, minutes, and seconds—once determined with an astronomer's eye on a telescope in a nearby dome, now transmitted from a physicist's atomic clock in a laboratory.

Over the centuries, clocks changed from luxuries to necessities and from rarities to ever-present machines. They also became more accurate. Mechanical clocks, invented in Europe just before 1300, were the basic timekeeping instruments until the twentieth century, when quartz and atomic clocks were invented. Requirements for navigation often stimulated improvements in timekeeping. Roughly speaking, the more accurate the clock, the better the positioning: In the eighteenth century, accuracy was measured in nautical miles, while in the twenty-first century it is measured in centimeters.

Information about time and place has played a crucial role in international politics. In their competition for empire, Western Europe's maritime nations recognized early the importance of technical control of time as a means of determining place. Beginning at the end of the sixteenth century, their generous cash prizes stimulated solutions to the problem of measuring longitude at sea. The hot and cold wars of the twentieth century likewise spurred nations to fund new navigation solutions that could work at all times and in all conditions. Governments around the world continue to devote huge sums to develop and deploy space-based systems for providing regional- and global-scale navigation services.

In concert with all these developments, the role of the navigator has dramatically changed through history. In the past, navigators served as elite practitioners with specialized equipment and training. In recent years, professional navigators have almost entirely disappeared from many fields, replaced by "black boxes" receiving ground- and space-based signals. The widespread availability of navigation services from orbiting satellites, however, has made it simple for ordinary people to determine position and obtain updated digital maps. Navigation has become more of a global utility than a specialized art.

This book explores these themes through history in different environments. It offers an illustrated history of how scientists and

LATITUDE

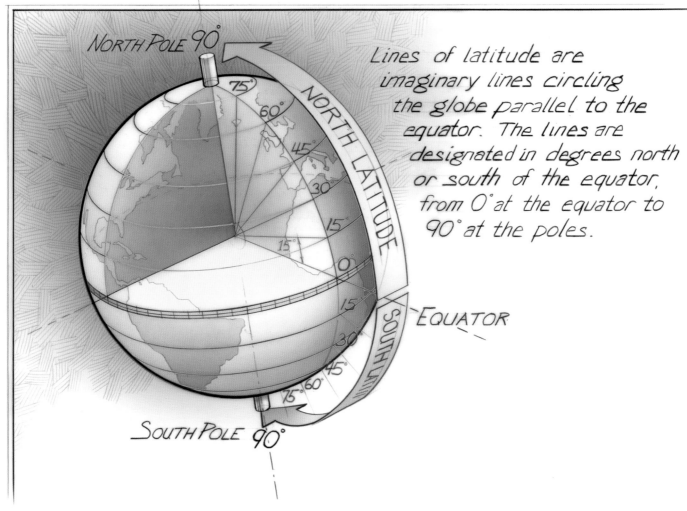

NORTH POLE 90°

75°
60°
45°
30°
15°
15°
0°
15°

NORTH LATITUDE

SOUTH LATITUDE

30°
45°
60°
75°

EQUATOR

SOUTH POLE 90°

Lines of latitude are imaginary lines circling the globe parallel to the equator. The lines are designated in degrees north or south of the equator, from 0° at the equator to 90° at the poles.

explorers invented a style of navigation—the process of getting from here to there—that combined timekeepers with other instruments and techniques for wayfinding. It explores the changing role of the professional navigator, relates improvements in timekeeping to the demands of navigation, and reveals how and why national interests have stimulated improvements in navigation.

The first part, "Navigating at Sea," focuses on the introduction of the sea clock and astronomical solutions for finding longitude in the eighteenth century, and it explores the consequences for the balance of power among the maritime nations of Europe and the young United States. Between the voyages of Columbus and the sleek clipper ships of the 1850s, shipmasters learned to use new tools to determine latitude and longitude at sea. The ability to use an accurate clock at sea was a turning point that set the stage for the clock's relationship to navigation in subsequent centuries—not only at sea, but also on land, in the air, and in outer space.

Lines of latitude have been used for thousands of years to define positions north and south, based on angles measured from the center of the earth. Lines of latitude circle the globe perpendicular to the axis of rotation.

LONGITUDE

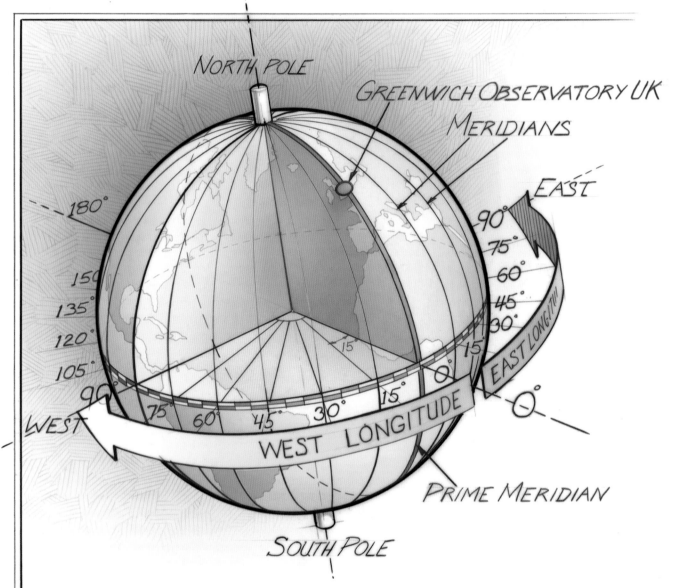

NORTH POLE

GREENWICH OBSERVATORY UK

MERIDIANS

EAST

180°
150°
135°
120°
105°
90°
WEST

90°
75°
60°
45°
30°

75° 60° 45° 30° 15° 0° 15°
WEST LONGITUDE

15 15
EAST LONGITUDE

0°

PRIME MERIDIAN

SOUTH POLE

Lines of longitude are imaginary lines circling the globe through poles. Also called meridians, they are designated in degrees east or west of a starting reference line from 0° at that prime meridian to 180° on the opposite side of the globe.

The second part, "Navigating in the Air," examines how aerial pioneers adapted techniques developed for navigating at sea for flying and how new forms of navigation used radio signals. When air navigation matured in the 1930s, it was much more reliant than maritime navigation on the interdependence between celestial navigation, radio navigation, and new dead-reckoning technologies. The demands of World War II brought the additional requirement of all-weather operations, anytime and anywhere. The shift from mechanical timekeeping of seconds to the frequency-based measurement of millionths of seconds became essential to postwar global navigation.

The third part, "Navigating in Space" shows how forms of navigation were extended and enhanced for guiding spacecraft into space and across the solar system. Astronauts used celestial techniques and sextants for some early space voyages to the moon. It was the use of radio transmissions, however, that became standard practice in space. Networks of powerful radio transmitters and receivers were constructed around the earth. Atomic frequency standards at these ground stations could measure billionths of a second. This allowed mission teams to navigate space by observing tiny changes in the frequency of radio signals from spacecraft. The principles involved inspired scientists and engineers to experiment with these solutions for navigation on the earth.

The fourth part, "Inventing Satellite Navigation," describes the U.S. military's development of space-based time and navigation services for use on the earth. Satellite systems such as the Global Positioning System were developed to meet the needs of global navigation. By measuring tiny changes in radio transmissions down to a few billionths of a second, engineers developed new systems to determine position anywhere. In its early years, GPS was used mostly by military personnel, professional surveyors, and other specialists. Today, people in all walks of life use GPS every day.

The final part, "Navigation for Everyone," explores the modern applications and implications of global time and navigation services for people all over the world. The use of precise positioning has revolutionized countless fields and professions. Advanced satellite technology is in the hands of farmers, truck drivers, commuters, shoppers—indeed, almost anyone with a need to find his or her way. As these technologies proliferated, new opportunities were created, just as new questions arose about how these technologies are coordinated and how they would continue to evolve.

Throughout the book you will meet navigators and innovators who made important advances, will see examples of navigation errors that led to improvements, and will discover what made many advances in navigational science possible. These explorations reveal the intriguing untold story of getting from here to there: the enduring connection between time and place.

OPPOSITE: Lines of longitude, measuring position east or west, are designated in degrees east or west of a 0° line called a "prime meridian." In contrast to latitude, the placement of the 0° longitude line is not determined by the orientation of Earth's rotational axis. It could theoretically be placed anywhere east or west on the roughly spherical Earth. Greenwich became the most commonly used prime meridian, and eventually the international standard. Because Earth rotates 360 degrees around in twenty-four hours, or 15 degrees per hour, the sun appears to move in the sky by 15 degrees longitude every hour. This connection between time and place allows anyone to determine their longitude on Earth—if they have an accurate time reference, that is.

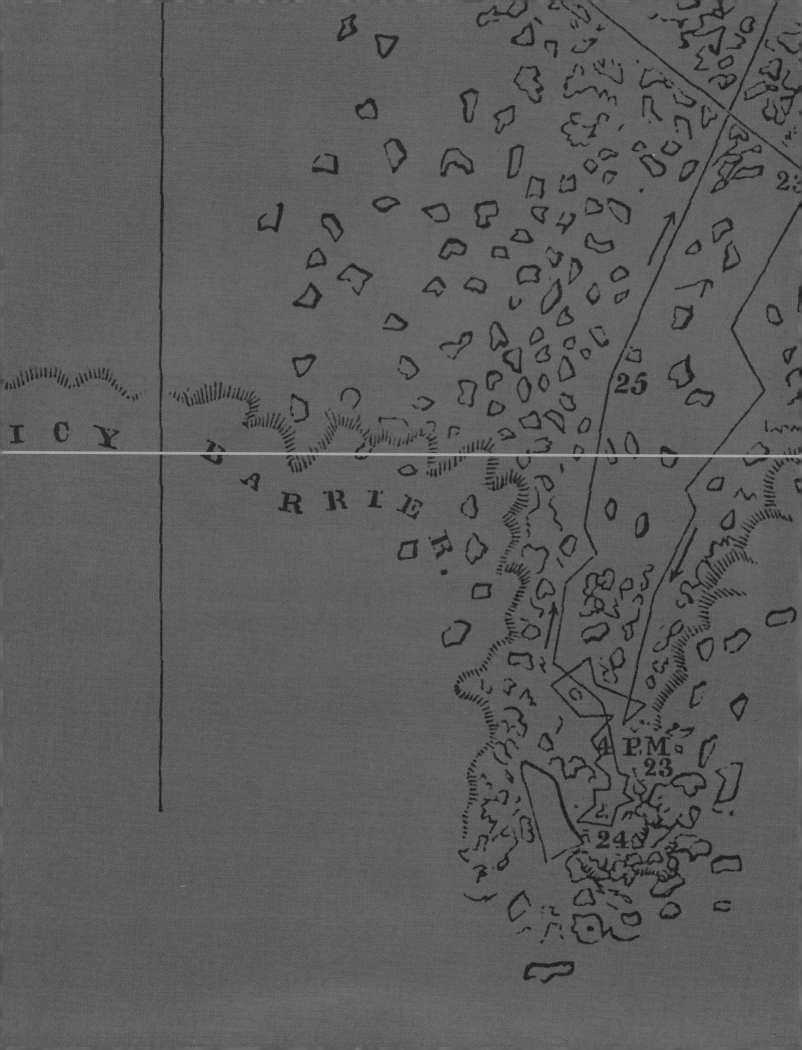

NAVIGATING at SEA

Instruments to find and keep time revolutionized the way mariners crossed the oceans.

By 1700, rival European nations were exploring the world's oceans in search of wealth, power, and prestige. But mapmakers knew only about half of Earth's surface with any detail. To make traveling dangerous waters safer, people developed better maps, navigation techniques, and clocks.

Scale.

20 Miles

NAVIGATING *at* SEA

They were alone and in trouble at the edge of the world. The crew of USS *Peacock* had sailed into the Antarctic bay to try to land. They knew that the icy barrier they had been following was in fact the shoreline of Antarctica, and they had a chance to be the first to ever set foot on the continent. Frozen floes covered the surface of the water in every direction around them, but straight ahead stretched an opening of smooth dark-green water. The weather was clear and pleasant, the wind light. Nearby an immense iceberg, higher than the masts, loomed like a protective wall. The men paused in the open water to take some soundings.

USS *Peacock* trapped against an ice wall in Antarctica in 1840. Engraving from artwork made by Alfred T. Agate.

Measurements finished, the crew brought the ship's head out of the wind to avoid a big block of ice that had moved under the bow. Instead of safe passage, they found terrible peril. The stern smashed into a floe so hard that the blow twisted the rudder. Ice began to grind the hull on all sides, and every timber groaned. Worst of all was a punishing crash into the iceberg itself. Only the rebound from the collision saved them. The shattered ship careened off the iceberg at an angle and moved off through a narrow channel in the ice.

The only way to safety lay back the way they had come, north to the open ocean. They attempted repairs underway, but no one believed they would survive weeks of crossing the seas to harbor in Australia. The other ships in their squadron had sailed away days before. The fair weather had departed, too. It was starting to snow.

Miraculously, the crippled ship and the entire exhausted crew reached Sydney twenty-five days later, reunited with the U.S. Exploring Expedition, and gave a detailed report of their harrowing escape from an icy death.

Although the *Peacock*'s situation had been dire, the crew could take some comfort in knowing they had never been lost throughout the ordeal. Because they had been able to make routine observations with onboard navigation instruments and timekeepers, they knew exactly when and where the accident had occurred. They understood the exact dimensions of the bay that had trapped them well enough to make a reliable map. Most important, they knew in which direction to sail to safety.

Map of Peacock Bay, Antarctica, showing the route of USS *Peacock* on January 23–26, 1840.

In the following pages, we will learn how voyagers met the problems of navigating across oceans and how the instruments used for finding time and location aboard the *Peacock* became standard on sailing ships by the 1830s.

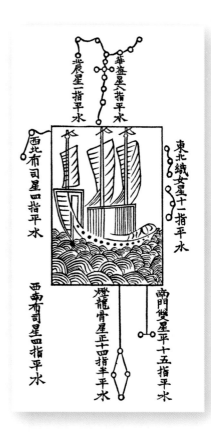

ABOVE: Star diagram for celestial navigation published with the nautical charts of Zheng He, who commanded seven sailing expeditions to South Asia, the Middle East, and East Africa between 1405 and 1433.

OPPOSITE: Arab ship illustrated in a thirteenth-century manuscript written by al-Hariri.

Who were the first peoples to navigate across open oceans? What tools and skills did they use? Tens of thousands of years ago, prehistoric inhabitants in the western Pacific began to explore their ocean's thousands of islands and migrate among them. More recently, within the past four thousand years, Egyptians and other peoples in the Mediterranean Sea, Persian Gulf, and Indian Ocean dared longer-distance sea travel. Early voyagers made more durable boats and sails, developed better methods for estimating position, and used their senses to navigate. A story from the *Jatakamala*, written about two thousand years ago, describes the Buddha in his incarnation as the ideal mariner Suparaga, and sums up the skills common to successful early ocean adventurers:

> *Knowing as he did the movements of the heavenly bodies, the Great One never lost his sense of direction. He recognized all the telltale signs around him—the usual, the unusual, and the dangerous—so that he could forecast how long good or bad conditions would last. From such clues as the fish, the color of the water, the type of terrain, the birds, and the rocks, he could easily plot his position at sea.*

With these same skills, prehistoric Polynesians migrated over vast distances and spread their culture across the Pacific. In the absence of written or archeological records, modern voyagers have attempted to recreate skills, routes, and canoes. They suggest that early Polynesian navigators sailed from island to island by observing the sun and stars, the wind and waves, and the behavior of birds and fish. They

الفرآن ثم أربعد أساطير ملاها ورخارف جللها وقال اركبوا فيها بسم الله مجراها

ومرسأها ثمّ بنفس تنفس المغرمين أو عباد الله للكرمين وقال لهم انا

Illustration of a Viking ship built about 890 CE and excavated from a burial mound in Gokstad, Norway, in 1882.

sailed into the wind, making use of southeast trade winds that blow constantly and year-round in that corridor of the Pacific.

In the harsh, stormy waters of the North Atlantic between 750 and 1000 CE, waves of peoples from Scandinavia collectively known as the Vikings sailed west to settle Britain, Iceland, Greenland, and even North America. Like the Polynesians, they hopped from island to island and made use of winds and currents. They used no charts, and they observed the birds, sky, and sea. Discoveries of buried ships in Norway and Denmark have yielded crucial material evidence that the Vikings built various sizes of wooden boats, each fitted with a sail and oars.

Ships carrying traders from the Arabian Peninsula and Persia traveled the vast Indian Ocean well before the coming of Islam. But with the influence of Muhammad (d. 632 CE), shipping flourished, and a major empire began to stretch from Spain to China. Science and learning were important in Islamic culture, and time and direction finding were especially vital to pious medieval Muslims. They had a deep interest in studying the heavens for divine guidance in both the spiritual world and for their earthly travels. The position of the sun influenced times of daily ritual prayers. Knowing the direction of the sacred shrine of the Ka'bah in Mecca in the Arabian Peninsula was essential for both prayers and orienting mosques. Navigation benefitted from Arab knowledge of astronomy, handbooks of recorded ocean routes, and instruments for finding latitude: the seagoing kamal and the land-based astrolabe.

China's medieval maritime power began to build with the construction of a large oceangoing merchant fleet in the Song dynasty (c. 960–1270). About 1040 CE, Chinese navigators began to use the compass, in the form of a magnetized needle floating in a bowl of water, for direction finding at sea. Emperors in the Yuan dynasty (c. 1271–1368) built a trade network with posts as far away as Sumatra and India. The Ming dynasty extended that reach in the fifteenth century. On behalf of the Chinese emperor Zhu Di, Admiral Zheng He (also called Cheng Ho) commanded seven sailing expeditions to South Asia, the Middle East, and East Africa between 1405 and 1433. Each voyage engaged huge ships more than four hundred feet long, supported by a flotilla of smaller vessels. Aboard the expedition's junks were tens of thousands of troops meant to enforce China's empire across the Indian Ocean, as well as repair specialists, diplomats, astronomers, medics, and navigators.

Zheng He's fleet navigators noted detailed compass directions for establishing sea routes on marine charts and used the stars for position finding and traveling along a line of latitude. Surviving star charts show ten constellations and the altitudes of stars above the horizon, measured by the number of finger-breadths with the hand held at arm's length.

By 1500, the Chinese emperor's successor deemed the expeditions extravagant. The navy disbanded, the voyages ended, and China, while keeping its trade routes intact, retreated from its position as the world's greatest sea power. At the same time, the global oceans became the setting for European explorations.

TOP: Hawaiians led by chief Kalaniopuu received Captain James Cook on January 26, 1779. Engraving of the event from a drawing by Cook expedition artist John Webber, published in 1784.

BOTTOM: *Hōkūleʻa*, a modern Hawaiian voyaging canoe, sailing off Kauaʻi in 2005.

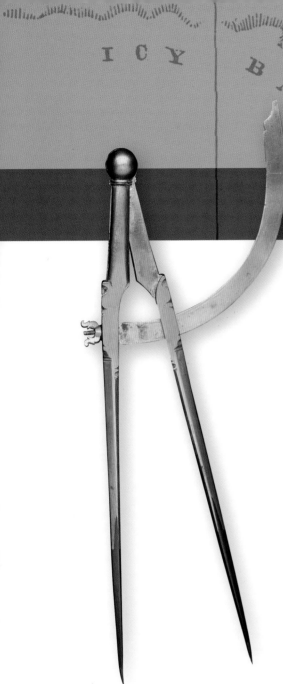

ABOVE: Navigational dividers, probably German, eighteenth century, used to measure the distance between two points on a chart to mark a ship's position.

OPPOSITE: Frontispiece to *The Mariners Mirrour*, a collection of sea charts from the sixteenth century. Navigation instruments (top to bottom down each side) are the quadrant, astrolabe, cross staff, dividers, and compass. Each male figure along the sides holds a lead line.

I
n 1300, medieval Europe was isolated and unaware of much of the rest of the world. By 1700, European maritime empires vied for wealth and power around the globe they were beginning to explore. Efforts to expand geographic knowledge, markets, and colonies in those four hundred years stimulated a revolution in navigation.

Beginning in the 1330s, Genoese and Venetian merchants and mariners from Catalan Majorca sailed out of the Mediterranean, past Gibraltar, and into the Atlantic. Some headed north after English wool, and others, carried by the Atlantic's winds, into previously unknown waters to the west and south. Exploration and detailed mapping followed in the central part of the eastern Atlantic Ocean. After 1453, with the fall of Constantinople to the Ottoman Empire, the new Muslim rulers cut off traditional lucrative trading routes to Asia from the Christian West, and European commercial interests stimulated a focused search for new routes to Asia.

Medieval European sailing had depended on the personal knowledge of known sailing routes. Most of those routes kept land in sight when possible. A shipmaster, the man in charge of a merchant ship, or pilot, a specialist skilled in navigation sometimes found on the larger merchant vessels, guided the ships. They learned their skills from other seamen and repeated travels.

Marine navigation had been based on what one nineteenth-century navigation expert has called "the three Ls," *log*, *lead*, and *lookout*: log for determining ship's speed, the lead and line for sounding or sampling the bottom, and lookout for the crucial attention required at all times. Two critical developments began to transform medieval navigation to modern navigation:

THE MARINERS MIRROVR

Wherin may playnly be seen the courses, heights, distances, depths, soundings, flouds and ebs, risings of lands, rocks, sands and shoalds, with the marks for then tring of the Harbouroughs, Havens and Ports of the greatest part of Europe: their seueral traficks and commodities:Together wᵗʰ the Rules and instrumēts of NAVIGATION.

First made Vset fourth in diuers exāct Sea Charts, by that famous Nauigator LVKE WAGENAR of Enchuisen. And now fitted with necessarie additions for the use of Englishmen by ANTHONY ASHLEY.

Heerin also may be understood the exploits lately atchiued by the right Honorable the L. Admeral of England, with her Maᵗⁱᵉˢ Nauie and some former seruices don by that worthy Knight Sᵗ. FRAN. DRAKE.

TOP: Using a compass for finding direction at sea, depicted by Flemish artist Jan van der Straet or Stradanus (1523–1605).

BOTTOM: A lead line could measure water depth and bring up a sample of the bottom. From Olaus Magnus, *History of Nordic Peoples*, 1555.

the introduction of the magnetic compass used with sea charts based on compass headings, and a simple form of astronomical navigation that permitted the finding of latitude.

Medieval navigation then evolved from mostly a coastal enterprise to sailing open oceans with the aid of astronomy in the fifteenth century. Portuguese sailors pioneered modern celestial navigation techniques beginning in the 1430s, when they began to sail down the African coast. By 1498, they had sailed to Brazil and the Indian Ocean. Royal support in first Portugal and then rival Spain generated amazing feats of marine navigation with only the simplest tools and launched the great European Age of Exploration. In the imperial competition, information about sailing routes became state secrets.

The magnetic compass became practical for European shipboard use in the fourteenth century, when the needle was balanced on a point, rotated freely, and indicated direction against a fixed paper scale marked off in a circle of thirty-two compass points. The compass was put in a box to protect it from weather and set in a gimbal, or pivoted support, to adjust its level as the ship rolled.

At about the same time, a revolution in European mapmaking meant that fanciful maps decorated with imaginary creatures and religious themes based on literary sources gave way to maps based on actual measurements of the earth. Pilot books, written sailing instructions created with compass readings, supplied firsthand sailing knowledge for accurate regional maps of Mediterranean coastlines and then the coasts of Europe and Africa.

Starting at a known or assumed position, a navigator used simple but reliable tools to track three things: the ship's compass heading; the ship's speed; and the time spent on each heading and at each speed. Sandglasses kept time. Columbus and most other seafarers in the Age of Exploration used this method, called dead reckoning.

Modern navigation began when a seafarer could find latitude at sea. Roger Bacon had proposed mapping the earth with latitude and longitude in his *Opus maius* (c. 1265), but it would take the publication of Claudius Ptolemy's *Geography*, written in the second century and translated into Latin in 1409–10, to show the entire world drawn with coordinates of latitude and longitude. By the early sixteenth century, nautical charts began to show those latitude lines.

DEAD RECKONING AT SEA

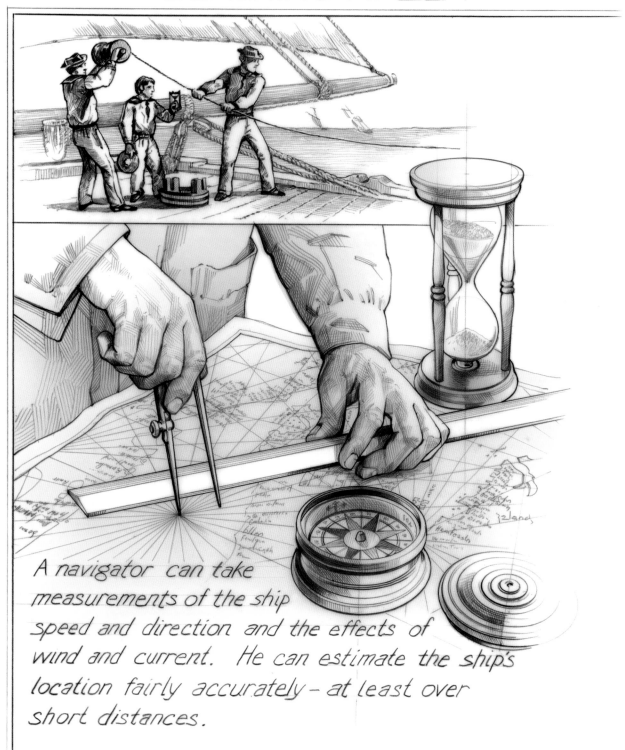

A navigator can take measurements of the ship speed and direction and the effects of wind and current. He can estimate the ship's location fairly accurately – at least over short distances.

CELESTIAL NAVIGATION AT SEA

NORTH STAR

Little Dipper

Big Dipper

Measured Angle = Latitude

HORIZON

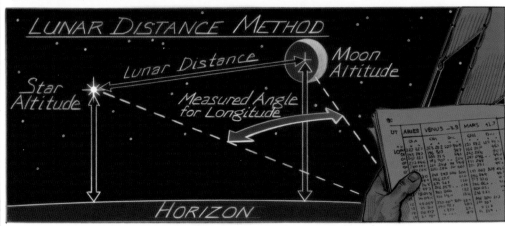

LUNAR DISTANCE METHOD

Lunar Distance

Star Altitude

Moon Altitude

Measured Angle for Longitude

HORIZON

FINDING LOCAL NOON WITH A SEXTANT

HORIZON   Maximum Angle at noon

To locate themselves on the open ocean, navigators can determine their position by observing the Sun, Moon, stars, or planets.

Mariners had always relied on the sun and stars to tell time and determine their place on the featureless ocean, but these had always been estimates. Using latitude made their efforts more accurate. On a starry night in the Northern Hemisphere, a mariner could easily calculate latitude by measuring the angle between the North Star and the horizon and referring to the latitude passing through his home port to calculate distance. On fair days, the sun also provided reliable readings. To find their latitude based on solar observations, navigators needed to know the sun's declination on the day in question, which published tables provided from the fifteenth century onward.

To find latitude, navigators relied on angle-measuring instruments, which became increasingly accurate toward the end of the 1400s. The earliest was the quadrant. The quadrant was made of a panel of wood or brass with degrees marked on the outer edge, a plumb line, and sight along one edge. The plumb line intersected the degree of the polestar above the horizon on the outer edge of the panel.

Another angle-finding instrument was the mariner's astrolabe. This maritime tool was simplified from an Arabic calculating device introduced to Europe in the tenth century to display the changing positions of many stars as time and latitude changed. Portuguese and Spanish makers dominated astrolabe making, but examples attributed to Dutch, French, German, and English makers also survive.

By the early seventeenth century, a mariner's astrolabe included a heavy bronze wheel held from a pivoted suspension ring; an arm, called the alidade, to rotate over a scale of degrees stamped on the upper quadrants of the instrument's wheel; and two sighting vanes on the arm, each with a pinhole, to align with either the polestar or the sun's rays. To use the device, the navigator held it at arm's length by its pivoted ring, rotated the alidade to sight a specific star or the sun, and read from the scale the resulting degrees of altitude indicated by the alidade pointer. The scale could be numbered to measure from either the horizon or the zenith. With the measured angle and astronomical tables, the navigator could then determine the ship's latitude.

Measuring the altitude of heavenly bodies for determining latitude would remain crucial for navigation. In the centuries to come, the astrolabe would give way to the cross staff in the sixteenth century and the octant and the sextant in the eighteenth century.

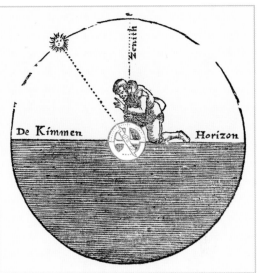

TOP: Using a cross staff.

BOTTOM: Using a mariner's astrolabe to measure the angle of the sun or a star above the horizontal.

The routes of the Spanish galleons.

CARRYING TREASURE *on the*
SPANISH GALLEONS

The four-hundred-year-old mariner's astrolabe pictured here was dredged up from the bottom of Manila harbor about 1917. Once the essential tool for navigating by the stars, the instrument is a reminder of the crucial role Manila played in Spanish control in the Pacific. From 1571, the city became the trade hub that linked China, the Americas, and Europe. The Spanish galleon, part cargo ship and part warship, began to sail once a year across the Pacific between Manila, the chief city of the Philippines, and Acapulco, Mexico. Silver, mined in Peru and coined into Spanish reales, went to China to pay for Asian luxury goods destined for Mexico, South America, and Europe. Cargo unloaded at Acapulco traveled overland to Atlantic ports and then sailed on to Spain. One observer in 1609 recalled seeing a galleon's riches:

Raw silk in bundles . . . quantities of velvets . . . woven stuffs and brocades . . . quantities of gold and silver thread . . . damasks, satins, taffetas . . . musk, benzoin and ivory; also pearls and rubies, sapphires and crystal . . . precious stones of all colors; pepper and other spices; and rarities, which, did I refer to them all, would never finish. . .

Such shipments made the galleons famous, but they also made them targets for raiders. British ships captured four of them, and others were lost to maritime hazards.

Spanish explorers had reached the Philippines in 1543 from the Americas, but they had repeatedly failed to find a reliable return route. They suffered terrible losses of life and cargo. That changed in 1565, when Andrés de Urdenata sailed north from Manila to the latitudes of Japan to find favorable winds, turned east for the Americas, and then sailed down the California coast to Mexico.

Even after Urdenata's success, the long voyages across the Pacific were grueling. Acapulco to Manila could take three months, the reverse trip often six months. Crews could determine latitude, but not longitude. This often required ships to follow lines of latitude, so no ocean crossing was truly direct. For centuries, it had been clear that longitude was a necessary component in navigation. At sea, though, an easy way to determine longitude remained elusive. ✺

TOP: Mariner's astrolabe from about 1600, found in Manila Harbor in 1917.

BOTTOM: Spanish silver coin with a value of fifty reales, dated 1659, from the reign of Philip IV, obverse and reverse.

LONGITUDE AND THE SEA CLOCK

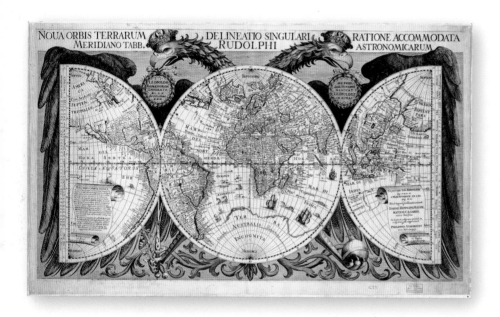

World map by Philipp Eckebrecht of Nuremberg, 1630, the first map to equate one hour of time to 15 degrees of longitude.

The importance of time and navigation information was apparent to Europe's major seafaring powers—Spain, the Netherlands, Portugal, the Venetian Republic, England, and France. Each offered vast prizes to stimulate innovation on the era's crucial problem: how to find longitude at sea. Such government prizes, which became a popular form of sponsorship in the eighteenth century, encouraged science and technology for useful ends.

The prizes inspired an inventive outpouring from both the greatest scientific minds and the humblest tinkerers. One promising but difficult direction for research was developing a clock that could go to sea. A Flemish mathematician named Gemma Frisius proposed in 1530 that using a sea clock to find longitude could be based on the knowledge that the earth tracks fifteen degrees of longitude relative to the sun in one hour. With a good seaworthy clock, mariners in theory could calculate longitude by comparing local time, using the sun, to a standard time on a clock brought from port. The trouble was, there was no such seaworthy clock. At the time of the earliest prizes, two offered by Spain in 1567 and 1598 and another a few years later by the Dutch Republic, no clock on land or sea could keep better time than within about fifteen minutes a day.

Galileo Galilei, the prominent Italian man of science, entered the contest for both the Spanish and the Dutch longitude prizes. To Spain he offered an astronomical solution based on observing the moons of Jupiter, which he had discovered with a telescope of his own design in 1610. He also devised a calculator to find the positions of those Jovian moons. For the Dutch prize, in 1641, Galileo proposed to make an accurate sea clock, the first clock ever to have a pendulum, but he died before constructing it. His son Vincenzo built a model in 1649.

In pursuit of a prizewinning sea clock, Dutch mathematician Christiaan Huygens changed timekeeping forever. He patented the first working pendulum clock in 1656 and later devised a watch regulator, called the balance spring. He began to receive support for his clock experiments from the French Académie Royale des Sciences, founded in 1666 under Louis XIV, to address a broad range of

Ludolf Backhuysen, *Ships in Distress off a Rocky Coast*, 1667.

TOP: Galileo Galilei.

BOTTOM: Galileo's pendulum clock design. Replica made by L. C Eichner in 1958.

scientific studies, but also, through mathematics and astronomy, to improve sailing charts and navigation. Huygens's inventions proved essential for keeping good time and endured as basic components in mechanical timepieces for more than three hundred years. Pendulum clocks immediately became the best timekeepers for use on land, and wealthy homeowners developed a taste for them.

Huygens worked with several Dutch clockmakers, including his neighbor Johannes van Ceulen, who made the table clock pictured here. It is one of the earliest clocks with a pendulum. Still, despite heavy subsidies from the powerful Dutch East India Company to Huygens to continue his work, several sea trials between 1662 and 1687 demonstrated that a pendulum clock would never work accurately on a heaving ship's deck.

In the wake of a devastating maritime tragedy involving the English fleet in 1707, Parliament passed the Longitude Act of 1714. Four ships under Admiral Sir Cloudesley Shovell had smashed on the rocks of the Isles of Scilly, and more than a thousand lives were lost. The outcry after this disaster demanded improvements in navigation. The legislation established a commission of experts to oversee rewards to encourage practical ways to find longitude at sea. The Board of Longitude, as the commissioners became known, would continue until 1828 and fund much research in navigation.

When the prize was established, the commissioners considered an astronomical solution based on lunar distances to be the most likely answer to the longitude problem. Astronomy, after all, was on its way to becoming, in the words of British philosopher of science William Whewell, the "queen of the sciences" in the eighteenth century. A clockwork solution seemed impractical given the challenges that sea voyages presented to delicate instruments— the unstable deck of a ship underway, uncontrolled temperature and humidity changes, periods of no maintenance for delicate instruments, and gravity variations.

In shaping the legislation, Parliament was greatly influenced by Isaac Newton, England's most prominent man of science. Newton mentioned that clockwork might be possible, but he supported the role of astronomy for finding longitude, recommended linking the level of accuracy for finding longitude to the size of the prize to be awarded, and suggested that sea trials be conducted.

Given the size of the top prize, well over a million pounds in today's currency, it is not surprising that an outpouring of proposals resulted, some outlandish, others demonstrating a real effort to grapple with the problem. The most famous applicant for the prize offered a stunning technical breakthrough. English carpenter and clockmaker John Harrison built five experimental sea clocks between 1735 and 1772, and with them he demonstrated the feasibility of accurate timekeeping at sea. With regular grants from the Board of Longitude and with the help of his brother, James, and his son, William, Harrison built three very large clocks beginning in the 1720s. These were test beds to address the technical issues of shipboard conditions. He completed his fourth effort, a large silver-cased watch, in 1759 and sent it on successful sea trials to Barbados and Jamaica in 1762. The watch reportedly ran just five seconds slow, the equivalent of an error of one nautical mile after one hundred seventeen days at sea. In 1765, Harrison received half of the total prize of the £20,000 that England had offered to anyone who could solve the longitude problem. The commissioners were unconvinced that this astonishing feat could be repeated and imposed new conditions for awarding the remainder of the prize, including the manufacture of copies of the successful watch.

Harrison believed that he had earned the entire prize, but only shortly before he died did he receive the balance, and then only because King George III himself intervened to encourage Parliament to complete the reward. Harrison had sent his last sea clock to George's private observatory in 1772, where the king witnessed its performance and deemed it prizeworthy.

In 1776, the year of Harrison's death, a copy of his timekeeper, commissioned by the board and made by British watchmaker Larcom Kendall, went to sea on its second voyage with Captain James Cook on HMS *Resolution*. Cook made three extensive voyages to explore the Pacific, the geography of which was still largely unknown in the eighteenth century. Cook came to rely on the timekeeper, which he called "our never failing guide." In reporting its performance to the Admiralty, Cook convincingly argued its feasibility for finding longitude at sea. The watch survived the third voyage, but Cook did not. He was killed in a skirmish with Hawaiians in 1779.

Skilled watchmakers who came after Harrison made the marine timekeeper the practical solution to the longitude problem. Harrison's timekeepers were ingenious, but they were difficult to reproduce accurately and affordably. Still, they guided the work of later watchmakers, whose modifications would standardize the portable timepieces that came to be known as marine chronometers. The term "chronometer" had been mentioned by English clockmaker and Royal Society fellow William Derham in 1713, but it came into use only gradually through the process of testing and defining the timekeepers offered for consideration of the Commissioners of Longitude.

TOP: Christiaan Huygens.

BOTTOM: Dutch table clock with pendulum made by Johannes van Ceulen around 1680.

NAVIGATION
GONE WRONG

A BRITISH FLEET RUNS AGROUND

While returning from Gibraltar in 1707, a squadron of British Royal Navy ships went badly off course near the coast of England, with disastrous results.

BELOW: *Sir Cloudisly Shovel* [sic] *in the Association with the Eagle, Rumney and the Firebrand, Lost on the Rocks of Scilly, October 22, 1707.* Artist unknown, eighteenth century.

WHAT HAPPENED

The weather had been overcast and stormy for days. On October 22, Admiral Cloudesley Shovell consulted with all his navigators to determine the fleet's position. Most believed they were sailing on the latitude of Ushant near France. Shovell set a course for home based on their advice.

THE CONSEQUENCES

They were wrong. Later that night, Shovell's flagship, *Association*, slammed into the rocks off the Isles of Scilly and sank within minutes. Three other ships and more than a thousand men, including the admiral, were lost to the sea.

LESSONS LEARNED

The tragedy, the worst maritime disaster in British history to that time, provoked demands for safer navigation. Parliament passed the Longitude Act of 1714, which created a panel of experts to oversee rewards for solving the problem of finding longitude at sea.

One of the key areas of improvement involved the timekeeper's escapement—its regularly beating heart, which transmits energy from the train of wheels to swing the oscillating balance wheel through small impulses. In England, John Arnold received an award from the Board of Longitude for inventing a simplified version of the chronometer escapement. This escapement features a detent, a small catch that detains the escape wheel until it receives an impulse. Thomas Earnshaw also received an award from the English Board of Longitude for his spring detent escapement, which featured a detent mounted on a tiny spring. In bitter written exchanges, Arnold and son John Roger Arnold, on one side, and Earnshaw on the other debated the merits of their respective innovations. In the end, it was Earnshaw's version that became the standard.

Like the longitude prize offered by the English government, a prize offered biennially by the French Académie des Sciences addressed the longitude problem. Count Jean Rouillé de Meslay, a wealthy lawyer, had bequeathed the Academy considerable funds in his will of 1714 for two prizes, one in celestial mechanics and the other in naval science. The Academy gave its first navigation prize in 1720. The winner best known to us today was the mathematician Daniel Bernoulli, whose prizewinning work included an essay on the best shape for sandglasses used at sea and another on improvements to pendulum clocks.

At roughly the same time as John Harrison, two craftsmen in France were independently developing their own versions of a sea clock and competing for the prizes. Pierre Le Roy began designs for a marine timekeeper in 1754, built numerous models, and submitted them for sea trials. He won the Academy's prize in 1769 and 1773. Ferdinand Berthoud, a Swiss clockmaker who had moved to Paris to further his horological education, also began to design marine clocks the same year as Le Roy, produced many examples, and published extensively. Berthoud was well connected within the French government. He had been part of a royal delegation sent to see John Harrison's work in the 1760s,

Cover, Longitude Act of 1714.

Portrait of John Harrison by James King, about 1766.

and he received a royal appointment to supervise the French admiralty's chronometer acquisitions.

Following up on Cook's efforts, French explorers in the eighteenth century were also interested in voyages to the Pacific for scientific and geopolitical reasons, and they were eager to try out the accuracy of the new sea clocks. Berthoud claimed that some fifty of his timepieces had traveled on eighty voyages. The boldest of those was probably the expedition of Jean-François Galaup de La Pérouse, who set out in 1785 to explore the Pacific for the fabled Northwest Passage and to better map the coastlines of Asia and America. In 1788, La Pérouse sent letters and other information back to France via a British ship he encountered in Australia. Then he and the crews of his two ships vanished; later evidence suggests that they wrecked on the Vanikoro reefs in the Solomon Islands. A description of a weight-driven Berthoud sea clock, taken on the ill-fated exploration, inspired the first American seagoing clock by William Cranch Bond (see page 40).

Despite their voyages of exploration, the French feared a loss of maritime power, especially to England. By 1795, the French government took steps to improve navigation and naval strength. The result was the Bureau des Longitudes, an institution still in existence today, established to focus on not just navigation but also on geodesy, astronomy, and time standardization.

The French concern proved true with regard to the chronometer industry. English chronometer making, a specialized branch of watchmaking, would come to dominate the world market for military and commercial chronometers. The innovations of Le Roy and Berthoud, according to one English expert on the history of sea clocks, did more to advance the design of the modern chronometer than did any of the English designs. Unlike Harrison, though, Le Roy and Berthoud had no followers to transform their complicated designs for industrial production.

Regardless of the origins, the appearance of the marine chronometer became standardized in the early nineteenth century.

The movement of the timekeeper fits into a brass bowl with a glass lid. The bowl is suspended in a pivoting brass gimbal. The gimbal fits into the wooden case to keep the chronometer level, regardless of the ship's rocking. Sometimes the wooden case fits into a wicker basket or additional box for extra protection.

In 1815, the *Arniston*, a British vessel carrying wounded soldiers from Ceylon to England, slammed into a reef near the Horn of Africa and killed some 340 people. After this infamous shipwreck, another ship's captain wrote: "In this age of science . . . it is indeed astonishing, that any ship should ever be permitted to set out on any voyage without a chronometer." Still, the diffusion of the chronometer for merchant ships and navies was relatively slow. It was not customary for British naval vessels to be issued chronometers until 1825. The French navy was a little better equipped: there were thirty-four chronometers on board its ships in 1815 and fifty-one in 1820. By 1832, twelve dozen naval chronometers equipped the French Navy. The U.S. Navy also adopted the instruments gradually and in small numbers—it owned fifty-four chronometers in 1835, which is not surprising, since even by 1851 there were fewer than a hundred vessels in the entire U.S. fleet.

Merchant vessel usage is harder to track, but by one account, the supply of chronometers exceeded worldwide demand until 1840. The main reason for resistance was cost. The chronometer was a relatively expensive instrument, and shipmasters were required to buy their own.

Only when more clocks actually went to sea in the nineteenth century did time revolutionize navigation. Europe's maritime nations began to realize their ambitions for power, capital, and empire. Fewer navigation errors at sea saved ships, cargo, and lives. Smoother sailing aided the flow of goods, wealth, people, technology, and social practices. The nineteenth century's phase of globalization ensued.

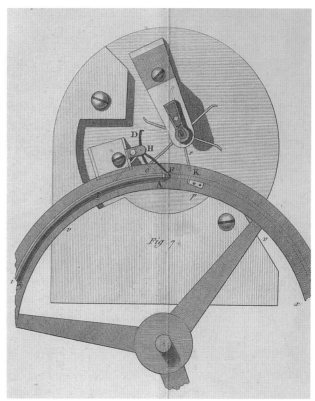

TOP: Ferdinand Berthoud's marine clock No. 24, 1782.

BOTTOM: Drawing of the escapement for Pierre Le Roy's marine clock.

Well before the 1714 British longitude legislation, astronomers were certain the solution to finding longitude at sea lay in observing the sky. But like the clockwork solution, the astronomical approach needed considerable research and new technologies to be practical for mariners. Better information about the movements of the heavens and better observing instruments would slowly emerge.

Astronomers had long known that the moon changes its position fairly quickly against the background of the sky and stars. It moves the distance of its own diameter in about an hour, a distance called a "lunar." In theory, it would be possible to determine the time at a particular reference place based on the angular distance between the moon and these other bodies. The difference between the reference time and local solar time aboard a ship at sea could be converted into a difference of longitude, with fifteen degrees of longitude equal to one hour of time. But in the seventeenth century, this was simply an idea—neither the moon's exact motions nor the positions of the stars were known with any certainty.

To supply the missing knowledge deemed so vital to navigation, King Charles II established an observatory at Greenwich in 1675. Astronomer John Flamsteed began forty years of observations with a large angle-measuring instrument and clock. The resulting star catalog, published in three volumes in 1725, contained tables of the movements of the moon and the positions of nearly three thousand stars at that meridian. A line of longitude through that observatory, established with

ABOVE: 1766 sextant, made by Jesse Ramsden in the last quarter of the eighteenth century.

OPPOSITE: Using lunar distances to find longitude. From Peter Apian, *Cosmographia* (1524).

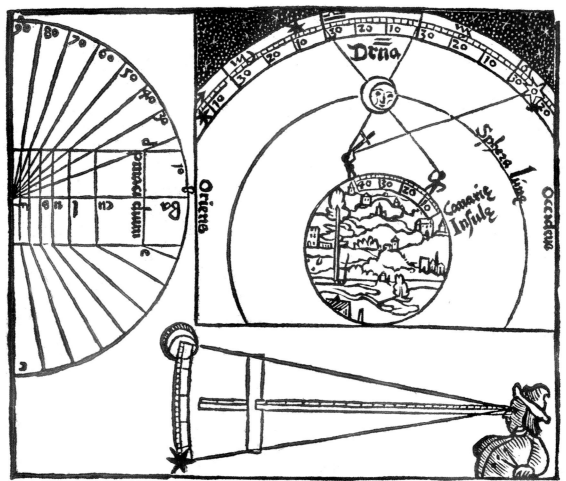

De partibus menſurae ſeu Speciebus Geometriae practicae. Caput vndecimum.

Enſura eſt longitudo finita: quae ignotam locorum diſtantiam ſenſibili experimento menſurat. Cuius ptes ſeu famoſę quantitates/quibus Geometer vtitur ſunt Granum hordei/Digit⁹/Vntia/palmus/Dichas/Spithames pes/Seſquipes/Gradus/paſſus ſimpler/paſſus dupler quē Geometricum appellare libuit/Cubitus ſeu vlna/pertica quem plures radium vocant/Stadiũ/Leuca/Miliare italicum/Miliare germanicum. ꝛc.

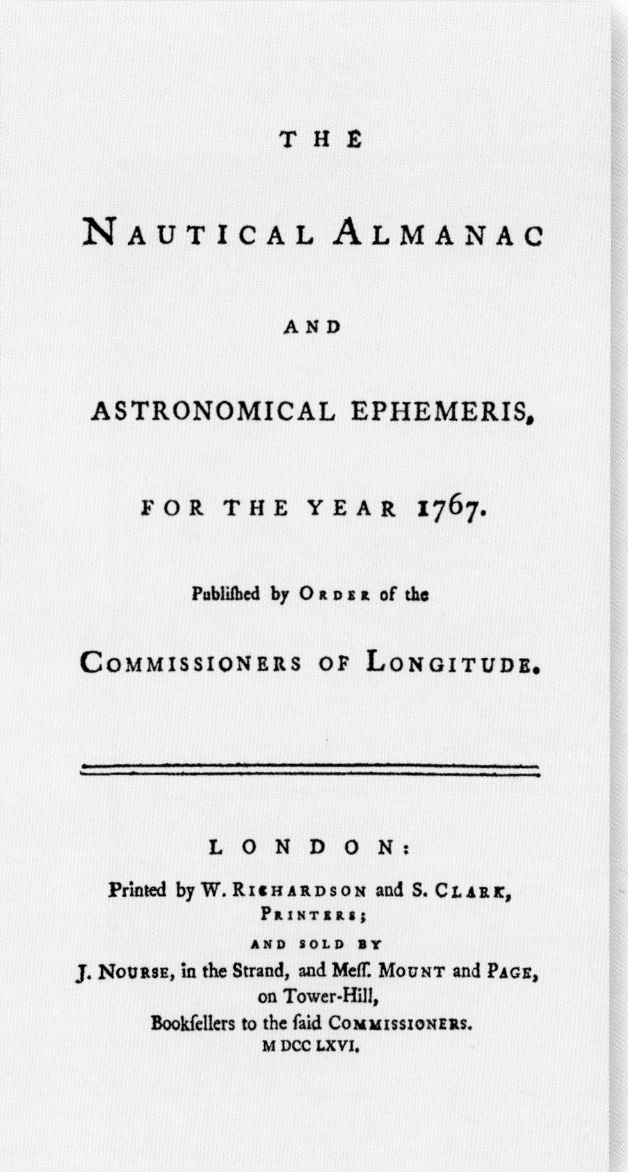

THE

NAUTICAL ALMANAC

AND

ASTRONOMICAL EPHEMERIS,

FOR THE YEAR 1767.

Published by ORDER of the

COMMISSIONERS OF LONGITUDE.

———————————————————

LONDON:

Printed by W. RICHARDSON and S. CLARK,
PRINTERS;
AND SOLD BY
J. NOURSE, in the Strand, and Meff. MOUNT and PAGE,
on Tower-Hill,
Bookfellers to the faid COMMISSIONERS.
M DCC LXVI.

The Nautical Almanac, first published in 1766.

painstaking precision, would later become Earth's prime meridian.

Under Flamsteed's successor, Neville Maskelyne, *The Nautical Almanac and Astronomical Ephemeris* was first published in 1766 specifically for aiding navigators at sea. To figure out local time, an observer noted how close the moon's edge was to a particular star. He then looked in the almanac tables to see the predicted time of that event at Greenwich. The difference between the two times could be used to calculate longitude. The Commissioners of Longitude approved the publication and rewarded a number of people for their work on it, including the widow of a German scientist, Tobias Mayer, who had calculated the accurate lunar tables before his death. In theory, the astronomers had given navigators at sea a way to know the time in two places simultaneously.

On his first voyage around the world, Captain James Cook tested the reference book and judged it useful. In his journal, he wrote that it offered "a method which we have found may be depended on to within a half a degree! Which is a degree of accuracy more than sufficient for all nautical purposes." Despite Cook's enthusiasm, in practice measuring "lunars," as lunar distances came to be called, was mathematically intense and laborious.

It was one thing for astronomers to know where they were at a fixed observatory, but quite another for navigators at sea to do so. Even with accurate tables predicting the motions of stars and the moon, they still needed better instruments for measuring lunar distances. In the early 1730s, John Hadley, vice president of the Royal Society in England, and Thomas Godfrey in Pennsylvania independently devised similar instruments for position finding. Initially known as Hadley's quadrant, the instrument is now more commonly called an octant, Godfrey's name for his instrument, which he based on its scale of 45 degrees, or one-eighth of a circle. This instrument was the first to make possible the measurement of lunar distances to the required precision at sea.

The octant inspired an even more precise instrument, the sextant, also used for measuring the altitude of a star or the moon above the horizon. London instrument maker John Bird and Captain John

Campbell worked with the Commissioners of Longitude to create an instrument based on a sixth of circle. Invented to improve on the arc of the octant, the sextant was initially seen as an aid for the lunar distance method of finding longitude. It became the standard for measuring latitude and the symbol of celestial navigation.

To use a sextant for finding the angle between the horizon and an object in the sky, a navigator would look through the eyepiece at the horizon. Half the field of view would show the horizon, while the other half would show part of the sky reflected by a moveable mirror attached to the sextant's arm. The navigator would move the sextant arm so the image of the sun or star aligned with the horizon, then read the angle from the sextant's scale.

At first, to make such instruments required a painstaking process to divide degrees of arc by hand, and for the first half of the eighteenth century angle-measuring octants and sextants were not produced in quantity. Beginning in 1767, Jesse Ramsden, another London instrument maker, devised a series of machines that speeded their manufacture and precisely marked the divisions on mathematical instrument scales. With Ramsden's circular dividing engine, for example, a workman could measure and mark out a sextant's 120-degree scale in just thirty minutes. Ramsden's invention won him an award from the British Board of Longitude. His instrument became the property of his successor, Matthew Berge, and Berge's successors, Nathaniel Worthington and James Allan. By the mid–nineteenth century, even small American instrument making enterprises had begun to buy dividing engines. The Philadelphia firm of Knox and Shain purchased Ramsden's dividing engine from his successors for their use. These dividing engines, found in Ramsden's shop and other instrument-making establishments, made accurate sextants more available and helped to revolutionize navigation.

Two competing proposals for finding longitude had first appeared in the same century—Peter Apian had suggested using lunar distances in 1524, and Gemma Frisius promoted the use of a good clock in 1530. Two competing solutions—the chronometer and the lunar distance method—emerged in the eighteenth century within a few years of each other. Although measuring "lunars" persisted into the nineteenth century, taking a good clock to sea eventually became the main way to keep track of position. This precedent continued for air and space navigation.

Dividing engine made by Jesse Ramsden, London, 1775.

THE UNITED STATES GOES TO SEA

This was the first American-made marine timekeeper taken to sea. William Cranch Bond, a twenty-three-year-old Boston clockmaker, crafted it during the War of 1812.

Oceans and waterways shaped the United States from the very beginning. As a young nation, the United States was eager to join the world's maritime powers. Although the Navy and Coast Guard remained relatively small, the country's commercial reach spread around the globe in the nineteenth century. Sail gave way to steam. American ships crossed every ocean. They carried immigrants to new homes, exotic goods from Asia, and prospectors to the California gold fields. American seaports flourished. Shipping grew faster, safer, and more reliable.

Intent upon contributing to the art and science of navigation, American innovators worked to lessen the dangers of seafaring by seeking better ways to find time and place. New Englanders, deeply influenced by their coastal setting, had key roles.

Edmund March Blunt opened a nautical bookstore in Newburyport, Massachusetts, in 1793, and went on to publish the two most important American navigational texts: Nathaniel Bowditch's *The New American Practical Navigator* and *The American Coast Pilot*. The latter, issued in 1796, was the first book of sailing directions for American waters published in the United States. The Coast Survey of National Oceanic and Atmospheric Administration (NOAA) still publishes a version. Blunt moved to New York in 1802 and opened a business "At the Sign of the Quadrant" to deal in nautical books, charts, and instruments. His sons, Edmund and George William, opened their own shop in New York in 1824, trading as E. & G. W. Blunt.

Bowditch, born in Salem, Massachusetts, sailed on merchant vessels as a young man and used his free time aboard to learn the

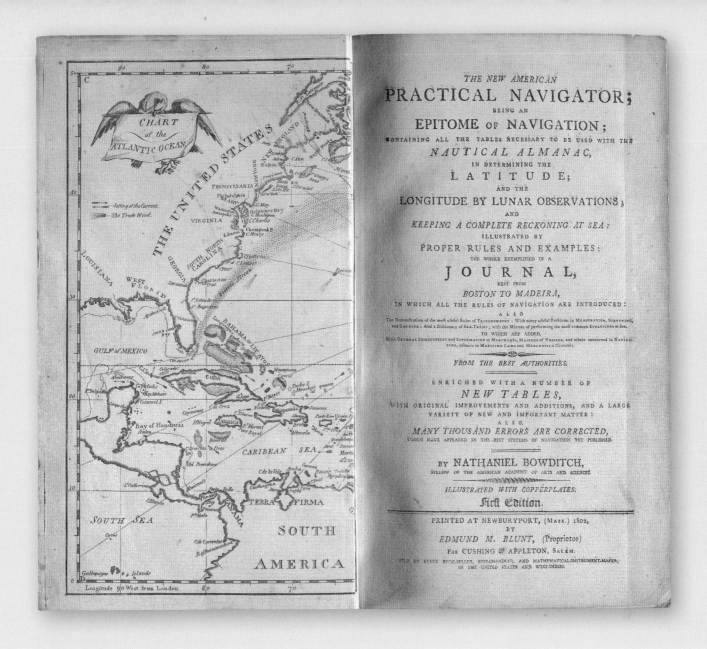

mathematics of celestial mechanics. His interest led him first to correct the astronomical tables in a popular English navigation handbook of the day, John Moore's *Practical Navigator*, and then to publish his own handbook with Edmund Blunt. *The New American Practical Navigator* has served American sailors since 1802. In that first edition, Bowditch provided instructions for how "to find the longitude by a perfect time-keeper" and for the lunar distance method. Bowditch went on to become a prominent astronomer, mathematician, and businessman remembered as the country's first insurance actuary. Popularly known as *Bowditch's*, the handbook remains today a useful guide with astronomical tables, meteorological information, and navigation instructions.

The New American Practical Navigator has served American sailors since 1802. Popularly known as *Bowditch's* for its first compiler, Nathaniel Bowditch, it remains a useful handbook of astronomical tables, meteorological information, and navigational instructions.

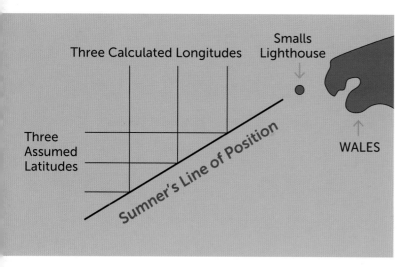

Three Calculated Longitudes

Smalls
Lighthouse

Three
Assumed
Latitudes

Sumner's Line of Position

WALES

The idea to navigate by "line of position" occurred to Thomas Sumner on a voyage in 1837. By measuring the altitude of the sun above the horizon and calculating three possible positions, Sumner realized he was located somewhere on a straight line. Later navigators regularly used this kind of technique by sighting stars, noting the time, and plotting the intersection of multiple lines.

Sharing an interest in astronomy with Bowditch was Boston's William Cranch Bond, who became the first director of the Harvard College Observatory. From 1839 to 1865, in the absence of a national institution, Harvard College Observatory under Bond and his successor, his son George P. Bond, met the U.S. government's needs for positional astronomy for determining basic latitudes and longitudes. As a twenty-three-year old clockmaker, Bond had constructed a sea clock during the War of 1812, when there was no chronometer industry in the United States and few instruments aboard American ships. Inspired by a description of a chronometer designed by Ferdinand Berthoud and used during the ill-fated voyage of French explorer Jean-François de Galaup La Pérouse, Bond's chronometer ran from the power of a falling weight rather than an unwinding spring. Tradition says that it was the first American chronometer to go to sea. Bond's instrument did so only once, on a voyage to Sumatra in 1818 aboard the U.S. Navy vessel *Cyrus*. William Bond & Son, the business begun by William Cranch Bond's father in 1793, became one of America's best-known chronometer dealers. During a brief period in the 1850s, the firm attempted to make chronometers of its own but found it impossible to compete with the established English industry.

Beginning in 1834, Bond had a contract with the U.S. Navy in the ports of Boston and Portsmouth to rate its ships' chronometers—that is, to determine how fast or slow they ran. With a private observatory in his home in Dorchester, Bond was the sole observer in New England with instruments accurate enough for determining local time to the U.S. government's satisfaction. In the late 1830s, his work for the Navy expanded to include supplying astronomical observations for longitude work to the Wilkes Expedition. Although Bond's role in the expedition was minor, his contacts and performance won him other federal contracts. He supplied similar observations for the U.S. Coast Survey's numerous longitude expeditions and the U.S. Topographical Engineers' boundary surveys with Canada and Mexico, and the Great Lakes. Even the British in Canada referred to the Cambridge meridian when they established the longitudes of their principal cities.

Another Bostonian, also trained in mathematics and astronomy at Harvard College, came up with an insight that altered the standard method of finding position at sea. While nearing land on his way to Scotland in 1837, Boston sea captain Thomas Sumner found that cloudy weather permitted only one sighting on the sun. With that limited information, he could calculate his longitude only based on estimates of his latitude. Sumner made three different calculations, assuming a slightly different latitude each time. Plotted on a chart, the results lay along a straight line. He realized that any ship seeing the sun at the same altitude in the sky must be located somewhere on that line. This was confirmed by sailing along that course until a lighthouse was sighted on the coast. Sumner published his method for determining what was later called a "line of position" in 1843 in his *New and Practical Method of Finding a Ship's Position at Sea by Projection on Mercator's Chart*, and it became standard practice for modern celestial navigation. Sumner's method to establish a fix did not catch on with others until thirty years later, when Marcq de Saint Hilaire of the French navy published a refinement. He determined that the difference between the altitude of a celestial body from a ship's true position and the altitude at the ship's position estimated from dead reckoning will be equal to the distance between the two positions.

The 1848 discovery of gold in California inspired efforts to speed the trip to San Francisco from East Coast ports, a sea trip around the tip of South America that averaged about six months. American shipbuilders began to craft slim vessels build for speed—the clipper ships. In 1851, the Boston-built *Flying Cloud* sailed from New York to San Francisco in an astonishing eighty-nine days, twenty-one hours. Three years later, the same vessel set a new record—eighty-nine days, eight hours—that stood for 135 years.

Josiah Perkins Creesy Jr. commanded the ship, and his wife, Eleanor, navigated. Almost no women were navigators, but as a child in Massachusetts, she had learned navigation skills from her seafaring father. She was among the first to follow new sailing directions, based on winds and currents, published by Matthew Fontaine Maury at the U.S. Navy's Depot of Charts and Instruments.

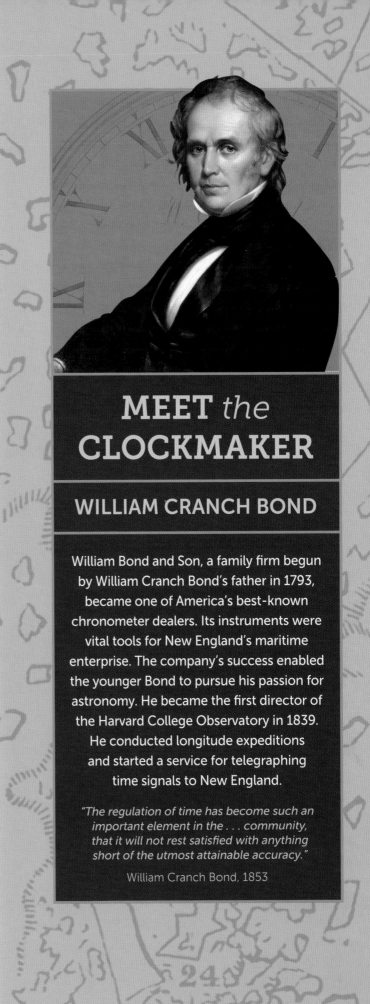

MEET *the* CLOCKMAKER

WILLIAM CRANCH BOND

William Bond and Son, a family firm begun by William Cranch Bond's father in 1793, became one of America's best-known chronometer dealers. Its instruments were vital tools for New England's maritime enterprise. The company's success enabled the younger Bond to pursue his passion for astronomy. He became the first director of the Harvard College Observatory in 1839. He conducted longitude expeditions and started a service for telegraphing time signals to New England.

"The regulation of time has become such an important element in the . . . community, that it will not rest satisfied with anything short of the utmost attainable accuracy."

William Cranch Bond, 1853

In 1851, the clipper ship *Flying Cloud* sailed from New York to San Francisco in an astonishing 89 days, 21 hours. Three years later, the same vessel set a new record—89 days, 8 hours—that stood for 135 years.

Established in 1830 in Washington, D.C., the depot's purpose was to improve navigation, specifically the navy's ability to find longitude with chronometers, between thirty and forty of which were in use by that time. The chronometer by then had demonstrated its ability to fix positions at sea routinely within tens of miles, not the meters we know today. In order to be reliable guides even to this margin of error, though, chronometers need to be rated, that is, tested to see how fast or slow they run, compared to a stable timekeeper. The source of time for that clock in the nineteenth century was astronomical observations. Better timekeeping and star positions brought better navigation.

The first officer put in charge of the depot was Louis M. Goldsborough, who was succeeded by Charles Wilkes until he went to Europe to outfit the U.S. Exploring Expedition with instruments. The activities of the depot grew into the U.S. Naval Observatory.

Maury became the first superintendent and remained from 1844 until 1861, when he left to join the Confederate Navy during the Civil War.

Beginning in 1847, Maury collected and published wind and current information, compiled from thousands of American ships' logs. After an international conference on marine meteorology in Brussels in 1853 that Maury organized, logs from European voyagers added to his data. These publications, along with sailing directions, helped navigators select routes to take advantage of favorable winds and currents. Sometimes these new routes shaved weeks from voyages, as demonstrated by the *Flying Cloud* and its competitors. The Navy discontinued Maury's work in 1861 but resumed it between 1885 and 1915. The final publication marked the official end of the Age of Sail.

Along with improving navigation with the Depot of Charts and Instrument, the Navy also sought to upgrade its navigation education. With a class of fifty midshipmen and seven professors, the Naval School began in 1845 in Annapolis. The curriculum included mathematics, navigation, gunnery, steam engineering, chemistry, natural philosophy, English, and French. Naval officer candidates could finally receive organized, comprehensive navigation instruction, theoretical and practical. In 1850, the school—now the U.S. Naval Academy—introduced new requirements for midshipmen—a four-year course of study and shipboard instruction every summer.

Most American contributions to the art of navigation occurred before the American Civil War. The reasons are complex, but they are mainly related to the changing nature of American shipping. In 1850, America's oceangoing fleet held a prominent position in international trading and nearly all American overseas goods—about 70 percent— traveled on American ships. The Civil War had a destructive and permanent impact. Confederate raiders not only destroyed American-registered ships, but they also drove shippers to shift cargoes to neutral ships. By the end of the war, about half of U.S. merchant shipping had fled to foreign owners, and the industry never recovered its former prominence. The war and the shift to petroleum-based kerosene nearly finished off New England's whaling industry, too, which at its peak around 1850 had dominated the world's fleets. Until the Civil war began, about six hundred American whale ships annually sailed the oceans and far outnumbered those of any other country.

Ironically, in the last half of the nineteenth century, as the United States grew in economic might and international trade rose, most of the country's imports, exports, and passengers traveled in foreign ships. By 1900, fewer than 10 percent of all international cargoes to and from the United States were carried in American vessels.

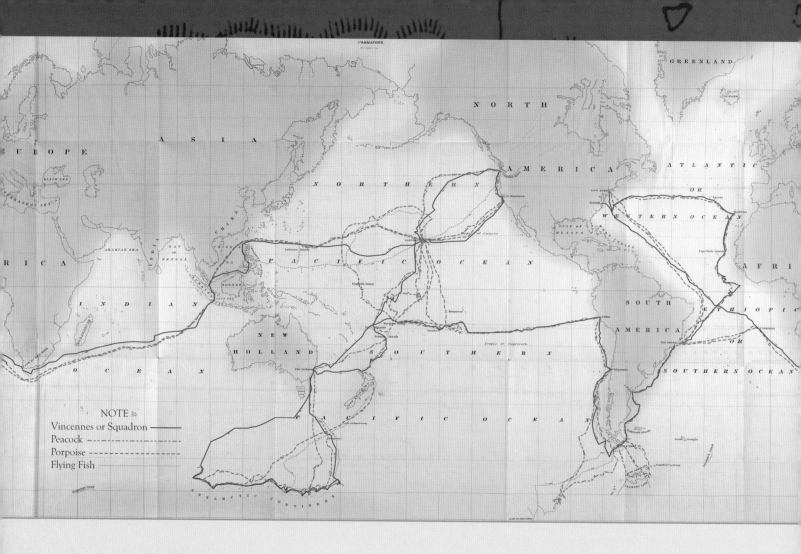

NOTE
Vincennes or Squadron ——————
Peacock - - - - - - - - - -
Porpoise - - - - - - - - - -
Flying Fish

SAILING *with the*
U.S. Exploring Expedition

In 1838, the United States dispatched an ambitious mission
to uncharted oceans. Six U.S. Navy vessels set out on a great
voyage of exploration. Aboard were 424 seamen and nine civilian
scientists under the command of Lieutenant Charles Wilkes.
Authorized by Congress, the U.S. Exploring Expedition (also known
as the Ex. Ex. or the Wilkes Expedition) was mounted to explore
and map the Pacific, Antarctica, and the northwest coast of the
United States. The four-year-long expedition covered nearly
87,000 miles (140,000 km), including a full circumnavigation of the
globe. A tremendous feat of navigation, the mission broadened

ABOVE: The routes of the U.S. Exploring
Expedition.

OPPOSITE: Kingfishers in Fiji, from the
volume on mammals and birds, U.S.
Exploring Expedition.

Captain Charles Wilkes led the U.S. Exploring Expedition, which sailed around the world between 1838 and 1842.

knowledge of uncharted areas of the world and helped expand American commerce, industry, and scientific knowledge.

Securing government approval for the expedition's costs had been controversial, as was the appointment of Wilkes. The Exploring Expedition's stated purpose was to assist American shipping, especially the whaling fleet, by surveying and making accurate charts of the Pacific. At the same time, the planned visit to the Pacific Northwest—what are now Oregon and Washington—was intended to strengthen U.S. claims to the territory.

Charles Wilkes was an experienced naval officer known for his expertise in surveying and charting. Before leading the U.S. Exploring Expedition, he headed the Navy's Department of Charts and Instruments (now the U.S. Naval Observatory), where he worked tirelessly on rating marine chronometers. For the expedition, Wilkes acquired the finest English-made navigation equipment at considerable expense. He outfitted his small squadron with twenty-eight box and pocket chronometers, twelve sextants, and many other astronomical and meteorological instruments, along with a scientific library for each vessel.

Accompanying the expedition was a formidable group of civilians to collect and catalog biological and cultural artifacts throughout the newly charted territories. Referred to as the "Scientifics," they included geologist James D. Dana, naturalists Charles Pickering and Titian Ramsey Peale, conchologist Joseph P. Couthouy, ethnographer Horatio C. Hale, botanists William Rich and William D. Brackenridge, and artists Joseph Drayton and Alfred Agate. Upon their return, the scientific corps published nineteen volumes on their findings. Wilkes himself contributed two volumes on meteorology and hydrology.

In the course of the voyage, two ships were lost, and several skirmishes with Pacific islanders ended in brutal deaths for both natives and explorers. A crew of eighteen aboard the Sea Gull vanished, presumably wrecked in a storm on leaving Cape Horn in 1839. Two years later, while exploring the Pacific Northwest, the *Peacock*, which had narrowly escaped destruction in the ice of Antarctica (see page 14) broke apart on shoals at the mouth of the Columbia River. The crew survived, but boxes of carefully collected specimens did not. South Pacific natives and two members of the crew, including Wilkes's nephew, died in a bloody confrontation in Fiji.

The expedition returned with nearly forty tons of specimens and artifacts. In 1858, most were transferred to the Smithsonian Institution in Washington, D.C., to become the foundation of national collections. The expedition also brought back living plants from around the globe, the basis of the U.S. Botanic Garden near the Capitol.

The expedition should have been recognized immediately as a valuable success when it returned in 1842. Instead, Wilkes's heavy-handed treatment of his crew resulted in his court-martial and a reprimand. English and French explorers disputed his discovery of Antarctica. Meanwhile, American attention turned from charting the sea to the continent of North America, as the annexation of Texas, war with Mexico, and settlement of the boundary of the Pacific Northwest with England resulted in the addition of 1.2 million square miles (3.1 million square kilometers) to the nation's territory. ☀

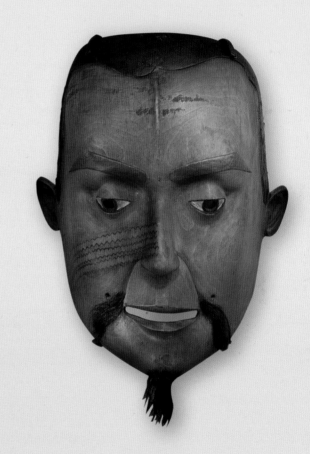

TOP: Shell trumpet from Samoa collected during the U.S. Exploring Expedition.

BOTTOM: Mask from Oregon Territory.

SYNCHRONIZING THE WORLD

Pocket watch made for Sandford Fleming, chief engineer for the Canadian Pacific Railroad, showing his system for dividing the globe into twenty-four zones identified by letters of the alphabet.

Organizing the globe using the spatial coordinates of latitude and longitude was already a common convention in Western Europe by the late Middle Ages. Latitude lines, with the zero-degree equator splitting the world into northern and southern hemispheres, had a mathematical basis in the line's angular distance from the equator. The longitude's zero degree line was arbitrary, however; the line going through the poles could loop the earth anywhere. In 1494, for instance, the Treaty of Tordesillas divided the world between the Portuguese and the Spanish empires with a meridian line between the nations. Multiple prime meridians came to exist, since any country could adopt its own national meridian, often reinforced by its own national observatory and mapmakers.

Coordinating time and space on a global scale is a relatively recent endeavor. Efforts to use the best timekeeping instruments to connect parts of the world had begun modestly in the 1840s. During 1843 and 1844, longitude measurements with chronometers transported across the Baltic, the North Sea, and the Thames determined the relative longitudes between key observatories at Greenwich, England; Altona, near Hamburg, Germany; and Pulkovo, near Saint Petersburg, Russia. In an effort to determine the exact longitudinal difference between the Harvard College Observatory in Boston and its counterpart in Liverpool, England, the astronomers at each institution exchanged marine chronometers carried aboard steamships crossing the North Atlantic in three separate expeditions in 1849–50, 1851, and 1855.

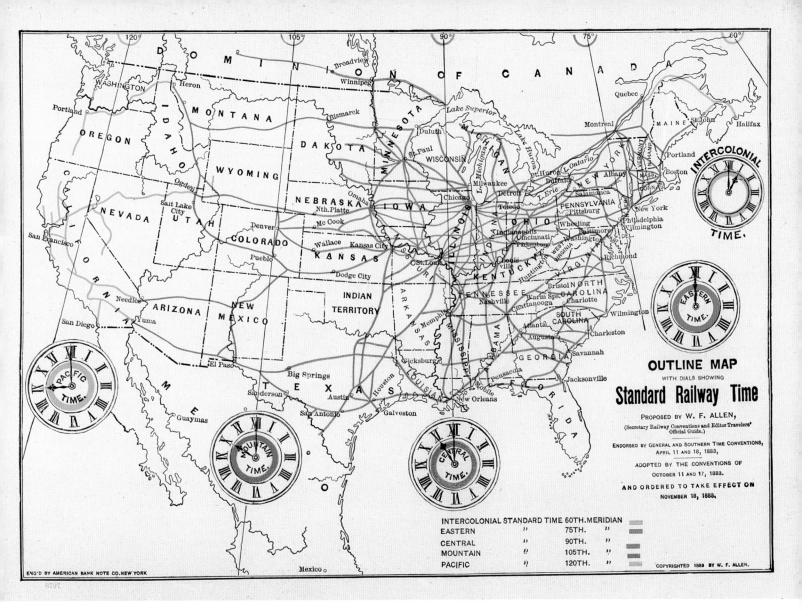

Map of proposed railway time zones for North America published by William F. Allen, 1883.

The expeditions had the support of the Astronomer Royal at the Greenwich Observatory, who sent comparative time by telegraph to Liverpool, and the U.S Coast Survey, which had developed a specialty in telegraphic longitude determinations after the method's utility was demonstrated by Charles Wilkes. Wilkes had sent the first time signals for determining the difference in longitude between Baltimore and Washington in June 1844, just seventeen days after Samuel Morse sent his famous message: "What hath God wrought." Repeated with time sent over the transatlantic telegraph cable, the experiments produced split-second refinements in 1866, 1870, 1873, and 1897. The formal measurement of the longitude difference between Harvard and Liverpool was 4h 44m 31s.046 ±0s.048—that is, four hours, forty-four minutes, and nearly thirty-two seconds.

Beginning in the 1870s, ideas to establish a common way of measuring time and space globally began to gather momentum,

Attendees at the World International Meridian Conference, Washington, D.C., 1884.

especially among professional communities dealing with astronomy, geography, and navigation. There were suggestions long before then for a unifying system. In 1870, Otto Struve, a prominent astronomer at Pulkovo Observatory in Russia, issued an especially influential report after undertaking a study of the multiple meridians in use for astronomy, geography, and navigation. He suggested making a prime meridian through Greenwich and an antimeridian in the middle of the Pacific Ocean.

The subject of a common meridian and common time, however, fell outside the concerns of national governments until much later. At the invitation of the French government, the Meter Convention of 1875 established the International Bureau of Weights and Measures (today the BIPM) through diplomatic means and became a model for future international cooperation in the science of measurement.

In the 1870s, there were no time zones as we know them. Towns and cities across the world independently set their own times by observing the sun. There were thousands and thousands of local times. Ideas for a coordinated universal system picked up speed and traction when North America's railroads, more than six hundred different lines, voluntarily adopted Standard Railway Time in 1883 and linked its time zones to Greenwich, England, as the zero meridian or 0° longitude.

Nations soon clashed over whose time and place should be the standard-setter. At the International Meridian Conference, held in Washington, D.C., in October 1884, diplomats and technical specialists from twenty-five countries met to act on numerous proposals for establishing a standard of time and longitude for the whole world. They recommended that the prime meridian (0° longitude) run through the Royal Observatory at Greenwich, England. The vote for Greenwich passed twenty-two to one, with only San Domingo (now Dominican Republic) opposed. Brazil and France abstained.

In doing so, they confirmed the utility of a process that had begun centuries ago with the establishment of the observatory at Greenwich, the construction there of accurate star tables, and the resulting charts for navigation. By the 1880s, nearly 75 percent of the world's shipping was using British charts and referencing Greenwich mean time.

The gradual introduction of radio time signals at the beginning of the twentieth century made nearly instantaneous global connections a reality and connected local times in a tighter network. The French saw an opportunity to balance the prime meridian at Greenwich with an international institution for world time based in Paris, and they hosted the International Conference on Radio Time in 1912. Technical representatives of the sixteen countries attending addressed a uniform method of determining and maintaining accurate time signals and transmitting them around the world. A year later, thirty-two countries gathered again in Paris and drew up guidelines for world time, but they were not ratified until after World War I.

In parallel with international developments, the U.S. national government's authority over time was growing. The government built and maintained public clocks, for example, and funded time finding and timekeeping at the U.S. Naval Observatory. Although there was no national observatory such as many European countries had, the U.S. Naval Observatory began to serve that role, providing time by telegraph to all of Washington, D.C., and then the entire country through an arrangement with Western Union. The U.S. Navy pioneered the use of radio and in 1913–14 conducted a set of definitive experiments to determine the difference in longitude between radio towers in Arlington, Virginia, and the Eiffel Tower in Paris. The official difference was 5 hours, 17 minutes, 36.653 seconds, ±0.0031 seconds.

Towers for U.S. Navy radio transmitters, Arlington, Virginia.

By 1918, Congress made time zones the law of the land, one that was administered first by the Interstate Commerce Commission and now by the Department of Transportation. In the radio age, the Department of Commerce's National Bureau of Standards also became an authority for time and frequency for the country. The partnerships between government institutions, commercial enterprises such as clockmakers and watchmakers, and a public eager to buy timepieces all contributed to a growing network of time and space.

By this time, airplanes had begun undertaking long-distance overwater flights. The stage was set for connecting time and place for navigating not just at sea but also in the air.

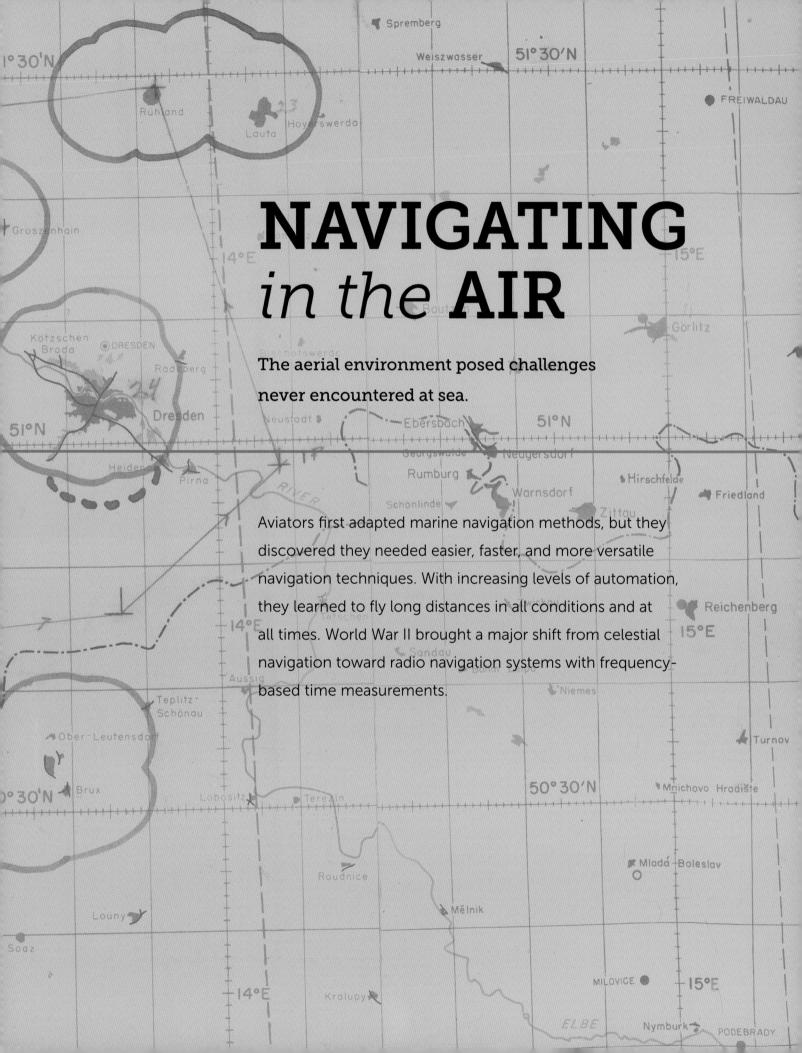

NAVIGATING
in the AIR

The aerial environment posed challenges
never encountered at sea.

Aviators first adapted marine navigation methods, but they
discovered they needed easier, faster, and more versatile
navigation techniques. With increasing levels of automation,
they learned to fly long distances in all conditions and at
all times. World War II brought a major shift from celestial
navigation toward radio navigation systems with frequency-
based time measurements.

NAVIGATING *in the* AIR

As they reached the target area, the fate of thousands hung in their hands. Between February 13 and 15, 1945, the dividing line between life and death for tens of thousands of people came down to the choice of navigational aid. As World War II raged in Europe, more than one thousand bombers of the British Royal Air Force and U.S. Army Air Forces flew missions to targets in eastern Germany. After flying across hostile territory, many aircrews found that clouds obscured their primary targets. In this situation, their orders were to seek secondary targets of opportunity. Hundreds of additional aircraft turned toward the city of Dresden.

U.S. Eighth Air Force B-17s bomb "blind" through cloud cover, using radar as the primary navigational aid somewhere over northwestern Europe. Military applications were the single greatest impetus in the development of air navigation systems.

Navigation was not the only reason for the bombing of Dresden, but newly available electronic equipment favored easily found cities over smaller targets. The raids devastated Dresden, killing more than twenty thousand civilians and displacing tens of thousands more. While raids on other cities claimed more lives, the bombing of Dresden has become one of the most contested incidents in discussions of ethics and morality in warfare.

The critical navigational tool at Dresden was radar. Radar operators on bombers generated navigational fixes with bearings from two principal types of prominent features: shorelines and urban areas. With the especially heavy cloud cover of the 1944–45 winter in Europe, radar for navigation and bombing became dominant over other methods. The dilemma for commanders was clear: to bomb cities, or not to bomb at all.

Navigation suddenly meant more than wayfinding. It gave a decisive military advantage to the Allies and affected the lives of millions. Radar was hardly the only new development. An alphabet soup of systems, such as Gee, LORAN, SHORAN, Oboe, and Sonne, guided airmen in all weathers with accuracies often better than celestial navigation. Technology replaced skill, an essential development for the tens of thousands of young navigators charged with guiding the Allied air forces with only scant weeks of training.

Before the war, cost, complexity, and weight had stifled development of air navigation technologies. The war eliminated these concerns and placed a premium on all-weather, easy-to-use solutions that worked over wide areas of the globe. The marriage of aviation and electronics that occurred in World War II has informed nearly all aspects of aerospace in the years since. ☀

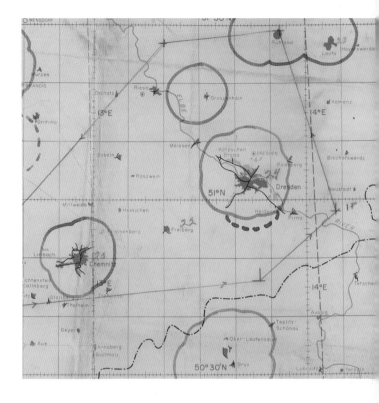

This 1945 radar navigation chart depicts an Eighth Air Force bombing raid that struck Dresden. Bombing by electronic systems such as radar imposed operational limitations with enormous human costs as accuracies decreased over visual bombing, making cities primary targets during the last year of World War II.

In the following pages, we will see how innovators first adapted marine navigation techniques for use in aircraft and over the decades met the distinct challenges of long-distance navigation for flying in all conditions and all times.

INTO THE AIR AGE

IMPERIAL AIRWAYS
EUROPE AFRICA INDIA FAR EAST AUSTRALIA

ONE OF THE 28 NEW 200 MILES AN HOUR TWO-DECKER EMPIRE FLYING BOATS

Long-range flying boats, like this British "Empire" C-class, heralded a new age in transport that promised fast and efficient global movements. Nationalized airlines with overwater routes were the most significant early consumers of advances in air navigation technology.

The air navigator was a member of a distinctly twentieth-century profession that has almost entirely disappeared, replaced by "black boxes" incorporating complex algorithms and receiving signals from a sophisticated ground- and space-based infrastructure. For over three decades, the air navigator served as an elite practitioner who helped create the popular conceptions of the Air Age, Jet Age, and Space Age.

Two distinct challenges defined innovation in air navigation. First, the crossing of oceans demonstrated the limitations of conventional navigation methods. Solving this puzzle required the creation of the profession of air navigator and the development of fast, reliable methods of navigation that were simpler than maritime techniques, even if slightly less accurate. This process yielded significant results during the 1930s as nations sought to use transoceanic flight to signify national power through demonstrations of commercial and military might. Individuals achieved glory by flights of exploration and record setting built upon this new navigational capability.

World War II was the second great challenge for innovators—one that placed a premium on global all-weather operations by young and inexperienced navigators. The intersection of the demand for easier-to-use techniques with the rising electronics industry resulted in complex systems combining highly accurate frequency-based timing with radio signals. The shift to electronic means has continually transformed the practice of navigation over the past seven decades.

If there is a singular moment in the history of twentieth-century navigation, it came in 1943, with the transition from mechanical timekeeping based on the measurement of seconds to frequency based measurement of millionths of seconds (microseconds). This contributed to the "miracle" of radar, as well as ground-based radio navigation, an important antecedent to the modern "miracle" of GPS.

At the dawn of the twentieth century, maritime navigation was a mature operational and technological field, but one that depended heavily on the ability to see the sky. However, these celestial techniques quickly proved inadequate for aircraft. The first limitation was speed. Lengthy computations meant longer times flying incorrect headings at high speeds, resulting in greater positional errors. Aircraft instability made celestial sightings inaccurate. Weather also posed numerous problems, ranging from obscured horizons to turbulence. Last, the cockpit environment was hostile to the process of navigation. A marine navigator in the relatively spacious confines of a vessel could compute a position fix in fifteen minutes, but an aviator in an open cockpit faced a different set of conditions. The cold air at altitude with relative wind speeds near 100 miles per hour (160 kph), combined with gloved hands and incessant noise and vibration, made position fixing an unreliable and often impossible task in early long-range airplanes.

Unfortunately for aviators, air navigation languished as a highly specialized field that received scant attention outside a handful of enthusiast innovators and practitioners. Most operated on the margins of the aeronautical industry, which prized aerodynamic and propulsive innovations above all else. For instance, when Charles Lindbergh sought to win the Orteig Prize by flying from New York to Paris in 1927, his primary interest was finding the right airframe and engine combination, with navigation as an afterthought. The subject received much more attention during World War II, when failures of navigation carried dire national consequences. The union of the aeronautics and electronics industries under wartime pressures brought about a change in perspective, but only at great material cost.

This late 1930s Japanese Air Transport Corporation poster vividly portrays the connection between commercial air transport and military air power.

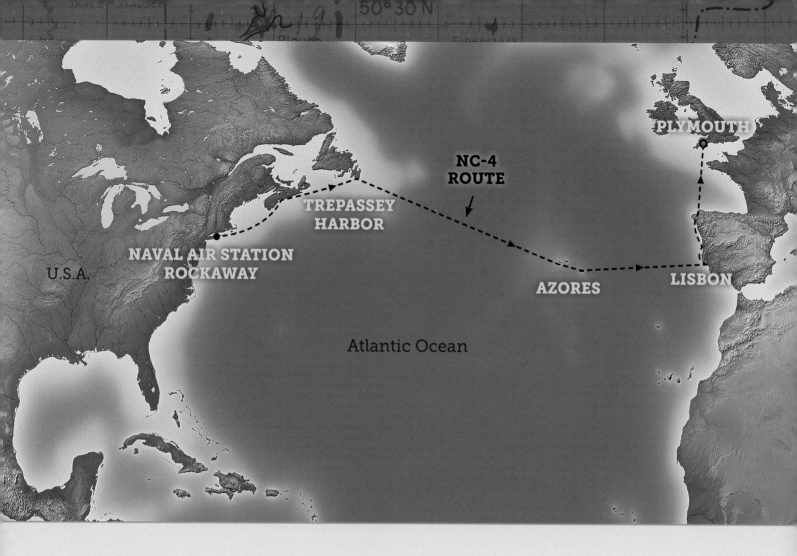

NC-4
ROUTE

PLYMOUTH

TREPASSEY
HARBOR

NAVAL AIR STATION
ROCKAWAY

U.S.A.

AZORES

LISBON

Atlantic Ocean

CROSSING THE OCEAN *with the*
NC-4

On May 31, 1919, a U.S. Navy NC flying boat with a crew of five reached Plymouth, England, after a two-week transit of the North Atlantic with stops in Canada, the Azores, and Portugal. This marked the first successful aerial crossing of the Atlantic. Lieutenant Commander Albert Read, the captain of the aircraft, designated *NC-4*, was justly proud of the achievement. However, the flight also vividly demonstrated that while airframes and engines could now carry humans above the roiling Atlantic seas, the technologies to guide them safely and reliably were far less effective than the aircraft that carried them.

ABOVE: The first crossing of the Atlantic by air followed an arduous, indirect route and required fifteen percent of the U.S. Navy's surface combatant vessels to serve in support. The Azores remained a popular stopping point for later transatlantic flights until the Jet Age.

OPPOSITE: Painting by Ted Wilbur titled *NC-4* depicting a challenging aerial environment. Albert Read, the plane's captain and navigator, made celestial sightings and drift observations in the nose exposed to wind speeds of 80 mph (129 kph).

TED WILBUR

TOP: Future polar explorer Richard Byrd guided development of this American aeronautical bubble sextant for use on the NC-4.

BOTTOM: Richard Byrd (center) demonstrates his sextant to Albert Read (left) and Walter Hinton (right) on a Felixstowe flying boat.

The problem with the Navy's transatlantic flight attempt was not a lack of interest in the navigational challenges facing the flight. On the contrary, Lieutenant Commander Richard Byrd and Lieutenant Walter Hinton developed an ad hoc laboratory to address the problems of celestial, dead reckoning, and radio navigation in flight. Byrd developed an improved bubble sextant for use when the horizon was not visible, a new wind-plotting computer, and a new drift sight. The aircraft's radio receiver incorporated advanced direction finding coils. While Byrd's preflight preparations were systematic and thorough, their limited scope did not allow for extensive field testing and refinement. They were all a disappointment in one way or another.

The Navy arrayed vessels in a line between major stops on the route at fifty-mile (80 km) intervals to serve as radio beacons to keep the NC flying boats on track, regardless of the weather. In reality, the interference generated by the unshielded spark plugs on the four-engine aircraft limited reception to an insufficient fifteen miles (24 km). These factors combined to cause the NC-1 and NC-3, two planes accompanying the NC-4, to become lost as they ran low on fuel, resulting in both alighting on the open ocean. The crew of the NC-1 made a lucky escape onto a passing ship, while the crew of the NC-3 navigated their way on the surface to the Azores. A compass error also nearly led to the loss of the NC-4.

The flight demonstrated that air navigation required a degree of reliability that ships at sea, which could reduce sail or steam as necessary in response to uncertainty of position, did not. Cloud

cover at critical moments when a celestial shot was needed could mean the difference between life and death over the open ocean, where fuel reserves were often measured in minutes rather than hours. Little would change over the next decade, but as transoceanic flight became increasingly tied to national prestige, solving the failings of the Navy's flying boats became a priority.

Between the flight of the *NC-4* and Charles Lindbergh's solo crossing of the Atlantic eight years later, Britain assumed leadership in the advancement of transoceanic flight, starting with the remarkable, but often overlooked, achievement of Alcock and Brown's nonstop crossing a mere two weeks after the *NC-4* arrived in England. The British succeeded again a mere two weeks later with the first westbound crossing (and return), made by the *R 34* airship as a harbinger of a possible commercial airship link between Europe and North America, a dream that ended with the destruction of the *R 101* in 1930. ✦

TOP: The *NC-4* was robust enough to cross an ocean, but the crew lacked the navigational tools to do it safely or reliably.

BOTTOM: After becoming lost, the crew of the *NC-3* had to put down on the open ocean, damaging it so heavily that it had to limp into the Azores on the surface.

Germany's Zeppelin raiders struggled consistently with navigation during World War I raids on English cities. Despite the development of an ambitious radio compass system, the Zeppelins were as inaccurate as they were vulnerable.

The airship and the flying boat were the primary long-range aircraft during World War I and the early 1920s. Both posed special challenges to the first air navigators. The enormous gasbags of airships made celestial navigation challenging, but at least they tended to be stable platforms. The flying boat was less affected by strong winds, but its instability still made sextant use a challenge and large biplane structures tended to obscure much of the visible sky. Nonetheless, British airships and flying boats waged a largely successful campaign against U-boats over the North Atlantic by establishing a "spider web" of patrols.

Britain employed a newly developed series of bubble sextants to locate the horizon, but these were only marginally successful. The major innovation of the World War I years was the broad implementation of two radio compass systems: the Bellini-Tosi radio direction finding loop system and the Telefunken directional transmitter. These systems served in Europe and North America during the war years.

This era established several individuals as key innovators. Perhaps the most prolific was Britain's Harry E. Wimperis, who authored the first significant treatise on air navigation and became an adept innovator in navigational technologies such as bubble sextants, drift sights, and bombsights. He also encouraged the development of radar. An American analog to Wimperis was Albert Hegenberger, who began by heading the instrument development section at the U.S.

ABOVE: Gago Coutinho (foreground) sits in the *Lusitânia* with his copilot Sacadura Cabral during their arduous aerial transit of the South Atlantic, which took three months and resulted in the loss of two planes.

LEFT: Albert Hegenberger demonstrating a bubble sextant in the celestial navigation hatch of the U.S. Army Air Corps Fokker C-2 *Bird of Paradise* before his milestone flight from Oakland, California, to Honolulu, Hawaii, with pilot Lester Maitland.

NAVIGATION GONE WRONG

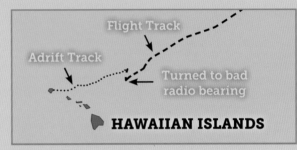

Pacific Ocean
San Francisco

⊗ HAWAIIAN ISLANDS

REACHING HAWAII BY AIR

The first attempt to fly to Hawaii from the mainland United States, in 1925, resulted in a fight for survival and an amazing feat of navigation and seamanship.

Flight Track

Adrift Track

Turned to bad radio bearing

HAWAIIAN ISLANDS

WHAT HAPPENED

The U.S. Navy's *PN-9-1* burned far more fuel than expected. After missing a supply ship due to a bad radio bearing, the aircraft ran out of fuel. Commander John Rodgers and his crew had to make a forced landing nearly 310 miles (500 km) from Honolulu.

THE CONSEQUENCES

Without a working transmitter radio to call for help, the five men had to improvise. They ripped fabric from a wing to make a sail, and Rodgers "sailed" his plane toward Hawaii. Almost ten days later, a submarine that had given them up for lost spotted them just off the coast of Kauai.

LESSONS LEARNED

Up to this point, U.S. Navy commanders had largely ignored the problems of air navigation, but some innovators, such as Lieutenant Commander P. V. H. Weems, now began seeking new methods and tools.

ABOVE: The U.S. Navy's *PN-9-1* aircraft barely survived its attempted flight to Hawaii.

BELOW: The damaged *PN-9-1* at anchor after drifting to Kauai. Note the wing fabric used for a sail.

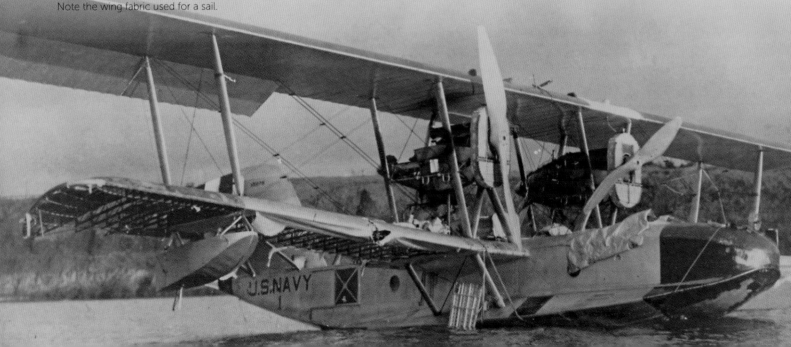

Army's McCook Field laboratory. There, he took a particular interest in navigation problems and incorporated new domestic and international developments into a broad systematic approach to the challenges of long-range flight. His most notable achievement came in June 1927 when he served as navigator for Lieutenant Lester Maitland on the first successful flight from the U.S. mainland to the Hawaiian Islands, employing a full range of instruments from bubble sextants and drift sights to radio compasses. Hegenberger continued as a significant innovator up to the World War II years.

Another example of the innovator-practitioner was Portugal's Gago Coutinho, who made the first aerial crossing of the South Atlantic in 1922. This was also the first truly successful long-distance flight that depended mostly on celestial navigation. Until P. V. H. Weems's advances of the late 1920s, Coutinho was the most successful innovator in adapting maritime celestial navigation to the aerial environment. He is most notable for applying the ideas of the "running fix" and "running down" a line of position to air navigation.

Other air navigators of the early 1920s used sextants with minor degrees of success. Arthur Whitten Brown, navigator on the first nonstop transatlantic flight in June 1919, used one, as did Major Gilbert Cooke, the navigator of the *R 34*, the first airship to undertake a transatlantic crossing. These flights did not prove the viability of celestial navigation in routine air navigation, but they showcased its potential in the absence of more effective methods. The near loss of the Navy's *PN-9-1* aircraft in the Pacific vividly demonstrated that this method still left much to be desired.

When Charles Lindbergh crossed the Atlantic in 1927 to enthusiastic international acclaim, the link between long-range flying and national prestige became starkly apparent, and the leading world powers redoubled their efforts to establish records. Some nations looked beyond such feats as mere tools of prestige and saw long-range aviation as the future of projecting power. The colonial powers of Europe, particularly the United Kingdom, embraced long-range flight as a more powerful thread with which to connect the jewels of their empires. The United States likewise used long-range flights to South America to promote its political interests in the Americas. Mussolini's Italy mastered the art of navigation as spectacle with military transoceanic formation flights from the late 1920s to the mid-1930s, led by a flamboyant air marshal, Italo Balbo. These demonstrations fueled an international public enthusiasm, even as economic depression enveloped much of the world. Many governments supported increasingly ambitious aeronautical voyages to instill national pride, even as domestic morale plummeted.

P. V. H. Weems served as America's leading air navigation authority in the late 1920s and 1930s. He simplified and sped up the process of airborne celestial position fixing so that it only took a tenth of the time of conventional maritime celestial techniques and with minimal loss of accuracy.

Between the world wars, transoceanic flight matured and the requirements for reliable long-range air navigation technologies rapidly expanded. Between the end of World War I and Charles Lindbergh's solo New York to Paris flight in 1927, air navigation technology in the United States and elsewhere developed slowly compared to other aeronautical technologies. There were some small successes. The U.S. National Bureau of Standards not only evaluated domestic and international air navigation equipment, but also worked to create improved tools such as the first truly practical bubble sextant to allow stable celestial sights. Practical radio direction finding aids also emerged out of government laboratories.

Other pioneers, such as Australia's Charles Kingsford Smith, demonstrated that with luck and the right airplane, tools, and crewmembers, even the formidable South Pacific could be bridged by air. Smith's 1928 and 1934 flights between the United States and Australia proved that aircraft could connect any population center in the world with another. In a less peaceful context, the 1932 formation flight of twenty-one Italian military flying boats from Italy to Chicago made Americans realize that the oceans no longer guaranteed their nation the protection they once did.

After the nearly disastrous results of its 1919 and 1925 oceanic flight attempts, the U.S. Navy would have been an ideal candidate to lead the charge for improvements in the field. This did not occur, possibly because of the maritime-oriented conservatism of the service. One exception was the Naval Research Laboratory, whose

In May 1928, Weems used this Bausch and Lomb sextant and these navigation logs during his tutoring of Charles Lindbergh in celestial navigation. Weems's *Star Altitude Curves* and *Line of Position* books, along with his second-setting watch, were integral to reducing the computations for celestial fixes.

aircraft radio section yielded some significant innovations in the 1930s that would become critical in the World War II years.

The most significant shortcoming in research and development was at the National Advisory Committee for Aeronautics in the United States, whose broad mandate covered nearly all aspects of flight technology. Unfortunately, both its advisory committee and professional staff were focused on fundamental aerodynamic research instead of research in other areas. This was especially true with regard to navigation, which was lumped together with cockpit instrumentation, communications, and meteorology. The few notable innovations that did occur during the early and mid-1920s were primarily improvements in sextants made in Portugal, the United Kingdom, and the United States. The result of this inconsistent investment in navigation was that when Lindbergh flew to Paris in 1927, he could justifiably look to the failed *PN-9-1* voyage, which had been conducted with the benefit of all the resources the Navy had to offer, and conclude that neither sextants nor radios were worth the weight penalty they incurred in exchange for their marginal utility.

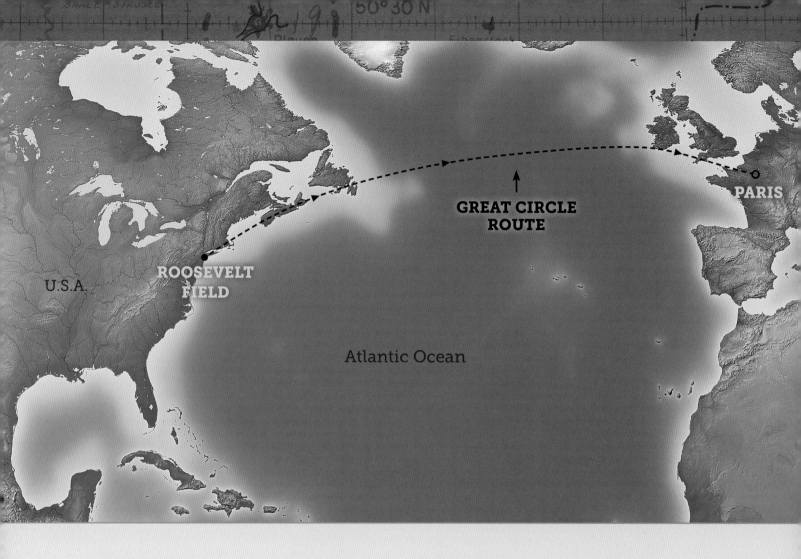

GREAT CIRCLE
ROUTE

PARIS

U.S.A.

ROOSEVELT
FIELD

Atlantic Ocean

TO PARIS *with* CHARLES LINDBERGH *and the*
SPIRIT OF ST. LOUIS

When Charles Lindbergh crossed the Atlantic from New
York to Paris in thirty-three and a half hours in May 1927, he
astounded the world—not because he had crossed the ocean
by air, something that had been accomplished many times
previously, but because he did it simply and economically.
However, Lindbergh's achievement was deceptive in that it
made navigation appear as a secondary concern that could be
easily dismissed.

Lindbergh's approach to navigation was simple dead
reckoning. While he was a seasoned military and airmail pilot,

ABOVE: Charles Lindbergh's route was
a straightforward great circle route,
providing the most direct path from
New York to Paris. He carried significant
fuel reserves to compensate for
navigational errors.

OPPOSITE: Charles Lindbergh with the
Spirit of St. Louis. The flight captured
popular imagination because it
demonstrated that transoceanic flight
was possible without direct government
involvement and minimal infrastructure.
Lindbergh made the feat look easier than
it was.

TOP: Lindbergh relied on this type of Pioneer earth inductor compass to maintain course during his Paris flight.

BOTTOM: Waltham eight-day clock used by Lindbergh to monitor his dead-reckoning flight path to Paris.

his skillset consisted almost exclusively of pilotage—navigating to fixed reference points on the ground. He taught himself to plot a great circle course, but he eschewed radio and celestial navigation. In the context of the *PN-9-1* debacle only two years earlier, this would have been a rational decision, but his decision to undertake the flight solo, made it even more so. Lindbergh later recalled:

> Since I could not take a sextant sighting at the same time I was flying my unstable Spirit of St. Louis, I saw nothing to be gained by buying and carrying a sextant.

His rationale for not taking a trained navigator was equally logical. Lindbergh noted:

> When I calculated the weight of a navigator and his cockpit to be equal to several hundred miles of range, and that, allowing for the greatest possible errors in navigation, I could not miss striking Europe's coastline somewhere, I decided to do my own navigating.

His navigation tools consisted of an earth inductor compass, a drift sight similar to that in use since World War I, and a clock. Lindberg encountered varying winds en route, but collectively they cancelled each other out. His landfall in Ireland within three miles (5 km) of his intended course lulled observers into thinking that his superb airmanship overcame shortcomings in navigational equipment or process. This would have disastrous result when many imitators attempted similar or even more difficult flights,

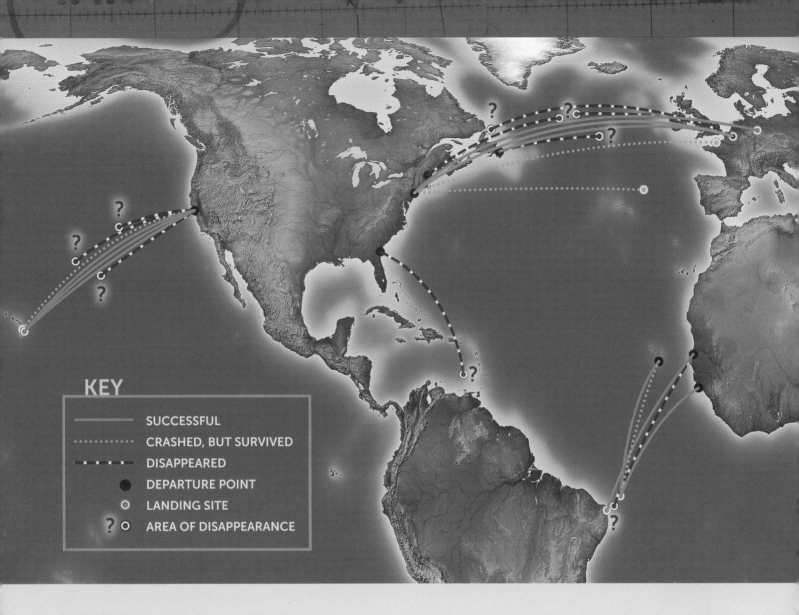

assuming that competence as an aviator could overcome navigational limitations.

The reality was far more complicated. While Lindbergh's approach to reaching Paris with his limited skills and equipment was relatively sound in the context of the time, it was not an effective method for long overwater flights. Two aircraft racing from California to Hawaii for a prize offered by pineapple magnate James Dole in August 1927 disappeared without a trace over the Pacific, as did an aircraft searching for them. These and similar losses forced Congress to regulate oceanic flight attempts. ✺

Charles Lindbergh's 1927 crossing of the Atlantic encouraged many imitators. As this map illustrates, many of the attempts that year ended badly, largely due to inadequate air navigation technologies. Government-funded expeditions typically fared better than private individuals setting out with limited training and equipment.

GREAT CIRCLE

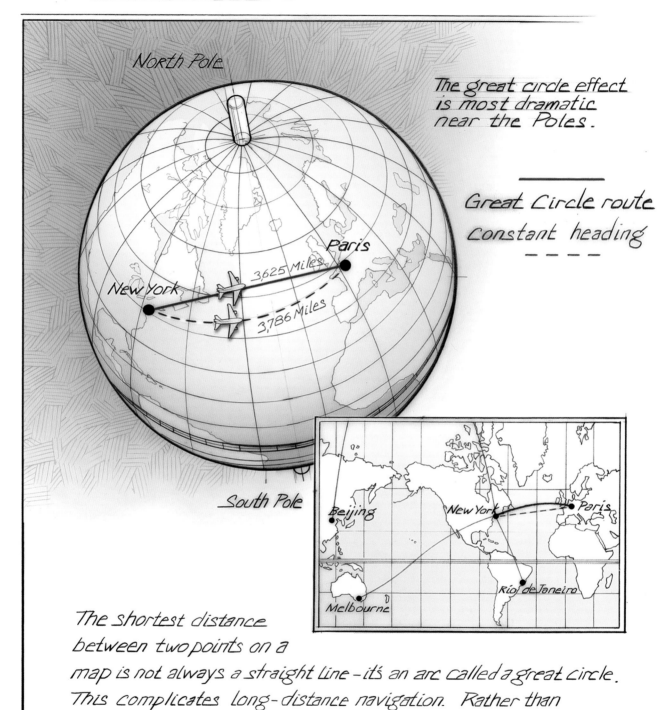

North Pole

The great circle effect is most dramatic near the Poles.

——— Great Circle route

constant heading
- - - - -

Paris

3,625 Miles

New York

3,786 Miles

South Pole

Beijing

New York

Paris

Rio de Janeiro

Melbourne

The shortest distance
between two points on a
map is not always a straight line – it's an arc called a great circle.
This complicates long-distance navigation. Rather than
stay on a constant heading, pilots must regularly adjust
their course to stay on the arc.

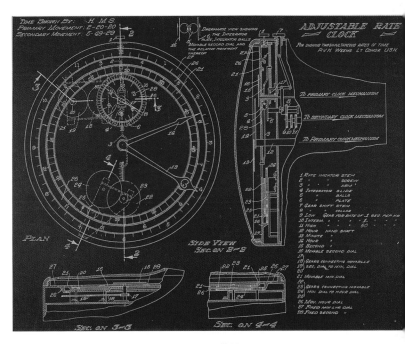

Better sextants and radios would only solve part of the problem. Aircraft were becoming faster at a time when computing a celestial fix required fifteen minutes under ideal conditions. To be practical in aircraft, air navigators needed much faster solutions for lines of position, even if they resulted in less accuracy. An Imperial Japanese Navy hydrographer, Shinkichi Ogura, developed a series of celestial sight reduction tables in the early 1920s that seemed to hold some promise of speedier calculations. In 1926, U.S. Navy Lieutenant Commander Philip Van Horn Weems, began exploring the possibilities of Ogura's work along with previously overlooked tables from Armistead Rust, a fellow naval officer. Weems launched his career as the most successful air navigation innovator of the interwar years with the development of his *Line of Position Book*, which repackaged Ogura and Rust's tables into a more aviator-friendly format. He soon followed that with his *Star Altitude Curves*, which provided quick graphical solutions for sextant sightings. This was not an entirely novel concept, but it was far easier to use than the Baker Navigating Machine carried on John Alcock and Arthur Whitten Brown's pioneering transatlantic flight of 1919.

Weems unofficially developed new tools during his appointment as navigation instructor at the U.S. Naval Academy. One of his most notable was a "second-setting" modification that allowed navigation watches to be "hacked" (or set via radio signal tone) to the second, which eliminated a small, but cumbersome, computation. He also aided development of an improved Bausch and Lomb aeronautical bubble sextant. Taken together, Weems's innovations, packaged as the "Weems System of Navigation," greatly reduced the time required for a celestial fix. An article in the August 1928 issue of *Popular Science Monthly* noted, "By ordinary methods it requires from fifteen minutes to half an hour to plot a position. . . . Weems' simplified method reduces this time to forty seconds on a starlit night, or two minutes by day." This simplification made celestial navigation practical in routine operations.

Naval commanders did not appreciate Weems's off-the-books efforts, and they censured him for operating outside his assigned field as a nonflying seagoing officer. However, by 1928, Weems's methods had begun to gain the notice of the aeronautical elite. Polar explorer Lincoln Ellsworth first sought out Weems for guidance.

TOP: Blueprint for a second-setting timepiece designed by P. V. H. Weems. The Waltham Watch Co. incorporated the features Weems proposed into one hundred watches made for navigation on Navy torpedo boats.

BOTTOM: One of the second-setting watches designed by P. V. H. Weems and made by Waltham Watch Co. This watch may have been a gift from Weems to Charles Lindbergh.

What solidified Weems's place in history was the attention of Charles Lindbergh. In February 1928, Lindbergh was flying his *Spirit of St. Louis* around Latin America and the Caribbean to promote commercial aviation when he became lost over the Straits of Florida after departing from Havana. He later recalled, "I had no notion whether I was flying north, south, east or west...I had flown at almost a right angle to my proper heading and it...put me close to three hundred miles off route!"

The incident forced Lindbergh to come to terms with the inadequacy of the navigational methods he had been using up to that point and he decided that before he again rejected the use of a sextant out of hand, he should at least know how to use it. Ellsworth suggested Weems as a tutor. Lindbergh placed a request through the White House for his temporary assignment as a personal navigation instructor in May 1928. Lindbergh became convinced that the Weems System was the only reliable method for overwater navigation. He later made this case to Pan American Airways when it began long-distance overwater operations.

News of Lindbergh's after-the-fact navigation training caused bemusement among some observers, with the *New York Times* wondering of him, "If the Colonel doesn't know how to navigate, who knows anything about anything?" The immediate outcome was that other distance flyers, explorers, and record setters approached Weems with requests for instruction. Through the interwar years, Weems ran a successful enterprise consisting of a navigation school and a mail-order navigational supply store. At first he did this with the help of his wife while he served at sea as executive officer aboard an oiler. The Navy never fully realized the asset it had in Weems and only briefly allowed him to serve as an air navigation expert in the Hydrographic Office in 1932, where he created the landmark *Air Almanac* supplement to the *Nautical Almanac*, which would prove crucial in World War II air operations.

Weems was a prolific champion of aerial celestial navigation, penning dozens of articles for the aeronautical trade press. In 1931, he wrote *Air Navigation*, which became the closest thing to a standardized textbook on the subject for the next decade.

TOP: Charles Lindbergh (second from left) poses in front of his Ryan B-1 Brougham, a plane of similar design to his *Spirit of St. Louis*, which it replaced. He underwent celestial navigation instruction in this aircraft with his tutor, P. V. H. Weems, in May 1928.

BOTTOM: P. V. H. Weems (center) stands with Charles Lindbergh and his wife Anne in 1930. Lindbergh's patronage launched Weems's air navigation business, while Lindbergh came to rely heavily on the Weems System of Navigation.

His voluminous correspondence with other navigational authorities and interested parties around the world established him as the nexus of a small, but increasingly significant, community of practitioners, which would become formalized after World War II as the Institute of Navigation. Through the 1930s, Weems attracted a steady stream of commercial, military, and private practitioners. Amy Johnson, the famed British aviator, remarked, "I consider [Weems] the best teacher in the world for that method, which is adapted to long flights." Richard Byrd, before setting off for his second Antarctic expedition, wrote Weems, requesting his services as navigator. When Weems demurred, Byrd responded, "Send me a list of the navigation equipment you think we should have. I want all those special gadgets and short-cut methods you believe in." Thomas Thurlow, the architect of the U.S. Army Air Forces wartime navigation program, maintained a steady correspondence with Weems and told him, "I preached the gospel of [the] *Air Almanac* and star curves and sold [my colleagues] on both." Even Fred Noonan, Amelia Earhart's hapless navigator on her final Pacific flight, was a pupil. Weems rushed to his defense after their disappearance, arguing, "Noonan has been flying for Pan American for many years and it was all in his day's work to hit smaller islands than Howland square on the nose."

Weems's other great contribution was as mentor to other innovators. The two most notable were Harold Gatty and Philip Dalton. Dalton was a fellow naval officer who had also been censured for innovating outside of channels. His expertise was in developing navigational plotters and manual flight computers, including the famed E-6B and the Mark 3 plotting board, which were produced in the tens of thousands during World War II. Gatty, an experienced marine navigator, became the manager of Weems's school while Weems was still away on sea duty. Whereas Weems was happiest as an innovator, Gatty became a master practitioner.

MEET *the* TEACHER

PHILIP VAN HORN WEEMS

Philip Van Horn Weems, a U.S. Navy officer, tutored Charles Lindbergh and other notable aviators of the 1930s in new techniques of celestial navigation, many of which incorporated his own improvements to the processes and equipment for fixing position. His greatest legacy was influencing the air navigation programs of U.S. airlines and the military. His techniques became the standard for long-range air navigation for three decades.

"Many flyers are really lost a good part of the time."

P. V. H. Weems

FLYING THE BEAM

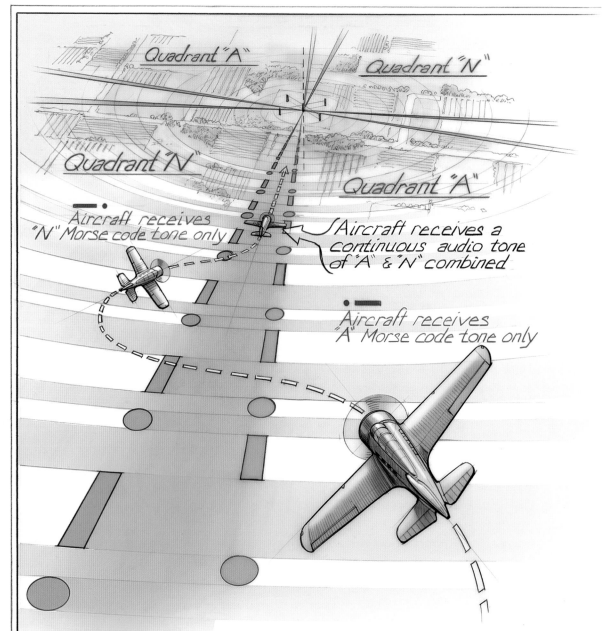

Quadrant "A"

Quadrant "N"

Quadrant "N"

Quadrant "A"

Aircraft receives "N" Morse code tone only

Aircraft receives a continuous audio tone of "A" & "N" combined

Aircraft receives "A" Morse code tone only

"Flying the beam" in the 1930s and 1940s meant using radio range stations to navigate. Pilots hoped to hear a steady tone on the radio that meant they were on course. If they drifted off course to either side, they would hear different sounds — a Morse code "A" or "N."

By 1931, he had already established himself as the leading air navigator for hire, supporting the efforts of such notable aviators as Roscoe Turner and Harold Bromley. When the adventurer Wiley Post approached him to serve as navigator for his 1931 around-the-world record flight attempt, the resulting fame brought Gatty to the attention of Albert Hegenberger and others in the Army Air Corps, who recruited him as the service's senior navigation engineer.

In 1932, Gatty helped establish a celestial navigation class as part of the Frontier Defense Research Unit at Rockwell Field, which was addressing the problem of navigating bombers toward naval targets in support of the coast defense mission that the Air Corps was determined to wrest from the Navy. An early student was Curtis LeMay, future chief of staff of the U.S. Air Force. While the Air Corps did adopt much of the Weems System through Gatty, it had its own innovator in Albert Hegenberger. While not as focused or as farsighted as Weems in the improvement of celestial navigation, he had a broader and more holistic approach to navigation. The noted navigator Harry Connor summarized that approach: "Precise navigation of long-range aircraft requires careful coordination of all three methods of navigation: celestial for position fixes, dead reckoning for flight between the fixes, and radio direction finding for getting into the airport on the nose and for radio bearings when the sky is not visible."

Perhaps the best indicator of Weems's importance came in the form of Charles Lindbergh's epic four-continent transoceanic airline route survey flight of 1933. Charles and his wife, Anne, who had learned celestial navigation from Gatty at Weems's suggestion while she was in the last stages of pregnancy, navigated their route in textbook form with the Weems System. They also designated Weems as the official chronicler of the flight.

Radio navigation emerged in prominence in the interwar years, and became especially important over land. In the cockpit, the new radio compass receivers of the 1930s could be used to display the heading to government-operated beacons and commercial broadcast radio stations. This required turning a loop antenna and

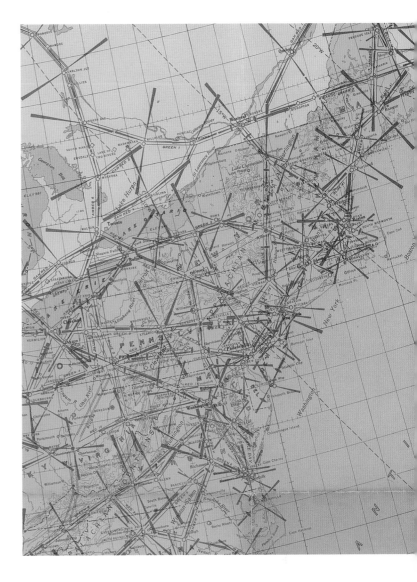

ABOVE: The electronic navigation infrastructure of the United States grew rapidly after 1930 in the form of the four-course Radio Range. Initially it primarily supported airmail routes. Busy regions like the Northeast were well served, but many Western states lacked effective coverage.

OPPOSITE: Radio Range navigation, or "flying the beam," took attention and skill, but it did not require a trained navigator. Before World War II, only international commercial flights regularly carried a navigator. Radio infrastructure placed government at the center of commercial air operations.

TOP: The massive single-engine ANT-25, used by the Soviets to dominate polar and long-distance flight records in the late 1930s. The 1937 Moscow–San Diego flight provided an ample demonstration that future wars would be shaped by the ability to navigate aircraft across great global expanses.

BOTTOM: The planned interception of the Italian liner *Rex* during a military exercise in 1938 demonstrated that the U.S. Army Air Corps had finally begun to master the problems of long-range overwater navigation.

charting the position of the aircraft based on the known location of radio transmitters on the ground. While celestial techniques enabled long-range navigation with some reliability, radio provided dependable all-weather guidance over shorter distances, and with less skill required and fewer opportunities for error. There were enormous operational differences between the two approaches. Celestial navigation required little financial investment, while radio navigation required extensive government subsidies for the necessary infrastructure.

In the United States and much of Europe, governments used subsidized airmail services to pave the way for passenger airline service, both internally and abroad. These services were viable only if they could sustain reliably scheduled operations, which meant safe navigation at night and in low visibility. The solution was the development of airways—the aeronautical equivalent of railways—in which ground-based beacons would guide aircraft point-to-point between principal airfields. Through the 1920s, airways consisted of lighted beacons to enable night navigation. Beginning in the early 1930s, all-weather radio beacons supplemented the lighted beacons for en route internal navigation. As a subset of radio navigation technology, new procedures and landing aids were developed for low-visibility landings. In the United States, the dominant technology from the early 1930s to the early 1950s was the four-course Radio Range for navigation and approach guidance. This line-of-sight system utilized overlapping audio tones to establish four directional courses radiating from the stations. While not ideal in accuracy or ease of use, the Radio Range served its purpose and allowed the rapid growth of reliable all-weather commercial service along internal domestic airways.

In Europe, nations preferred high-powered nondirectional beacons to the Radio Range and supplemented them with a sophisticated network of ground-based direction finding stations. These determined a plane's position based on its transmissions and then radioed the plane this triangulated position. This cumbersome predecessor to modern air-traffic control radar illustrates a tension that has persisted between navigational methods that emphasize pilot discretion and those that favor centralized control.

Transoceanic airline service was still a novelty at the start of World War II, but it was the one area in which long-range air navigation had become routinely reliable. While military air forces around the world were struggling with the place of the air navigator and what tools they would use, the flying boats of Pan American and Imperial Airways paired competent celestial navigators with radio operators. When America entered World War II, the first classes of military navigators came through the Pan American Airways Navigation School.

Despite these successful demonstrations of technical prowess, air navigation in the late 1930s remained an uncertain art. As British navigational authority Sir Francis Chichester noted in 1939, "At a conservative estimate, 50 percent of the [aircraft] accidents in the last five years have been due to bad navigation." Many of these accidents were due to disorientation in poor weather, typically in descending to the airport, which was as much a problem of control as it was navigation.

The lack of universally reliable techniques continued to frustrate practitioners on both sides of the Atlantic as war broke out. Frederick "Dickie" Richardson, who helped bring the Royal Air Force's navigation program to fruition at the beginning of World War II, recalled, "Not surprisingly, the USA, land of 'Riding the [Radio] Range,' had little to offer on navigating in an air war. Without radio ranges, they would at least need daylight to see where they were going in Europe. Capt [sic] Weems USN apart, I couldn't put my hands on a single innovative publication from North America." Perhaps the most important contribution of Weems to the Royal Air Force was the *Air Almanac*, which had not been published since its trial run by the U.S. Naval Observatory in 1933. The British government began printing new editions on the eve of World War II.

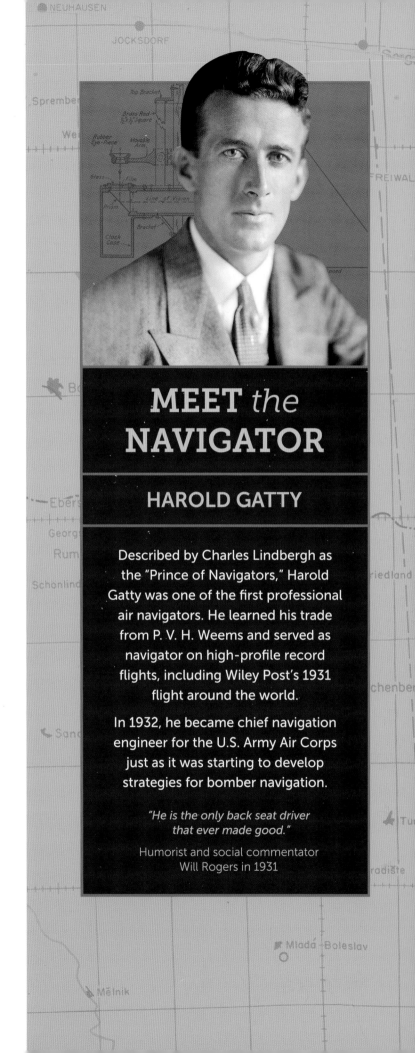

MEET *the* NAVIGATOR

HAROLD GATTY

Described by Charles Lindbergh as the "Prince of Navigators," Harold Gatty was one of the first professional air navigators. He learned his trade from P. V. H. Weems and served as navigator on high-profile record flights, including Wiley Post's 1931 flight around the world.

In 1932, he became chief navigation engineer for the U.S. Army Air Corps just as it was starting to develop strategies for bomber navigation.

"He is the only back seat driver that ever made good."
Humorist and social commentator Will Rogers in 1931

NAVIGATION
GONE WRONG

HAWAIIAN
ISLANDS

Pacific
Ocean

⊗

HOWLAND
ISLAND

AMELIA EARHART DISAPPEARS

During an around-the-world flight attempt in 1937, Amelia Earhart and her expert navigator, Fred Noonan, vanished in the South Pacific.

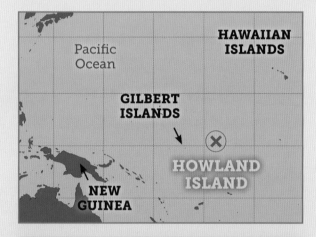

Pacific
Ocean

HAWAIIAN
ISLANDS

GILBERT
ISLANDS

⊗

HOWLAND
ISLAND

NEW
GUINEA

WHAT HAPPENED

The Lockheed Model 10E's limited range forced them to use tiny and remote Howland Island as a refueling stop. Missing it would guarantee disaster. Their eastbound route led them into headwinds that cost them fuel. Clouds hampered their navigational sightings. The plane was poorly outfitted for navigation and long-range communication, and neither Earhart nor Noonan knew Morse code, critical for the ship-based radio direction finding system the Navy used to support their flight. They overflew the Gilbert Islands, their best means of fixing position, in the dark.

THE CONSEQUENCES

Their flight required an effective blend of dead reckoning, celestial navigation, and radio direction finding, but poor planning, inexperience, and circumstance compromised all three. They never reached Howland Island and likely perished in the ocean.

LESSONS LEARNED

The exact errors that caused Earhart and Noonan to miss Howland Island may never be known, but their disappearance served as a warning to other aviators not to take navigation lightly.

ABOVE: Amelia Earhart and Fred Noonan vanished on June 2, 1937, between New Guinea and Howland Island.

BELOW: Earhart and Noonan take off from Caripito, Venezuela, in their Lockheed Model 10E.

Several flights in the late 1930s pointed to the potential of effective military air navigation. In July 1937, a Soviet single-engine ANT-25 made a successful 7,100-mile (11,425 km) nonstop flight from Moscow to southern California by way of the North Pole. A survey of the plane's navigational equipment revealed a detailed awareness of the Weems System equipment and methodology. Of all the interwar distance flights, this was the most challenging. The area above the Arctic Circle is largely devoid of navigational aids, the problem of magnetic variation between the geographic and magnetic north poles greatly complicates navigation, and Mercator charts typically used in aviation are so distorted near the poles that they become useless.

In May 1938, future airpower architect Lieutenant Colonel Ira Eaker dispatched a flight of Boeing Y1B-17 bombers to intercept the Italian liner *Rex*, which was sailing some six hundred miles (965 km) off the East Coast as part of a demonstration during a military exercise. This complex navigational test was led by Lieutenant Curtis LeMay, Harold Gatty's former student. While LeMay was intercepting the *Rex*, another milestone navigational achievement was underway. Howard Hughes, another Weems-trained aviator, was smashing the around-the-world speed record using the latest navigational techniques with noted airline navigator Harry Connor and military navigational authority Thomas Thurlow. Among the lessons the flight revealed was a need for an astrodome, a clear aerodynamic dome to facilitate celestial observation from within the aircraft.

Technical tweaks alone would not be sufficient to meet the military demands of World War II. Weems's techniques proved essential for many long-range operations during wartime, particularly in the Pacific, where celestial navigation was well suited to the more favorable weather conditions. Over Europe, an entirely different problem emerged for which Weems and Hegenberger had little to offer. Guiding large formations to targets in poor weather and through heavy anti-aircraft fire was not possible with celestial navigation—a fact that precipitated a technological crisis.

TOP: The Fairchild-Maxson Mark I Line of Position Computer of 1938. *Nautical* or *Air Almanac* data sets were coded onto cams in the cassette on the left. This was a remarkable attempt to automate line of position computations, but it was too expensive and heavy for regular use.

BOTTOM: Howard Hughes's Lockheed 14 was a showcase of the latest navigational techniques, many of which would soon be standardized into wartime service.

The map shows labeled locations along the route: NOVOSIBIRSK, BLAGOVESHCHENSK, IRKUTSK, KHABAROVSK, SOLOMON, FAIRBANKS, EDMONTON, CLEVELAND, HARBOR GRACE, NEW YORK, CHESTER, BERLIN, HANNOVER, MOSCOW.

CIRCLING THE WORLD *with the*
WINNIE MAE

From June 23 to July 1, 1931, one-eyed aviator Wiley Post and his navigator, the Tasmanian-born Harold Gatty, circumnavigated the northern hemisphere in eight days and sixteen hours aboard the Lockheed Vega 5C *Winnie Mae*, shattering the twenty-one-day speed record set by the *Graf Zeppelin* airship two years earlier. The flight was most significant because it showcased a mature form of air navigation, with significant advances in celestial navigation and dead reckoning, that was not present in aviation when Charles Lindbergh had crossed the Atlantic a mere four years before.

ABOVE: Wiley Post and Harold Gatty shattered the around-the-world speed record. Later, the standards for circumglobal flight records were strengthened to reflect equatorial circumnavigation distances.

OPPOSITE: Wiley Post (right) and Harold Gatty (left). Post's roughneck personality made him an ideal Depression-era hero for America. Gatty's polished persona completed the odd pairing, but the combination worked surprisingly well and brought them both great fame, if not fortune.

There is little doubt that at the time of the flight Harold Gatty was the most capable air navigator in the United States, and perhaps the world. A former maritime navigator, he studied under P. V. H. Weems and was soon manager of the Weems System of Navigation and chief instructor at his school. While Weems was a great innovator, Gatty was the master practitioner who instructed most of the school's elite clientele in the early 1930s.

Gatty was an avid inventor with a particular interest in developing new drift indicators. When he signed on with Post for the flight, he brought a very thorough and methodical approach to navigation. Post, in turn, was willing to gamble on a number of modifications and pieces of new equipment for the flight. This included a celestial observation hatch cut into the cabin roof and a slot for Gatty's prototype drift indicator in the side of the fuselage. Gatty was most dependent on an E. S. Ritchie aperiodic compass and a Weems-improved Bausch and Lomb sextant. He also carried Weems's *Line of Position* and *Star Altitude Curves* books.

An important requirement for any navigator is a stable platform for observations, and Post benefitted from a revolution in cockpit instruments. This was the first overseas distance flight undertaken with the new Sperry gyroscopic artificial horizon and directional gyro. These were essential as weather prevented Gatty from conducting many celestial observations during the transatlantic crossing.

TOP: Lockheed Vegas, like the *Winnie Mae*, were popular aircraft among distance fliers and record setters during the late 1920s and early 1930s, because of their speed, range, and ruggedness.

BOTTOM: Harold Gatty developed this drift indicator while at the Weems System of Navigation. This type became an industry standard for determining ground speed and wind correction angles.

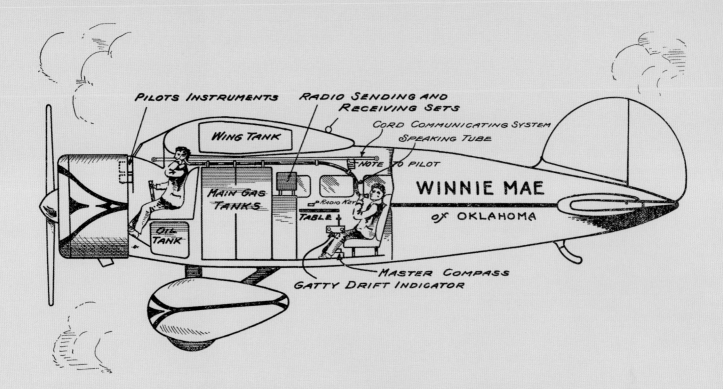

PILOTS INSTRUMENTS
RADIO SENDING AND RECEIVING SETS
CORD COMMUNICATING SYSTEM
SPEAKING TUBE
WING TANK
NOTE TO PILOT
WINNIE MAE
of OKLAHOMA
MAIN GAS TANKS
RADIO KEY
TABLE
OIL TANK
MASTER COMPASS
GATTY DRIFT INDICATOR

Post and Gatty received a raucous welcome on their return to New York, and President Herbert Hoover awarded both with the Distinguished Flying Cross. Gatty's citation read:

Mr. Gatty, as navigator, made an airplane flight around the world . . . not only eclipsing in time all previous world flights but also by his intrepid courage, remarkable endurance, and matchless skill materially advancing the science of aerial navigation.

In 1933, Post undertook a second circumnavigation, but this time he flew solo. It was also a great technical achievement, showcasing the world's first practical autopilot and a superb new radio compass; however, it must also be seen as remarkably reckless. Post's faith in technology over skill won out in that instance, but many other aviators would perish doing the same. ❁

TOP: The *Winnie Mae* was a flying laboratory for new aeronautical technologies. Post converted the aircraft a number of times during his five years of ownership.

BOTTOM: Harold Gatty, an Australian, receives the Distinguished Flying Cross from President Herbert Hoover at the White House on August 18, 1932. This was an exceptional honor for a noncitizen.

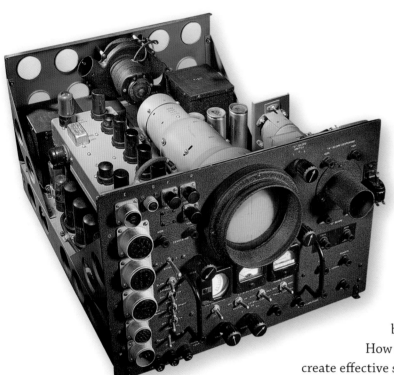

This AN/APS-2 Receiver and Plan Position Indicator (PPI) generated cathode ray tube images of terrain and vessels within the line of sight of the Navy patrol aircraft that carried it. This was particularly useful when operating in coastal areas.

World War II posed unprecedented challenges for air navigators. Of all the combatants, the United States faced the greatest obstacles, since it had to project power across two oceans and operate above trackless deserts and jungles as well as cities and settled areas. However, air navigation was a human problem as much as a technical one. Both the U.S. Army Air Forces and the U.S. Navy started the war with less than one hundred competent celestial air navigators between them, but ended the war with nearly 100,000 trained. How did the United States and its British allies come to create effective systems of global navigation? And how did tens of thousands of nineteen-year-olds with less than two months of training accomplish what only a few dozen had done before?

Most Allied air operations were not significantly hamstrung by navigational errors, an indication of both military-sponsored technical innovation and the enormous resources invested in the problem. While dead reckoning and celestial navigation remained critical and underwent evolutionary cycles of improvement, the real revolutions in navigation occurred in radio. Specifically, the combination of quartz oscillators, microwave emitters, and cathode ray tubes enabled the development of an entirely new class of electronic navigation aids. The ability to time signals electronically to millionths of a second for the purpose of positioning not only transformed the process of navigation, but it also revolutionized the science of destruction.

Most significant among the new technologies for the war effort was radar. While initially used primarily as an air defense tool for locating aircraft, the development of the cavity magnetron for emitting microwave signals enabled development of British and American navigation radars that could map landforms while airborne. This electronic form of all-weather, medium-range pilotage operated independently of ground-based transmitters. While this was of little use over open oceans, deserts, or polar regions, in areas such as northwestern Europe the often-overlooked innovation of navigational radar provided a potent weapon for the Allies that far surpassed the destructiveness of the vaunted jets and rockets of Nazi Germany.

The consequences of this transformation were profound. Before radar-guided strategic bombing missions began in earnest in 1943, frequent cloud cover prevented attacks. Radar allowed the process of "bombing through overcast," but it limited targets to those areas that most effectively reflected radar signals, which were large concentrations of buildings. In other words, when cloud cover limited the visibility of individual industrial or military targets, cities became the de facto overcast target of choice, even if their military value was not obvious. Given the choice between aborting missions on cloudy days or striking population centers with radar to keep the pressure up on the enemy, British and American commanders nearly always chose the latter.

The addition of sophisticated electronic systems like radar complicated the experience of the navigator. Given that interpreting radarscope images was perhaps more art than science, bombers and patrol aircraft carried an additional crewmember, nicknamed "Mickey," to run their navigational radar. Additionally, a radio operator was usually responsible for monitoring radio beacons in Allied territory. Thus, the navigator had to manage inputs from other crewmembers as well as his own equipment.

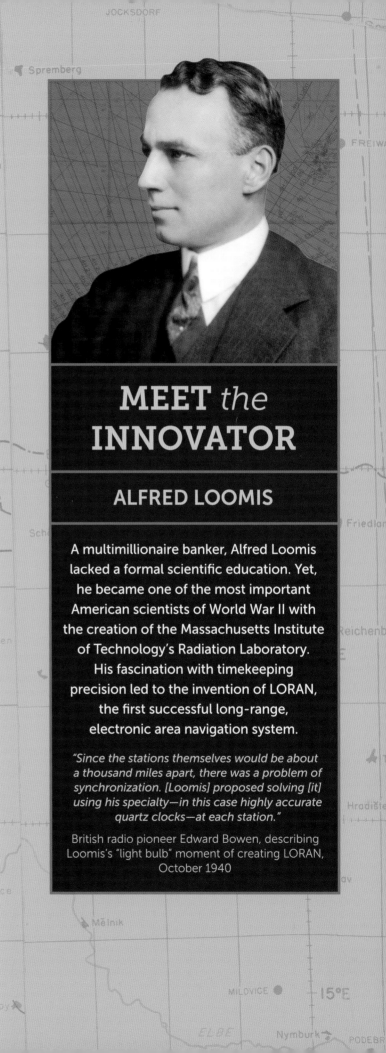

MEET *the* INNOVATOR

ALFRED LOOMIS

A multimillionaire banker, Alfred Loomis lacked a formal scientific education. Yet, he became one of the most important American scientists of World War II with the creation of the Massachusetts Institute of Technology's Radiation Laboratory. His fascination with timekeeping precision led to the invention of LORAN, the first successful long-range, electronic area navigation system.

"Since the stations themselves would be about a thousand miles apart, there was a problem of synchronization. [Loomis] proposed solving [it] using his specialty—in this case highly accurate quartz clocks—at each station."

British radio pioneer Edward Bowen, describing Loomis's "light bulb" moment of creating LORAN, October 1940

HYPERBOLIC SYSTEM

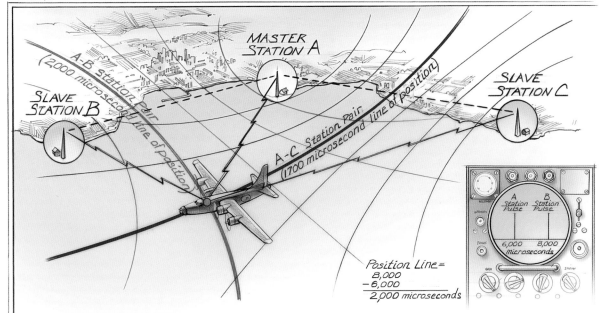

MASTER STATION A

SLAVE STATION B

SLAVE STATION C

A-B station Pair
(2000 microsecond line of position)

A-C Station Pair
(1700 microsecond line of position)

A
Station Pulse

B
Station Pulse

6,000   8,000
microseconds

Position Line=
8,000
−6,000
2,000 microseconds

In a hyperbolic system like LORAN, a receiver on an aircraft or ship picks up radio signals broadcast by one or more pairs of radio stations spaced hundreds of miles apart. The system works by measuring the time difference between signals from the two stations. By tuning in different pairs, the navigator could plot lines of position in the form of hyperbolas (arcs) that intersect to give a precise location.

Crystal oscillators facilitated development of hyperbolic systems that had enormous implications for wartime military operations. This line of technical development continues today through satellite-based systems such as GPS.

The same mix of technologies that enabled radar also facilitated another class of electronic positioning dependent on measuring very tiny units of time: hyperbolic area navigation systems, named for the hyperbola, or curved lines, that resulted from plotted lines of position on a chart. Unlike navigation radar, these systems required a complex ground-based infrastructure. They worked by establishing lines of position based on the time difference in signal reception from a pair of stations: a master that initiated a pulse, and a slave station that transmitted once it had received the master's pulse. Principal wartime forms were Gee, LORAN, Decca, and SHORAN. Gee was a shorter wavelength system that was primarily line of sight, which worked well over land. LORAN (Long-range Navigation) used longer wavelengths to provide ground wave coverage over water of more than three hundred miles (500 km) in daytime and upward of one thousand miles (1,600 km) at night using skywaves. An evolution late in the war known as Skywave Synchronized LORAN (SS LORAN) extended better-than-celestial fix accuracy to ranges of one thousand miles at night,

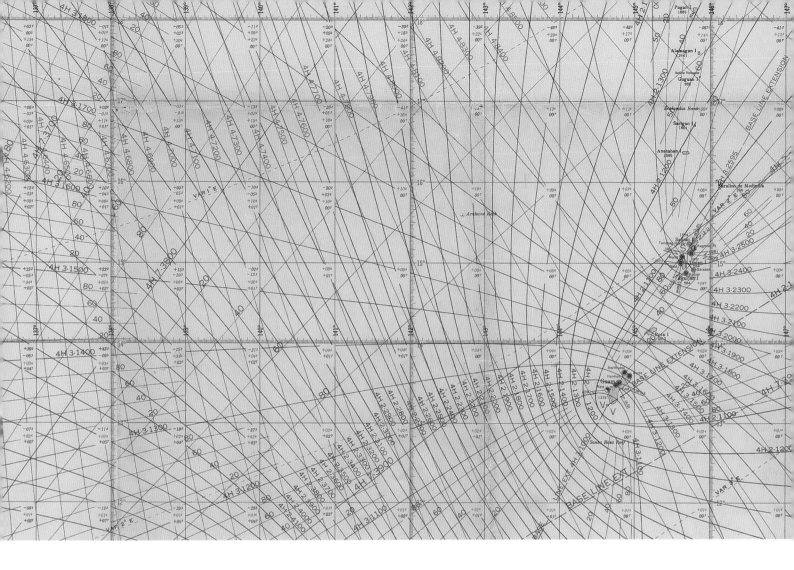

ABOVE: The hyperbolic chart was critical to locating a LORAN Line of Position (LOP). The operator would interpret oscilloscope amplitudes as time delay intervals from transmitting station pairs and then match that time delay to a corresponding hyperbolic line on the chart.

LEFT: LORAN station in Adak, Alaska. LORAN stations were often positioned several hundred miles apart (and farther still for Skywave Synchronized LORAN), frequently resulting in their placement in remote and inhospitable locations.

Gil Cohen's painting *The Regensburg Mission* depicts Harry Crosby, lead navigator of the "Bloody" 100th Bomb Group, at his plotting table in the nose of a B-17 bomber. During this August 17, 1943, strike on German factories, Americans suffered one of the worst aerial losses of the war, with six hundred men in sixty planes shot down.

even over land. The Gee ground infrastructure could also be repurposed as a pulsed beaconing system to be used with the oscilloscopes for Gee (Gee-H) and radar (Micro-H). These "beaconing" systems facilitated blind bombing system with accuracies similar to radar, but which could be employed against targets that lacked sufficient radar definition. SHORAN, a system that emerged out of RCA's early experience with television, provided blind bombing accuracies better than most navigational radar, allowing for the targeting of viaducts and other small structures, regardless of the weather.

These electronic systems were complex, expensive, heavy, and prone to failure. They also left vast gaps in coverage that could be filled only by competent dead reckoning and celestial fixes. Averaging sextants and cabin top astrodomes made sights more reliable, and kept celestial navigation as the preferred backup technique. Electromechanical analog computers helped reduce the negative effects of calculating fixes at faster airspeeds. The most prominent of these was the Air

Position Indicator (nicknamed "the brain"), a British invention that continuously resolved latitude and longitude based on inputs from airspeed and gyro compass sensors and corrected for estimated winds. Though far from the capability of Cold War inertial navigation systems, these wartime innovations increasingly moved navigational practice from an art performed by select and highly experienced individuals to a kind of science in which technicians managed an array of complex electronic systems.

New technologies also shaped the training of tens of thousands of navigators. While nothing compared to actual in-flight training, a variety of sophisticated ground trainers offered procedural experience. P. V. H. Weems once again came to prominence as he worked closely with Edwin Link to develop a complex multicrew simulator, called the Celestial Navigation Trainer (CNT), which provided a moving collimated star field, moving photographic terrain depictions and simulated radio signals. Navigators could practice on equipment ranging from drift sights, astrographs, sextants, astrocompasses, and LORAN receivers with the CNT.

The U.S. Army Air Forces and U.S. Navy employed a full range of dedicated aircraft to train their navigators. This was especially important because of the unique physiological demands incurred as navigator. Often riding backward and looking down through drift sights while in turbulence, the navigator was the crewmember most likely to suffer from airsickness. Most navigators were "washed-out" pilot candidates who failed to complete training but showed strong mathematical aptitude. Those without that inclination often became bombardiers.

Each theater imposed its own unique set of challenges for navigators. Writing in his memoir *A Wing and a Prayer*, 100th Bomb Group lead navigator Major Harold Crosby noted the problems in navigating in the European theater before radar and Gee became widespread as navigational aids: "The Army Air Forces was stressing celestial navigation and crews were able to make the Atlantic crossing better than I did, but in our supply shop, octants began to pile up as new navigators realized they could not be used on missions and they got in the way in the barracks." Celestial navigation was not used over

Unlike pilots, few navigators became renowned for their exploits. Harry Crosby is one of the exceptions. His memoir *A Wing and a Prayer* is often regarded as one of the best accounts of the daylight bombing campaigns over Western Europe.

ABOVE: ZB-1 Radio Homing Adaptor, one of the most critical tools for carrier-based navigation. It provided a method for direction finding that did not reveal the carrier's location to the enemy.

OPPOSITE: Marine Corps Corsair pilot Reinhardt Leu used this YE-ZB chart and code sheet during 1943 in the New Hebrides islands of the South Pacific.

FOLLOWING: World War II marked a new era in navigation as electronic systems came to dominate operations over much of the globe. As this 1944 Royal Air Force training poster indicates, these systems performed many functions over a wide range of operations.

Europe, since the need to avoid flak and fighter concentrations made for frequent course changes that were not amenable to stable celestial navigation. It played a far greater role in overwater operations in the Pacific and Mediterranean.

Crosby also recalled that radio navigation and dead reckoning were highly problematic in the crucial months of 1943, when the bombing campaign over northwestern Europe hit its stride: "In Germany and France the Germans changed their transmitters irregularly, and we could never depend on a radio fix. During much of our flying we were over the clouds. . . . With pilots having to jiggle their airspeed and headings to keep in formation, the navigator could not dead reckon." Thus, for many combat operations, navigators did little more than pick out landmarks and guess the wind. Of course, many aircraft (single-seat fighters, for instance) did not have the luxury of either a navigator or sophisticated equipment. With the wide range of diverse and identifiable landmarks in northwestern Europe, this was a tolerable situation. In poor weather, the hapless pilot hoped to come within range of ground control radar if he became lost. After the invasion of France in 1944, this became far less of a problem as ground-based radar coverage rapidly extended eastward. Navigating a single-seat fighter from a carrier that moved in a different direction after departure was an entirely different kind of problem.

The distinct problem of navigation in carrier-borne aircraft was also solved principally in electronic form, although in one that was more elegantly simple than radar or hyperbolic navigation systems. On the eve of America's entry into World War II, the Aircraft Radio branch of the Naval Research Laboratory implemented the YE-ZB system to guide naval aircraft. The system consisted of a transmitter on a ship or island airfield and a radio homing adapter that plugged into the aircraft's standard communications equipment. The transmitter used double modulation so that it would not be detectable without the homing adapter. When received, the signal came out as a single letter Morse code identifier. With a coded reference sheet that changed daily, the pilot could instantly determine a thirty-degree sector of bearing from the transmitter and plot a reciprocal course. Other naval innovations included a plotting board that allowed tracking of relative movements from the airplane's home carrier.

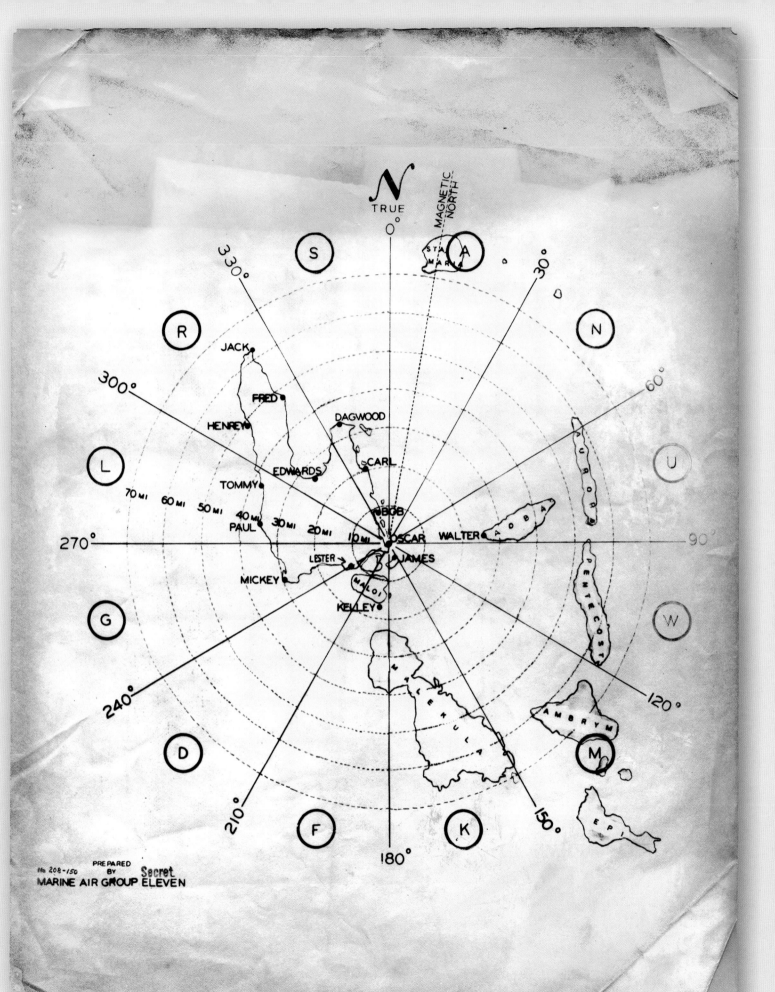

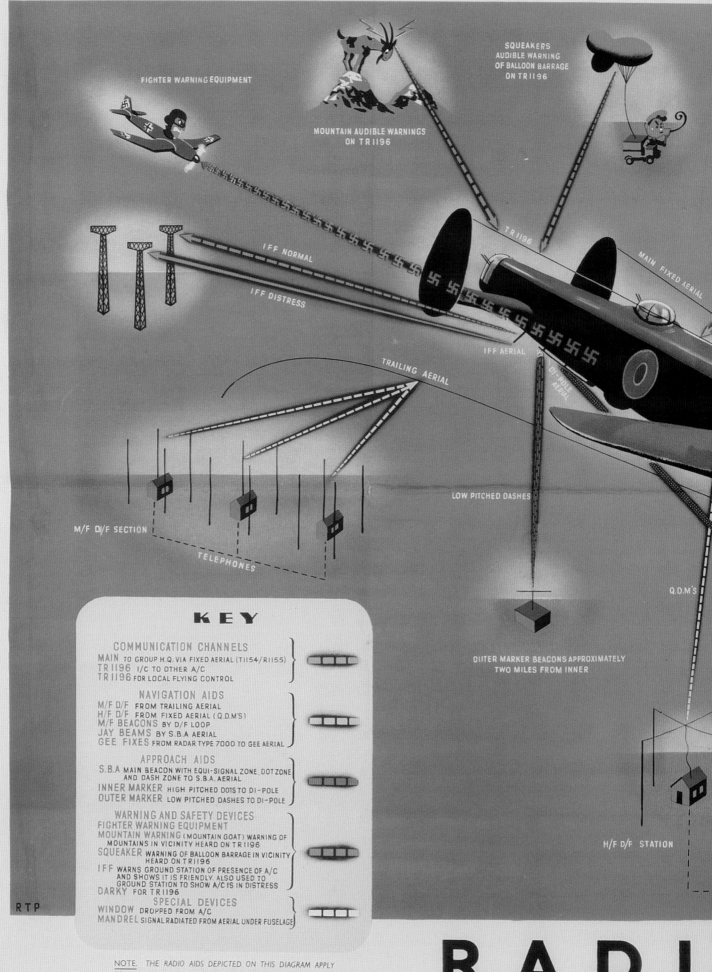

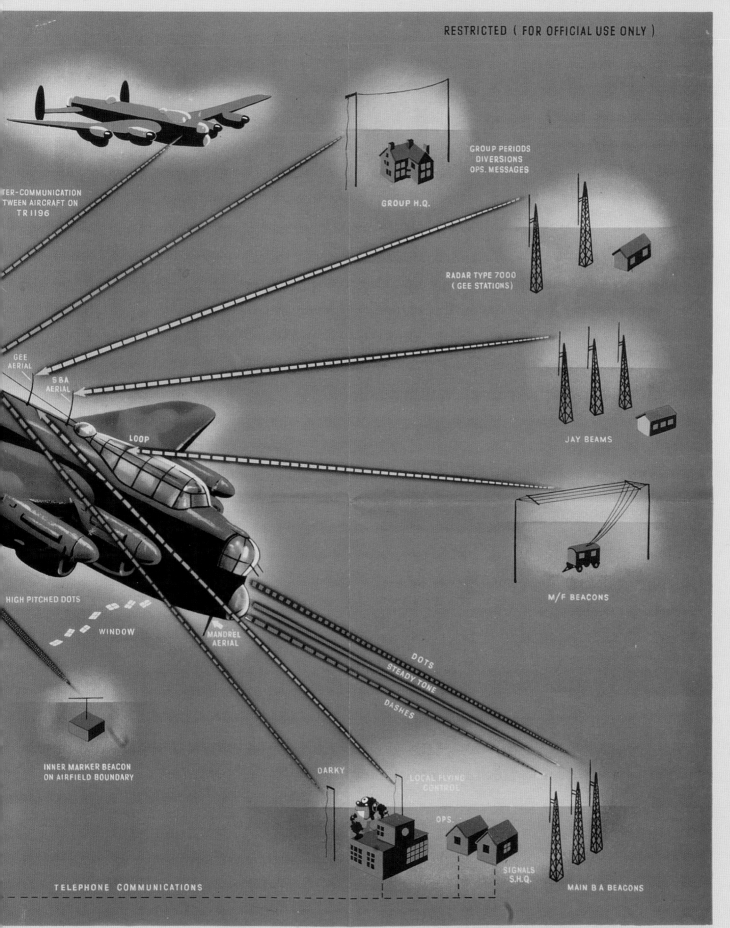

This K-system electromechanical computer integrated inputs from data sensors, radar, and the plane's bombsight to navigate to a target and deliver a nuclear bomb from a B-47 or early model B-52.

The trends toward automation and electronic guidance that began in World War II proliferated during the Cold War. Military requirements continued to stimulate the greatest innovations, but many of these technologies also evolved in the civil sector. Jet aircraft operating at high subsonic speeds above the Arctic Circle posed new navigational challenges, as did the need to guide ballistic and cruise missiles to their targets. The most effective solutions were those that integrated multiple approaches, including Doppler radar, autonomous celestial fixes, and inertial navigation systems. Many wartime electronic navigation systems also evolved into accurate and reliable civil navigation systems.

The rise of the Soviet Union as the principal American adversary made investigation of the problems of polar navigation a top priority in the early postwar years. The B-29 units assigned to explore this problem were carrying three navigators and one thousand pounds (450 kg) of navigational gear. New jet bombers like the Boeing B-47 traveled twice as fast, but they could accommodate only a third of the crew of a B-29. This resulted in the K-system, often described as a "magic black box," that integrated bombsights, radar, and air position computers. This system did nothing to eliminate the weight, cost, or complexity of the earlier equipment and often increased it, but it did allow a single crewmember to navigate effectively during high-speed, low-altitude operations over polar regions without external radio aids. New techniques of navigation came into widespread use, such as Polar Grid, which eliminated difficulties of using rapidly changing

compass headings near the pole, and Pressure Pattern Flying, a new way of plotting courses to follow favorable wind patterns high in the atmosphere. The advent of autonomous celestial astronavigation systems in the late 1950s, combined with inertial navigation units, built on the early 1950s advances of the K-system to create a truly robust global navigation system on the most sophisticated strategic aircraft.

However, the vast majority of military and commercial aircraft operated without the enormously expensive and heavy K-system type components, instead of relying on improvements to more conventional technologies. As transoceanic airline service became regular in the early postwar years, former military navigators brought their considerable skillsets to their peacetime occupations, including celestial navigation. With the introduction of pressurized airliners, a new concern emerged. The wartime astrodomes that facilitated celestial observation were not structurally sound under pressurization as was vividly illustrated

Republic F-84F, named *Excalibur IV*, flown by Charles Blair as his personal navigation research aircraft during the mid-1950s while working on long-range single pilot navigation problems.

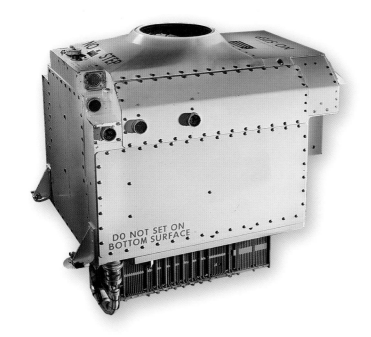

TOP: Nortronics NAS-14V2 Astroinertial Navigation System. It provided better than 300-foot (91 m) accuracy at speeds of 2,200 mph (3,540 kph) for Lockheed SR-71 crews, who nicknamed it "R2-D2."

BOTTOM: Lockheed SR-71. Autonomous astroinertial systems used on aircraft like this are still in use today on sensitive strategic systems such as the Northrop B-2 bomber.

in a 1947 incident in which a TWA navigator was sucked from a Lockheed Constellation at altitude over the Atlantic. The solution came in the form of the Kollsman periscopic sextant, which eliminated drag when not in use and did not compromise the pressure integrity of the cabin.

LORAN and Decca emerged from World War II as effective commercial navigation systems, but the International Civil Aviation Organization (ICAO), under pressure from the United States, ultimately adopted the American Very High Frequency Omni Range (VOR) and Distance Measuring Equipment (DME) systems as the core navigational technology for land-based navigational infrastructure. While the early four-course Radio Range had only four defined bearings emanating from the stations, VORs broadcast in a full 360 degrees, taking advantage of the rapid improvements in crystal oscillators. DME made precise positioning possible by giving distance on VOR bearings. This was not true area navigation, but it provided a greatly enhanced functionality and reliability in the context of the established airway system.

Inertial navigation migrated from submarines to aircraft by the late 1950s, though the first systems for civil aviation followed a decade later. Inertial navigation could provide reliable short-term guidance without correction for only thirty minutes or so. In the case of high performance strategic aircraft like the Lockheed SR-71 reconnaissance aircraft, when coupled with a highly accurate astronavigation system, inertial guidance could yield accuracies of 200 feet (61 m) while traveling at 2,200 mph (3,540 kph). Such systems required a clear view of the sky. In the case of the SR-71's cruising altitude of at least 80,000 feet (24,385 m), this was never a problem. Most aircraft navigation used far less exotic equipment. The trend away from the vacuum tubes of the mid–twentieth century toward solid-state circuits and, by the early 1980s, microprocessors, yielded steady improvements in accuracy and reliability in subsequent decades. By the 1970s, the navigator had disappeared from commercial aviation, as electronics became more capable. Older military aircraft, like the Boeing B-52, have retained a crew position for a navigator, but with the gradual retirement of these aircraft from service, the profession of air navigator will be at an end.

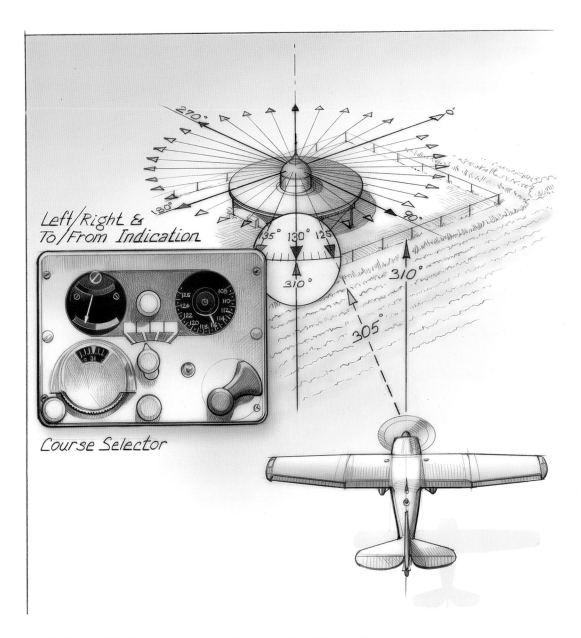

Left/Right & To/From Indication

Course Selector

Nonetheless, Cold War electronics and automation did not eliminate the need for human judgment in navigation. As Charles Blair succinctly noted in 1953: "Today's electronically guided airman is still a human. He does not think he is a superman. If he does, he doesn't stay with us very long." This problem persists as twenty-first-century airline events have revealed the interface between human flight crews and automation to be the most consistent source of major airline accidents. As the use of unmanned aerial systems proliferates, these concerns become increasingly relevant as artificial intelligence has yet to demonstrate the mix of wisdom and intuition critical to aeronautical decision making.

Many challenges remained for navigation in the air. By this time, radio navigation techniques were being enhanced for use in an even more difficult environment: navigating into space.

Very-high frequency Omni Range (VOR) stations began replacing the four-course Radio Range stations in the early 1950s. They are only now slowly giving way to GPS-based navigation and approach systems.

FAIRBANKS,
ALASKA

45°

60°

Arctic
Ocean

75°

→ NORTH
POLE

→ BARDUFOSS,
NORWAY

ACROSS THE ARCTIC *with*
CHARLES BLAIR

In May 1951, Charles Blair flew a single seat North American P-51C Mustang named *Excalibur III* across the North Pole from Bardufoss, Norway, to Fairbanks, Alaska. He carried just over a hundred pounds of navigational equipment at a time when U.S. Air Force B-29 crews conducting similar flights carried multiple navigators and hundreds of pounds of navigational equipment.

In his career as a transatlantic airline and charter pilot, Blair had consulted previously with P. V. H. Weems, but he was a largely self-taught navigator. His method centered on the mostly original idea of "pre-comp" navigation, which used a series of sun or

ABOVE: Charles Blair was not the first pilot to cross the North Pole, but he was the first to make it look easy.

moon lines computed in advance based on specific departure times. While an autopilot stabilized the plane, Blair took simple sun or moon sights with a twelve-dollar war surplus astrocompass and compared them with predicted sights for offset tracks at that particular time to determine a correction.

Blair employed Weems to do much of the computation. The planning worked nearly flawlessly, and Blair told reporters covering the flight that it was easy. An irritated Weems then cautioned Blair:

> *That kind of navigation is still complicated, and if you tell people there's nothing to it, they'll try to fly over the pole in ignorance of all the ins and outs of celestial, and kill themselves!*

The Air Force quickly hired the civilian Blair as an active-duty colonel to develop navigation technologies for tactical jets that could deliver nuclear weapons deep into Soviet airspace. To solve this problem, Blair automated his pre-comp techniques and created celestial astrotrackers that became a mainstay on strategic bombers and reconnaissance aircraft. Blair also advanced inertial navigation systems for tactical aircraft, facilitating development of the Republic F-105.

Blair's polar flight demonstrated that celestial navigation not only was adaptable for the Jet Age, but that it also was essential for strategic defense. His second great feat of navigation occurred on April 18, 1956, when he made the first transatlantic crossing with single engine jet fighters by leading a flight of F-84Fs (code named Operation Shark Bait). Using the new technologies of Doppler radar, autonomous star trackers, and inflight refueling, Blair ushered in a much more flexible form of nuclear defense, since now even fighter planes could be strategic nuclear bombers. ✺

TOP: The war-surplus Mark II Astrocompass that Charles Blair acquired for a mere $12. It was his primary navigational instrument for crossing the North Pole.

BOTTOM: Charles Blair (left) checks his Mark II Astrocompass before climbing into *Excalibur III* for his departure from Norway to cross the North Pole.

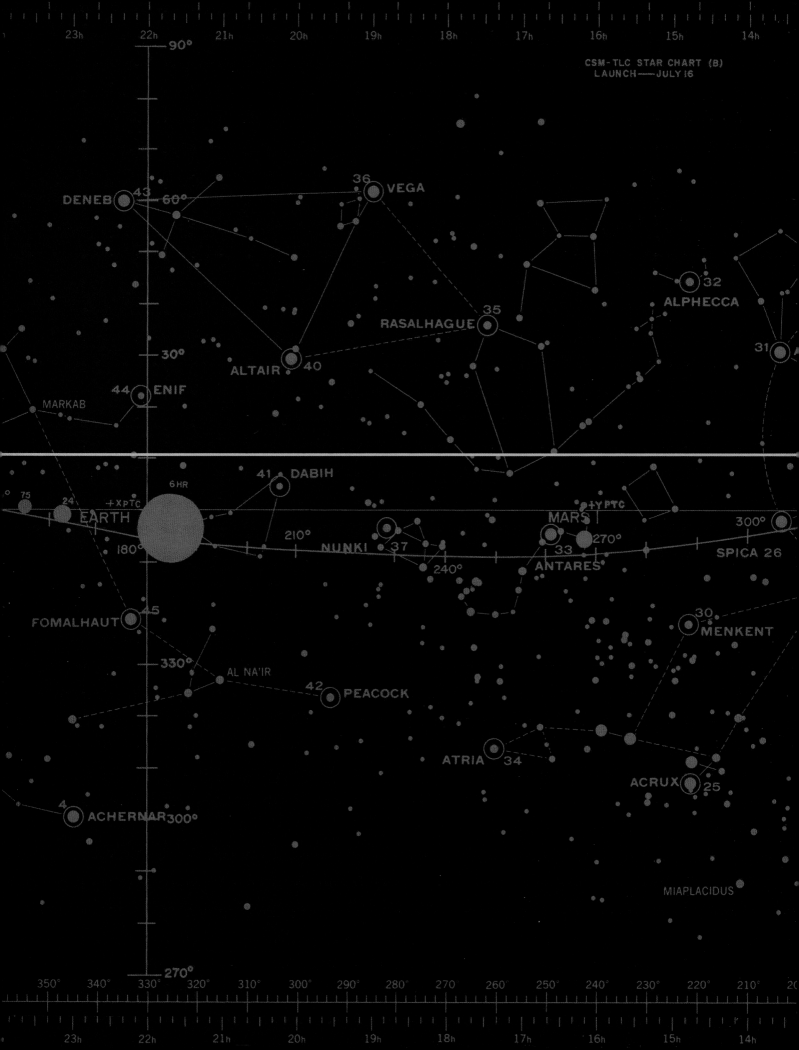

NAVIGATING
in SPACE

To journey across the vast expanses of space, navigators
drew on age-old methods and invented new ones.

To send humans to the moon and spacecraft across the
solar system, space navigators had to invent a new science of
space navigation using not just star sightings but also precise
timing and radio communications. The great distances
spacecraft had to travel called for greater precision in timing
and positioning than ever before.

NAVIGATING *in* SPACE

They boldly left Earth behind, pushing the limits of navigation. On Christmas Eve of 1968, Apollo 8 astronauts Frank Borman, William Anders, and James Lovell were on the far side of the moon, out of contact with Earth. A rocket engine boost was required to slow the spacecraft down and enter lunar orbit. Too much of a burn and the spacecraft would crash into the surface, out of any contact with Earth. Too little and the crew would be sent off into a wandering trajectory that might have prevented their ever returning home. The maneuver, perhaps the riskiest of the whole mission, was executed perfectly. After a journey of almost a quarter of a million

James Lovell looks through the telescope in the Apollo 8 command module. His right hand is over a button that he pressed when a particular star was centered on the telescope's crosshairs.

miles (402,000 km), it hit its target: an altitude of about sixty nautical miles (112 km) above the lunar surface. The mission was a success in every respect, and it gave a measurable boost to the U.S. space program.

This was the first time that humans ventured away from Earth's immediate vicinity. Accomplishing this mission required learning how to navigate a spacecraft to a pinpoint orbit around another celestial body. The solution developed included traditional forms of celestial navigation and radio navigation using signals from Earth. During the outward journey, the Apollo 8 crew sighted stars and the edge of the earth with their sextant, updated the computer, and compared onboard calculation results with ground-based position data computed by NASA. Throughout the mission, the astronauts continued to take sextant sightings to gain familiarity with the celestial system, correct for drift in the onboard gyroscopes, and check the accuracy of the ground-based data. By the end of the mission, they found that the two methods of navigation were in almost perfect agreement.

Apollo 8 was a unique turning point for space exploration. The Apollo 8 crew briefly had the opportunity to navigate using sextants in the manner of eighteenth- and nineteenth-century sea captains. It proved to be the last time humans extensively tested traditional celestial navigation techniques in space flight. For Apollo 8 and other missions, NASA decided that the ground-based radiometric positioning would take precedence over the onboard celestial/inertial system. Future space missions used radio transmissions and time measurements to tiny fractions of a second to navigate through space. ✳

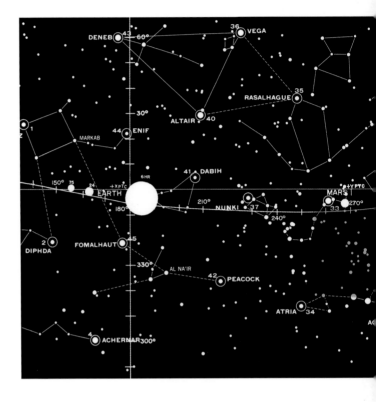

Apollo 11 astronauts used this star chart while training for their 1969 lunar landing mission. It shows the locations, names, and code numbers for a select group of stars. The astronauts would key those numbers into their Apollo Guidance Computer while taking readings with a sextant.

In the following pages, we will read how a new art and science of space navigation developed. By both recording images of the sky and measuring radio transmissions, humans and machines reached into orbit, to the moon, and to other worlds in the solar system.

INVENTING SPACE NAVIGATION

Pioneer 4 was the first U.S. spacecraft to escape Earth's gravity and reach the vicinity of the moon in 1959. Using timing accurate to one thousandth of a second, mission planners hoped to pass within 20,000 miles (32,000 km). Pioneer 4 had no ability to change its course once its booster rocket cut off, and it did not come closer than three times that distance.

I n the years following the end of World War II, people realized that the V-2 ballistic missile, developed by the Germans as a weapon of war, showed a practical way to achieve enough velocity to journey to outer space. That was only a crude first step, though. Once in space, how could one control and navigate a spacecraft to get to a desired location, and in the case of spacecraft carrying human passengers, how could one get it back to Earth safely?

In 2001, Stephen Ambrose and Douglas Brinkley interviewed Neil Armstrong about his experiences as an Apollo astronaut. They asked him which were the major challenges that had to be met to conduct such a mission successfully and safely. Armstrong replied that what concerned him greatly was "whether our navigation was sufficiently accurate, that we could, in fact, devise a trajectory that would get us around the moon at the right distance without, say, hitting the moon on the back side or something like that." Before Armstrong and other astronauts landed on the moon, it was not clear how navigation would be performed on the difficult journey. Just like in previous centuries, it was possible to determine location in space using a sextant and chronometer. Newer techniques based on measuring frequency shift of radio transmissions promised a different type of solution.

Just as the pioneers of aerial navigation drew on the tools and techniques of seafarers, so, too, did the early pioneers of space travel draw from navigation in air and at sea. But there were significant differences, and many of the techniques, such as using a sextant to take a fix on the stars, had to be abandoned or modified. Among the many differences, several set the tone for space navigation.

ABOVE: Left to right: Wernher von Braun, head of rocket development for the U.S. Army; John Casani of the Jet Propulsion Laboratory; and James Van Allen, a space scientist at the University of Iowa, inspect Pioneer 4 components.

LEFT: Engineers on the night of the Pioneer 4 launch at the Jet Propulsion Laboratory in Pasadena, California.

ABOVE: Dish antenna used for communicating with Pioneer 4 at Goldstone, California.

RIGHT: Engineers at Goldstone prepare for the launch of Pioneer 4.

The first is that the distances one encounters in space travel are enormous. Our closest heavenly body, the moon, is a little less than a quarter million miles away; Mars is millions of miles distant. At distances beyond the moon's orbit, which informally defines the beginning of "deep space," the time it takes a radio signal to travel, at the speed of light, becomes significant. Direct radio monitoring and control is thus not practical. And in space, everything is moving: the earth is rotating around its axis; it is moving around the sun; the moon is moving around Earth (and indirectly also around the sun); Mars is moving around the sun; and so forth. It was the requirement that Apollo astronauts navigate to a "window" on the far side of the moon, out of radio contract and only about a hundred miles (160 km) above the moon's surface, which was of concern to Neil Armstrong and his fellow Apollo astronauts. There were historical analogies to these challenges: The vast distances of the Pacific Ocean challenged seafarers who wished to cross it, and aircraft navigators knew that in the time it took them to take a fix on a star, their aircraft would have traveled a long way. Nevertheless, the scale of the solar system was a challenge that had to be faced.

A second factor was the lack of an atmosphere. A captain must propel and steer a ship continuously as it moves through the water; a pilot does the same as an aircraft flies through the air. With only a few exceptions, a spacecraft coasts for most of its voyage, its trajectory having been set by a carefully controlled burn of its rocket engines at critical moments during a journey. There is no atmospheric friction to overcome (although there are other very small forces of solar and other radiation that can affect a trajectory over long voyages). Navigation in space is not a continuous process, although during the journey it is necessary to track the craft to make sure it is on course.

A third property of navigation in space is that it is truly a three-dimensional problem. Ships remain at sea level and need to know their latitude and longitude. Aircraft must also know their altitude (and submarines their depth), but that number can be treated separately from the other two dimensions. In space, especially for missions beyond the moon, all three dimensions of position as well as movement in three directions must be considered equally. When dealing with space navigation, one refers constantly to a six-term "state vector": numbers that represent the craft's position in the

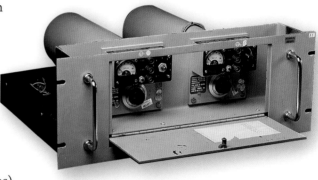

TOP: Replica of Ranger 7 lunar probe made from parts of test vehicles.

BOTTOM: Beginning in 1961, NASA used this pair of quartz oscillators as the main timing and radio frequency standard at the Goldstone tracking station. It improved the accuracy of velocity measurements from tens of meters per second to about 50 millimeters per second.

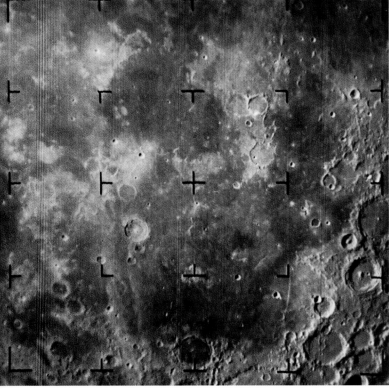

TOP: The Jet Propulsion Laboratory control room in Pasadena, California, as it appeared in 1964 during the Ranger missions.

BOTTOM: The first picture of the moon by the U.S. spacecraft Ranger 7 in 1964.

x, y, and z axes and its velocity in those three axes at any given time.

At the dawn of the Space Age in the late 1950s, little of this was understood, but a series of "firsts" from the Soviet Union meant that American scientists and engineers could not afford to take their time to develop a system of space navigation. The Soviets were the first to send an unmanned probe to the moon in 1959. The United States, after several failures, followed with Pioneer 4, launched on an Army rocket.

Although Charles Draper's MIT laboratory had studied the problem of navigating a spacecraft to Mars, most of its work centered on guidance of ballistic missiles, aircraft, and submarines, which relied not so much on celestial observations but were self-contained. These techniques, gathered under the name "inertial" guidance and navigation, relied on the properties of gyroscopes, accelerometers, and other devices to compute one's position without reference to the outside world—not sighting stars or receiving radio signals or any other reference to the outside world. The term "inertial" was derived from an application of Isaac Newton's three laws of motion, which described the tendency of a body to continue in motion and the forces required to change either its direction or speed. Inertial navigation has been called "astronomy in a closet." It uses gyroscopes to replicate the stable earth reference of traditional navigation and accelerometers to measure the change in motion of the craft. A computer uses those measurements, combined with signals from an internal clock, to calculate the vehicle's position and velocity. Its primary advantage was military: It could not be jammed by an enemy, nor did the vehicle being guided need to give away its position by, say, an aircraft sending out a radar signal or a submarine coming to the surface to take a reading from the stars.

Inertial techniques had several drawbacks, however. Although Draper's laboratory had improved the precision of mechanical gyroscopes by several orders of magnitude in the years following World War II, the systems tended to drift off-course due to friction in the

GUIDANCE, NAVIGATION, AND CONTROL

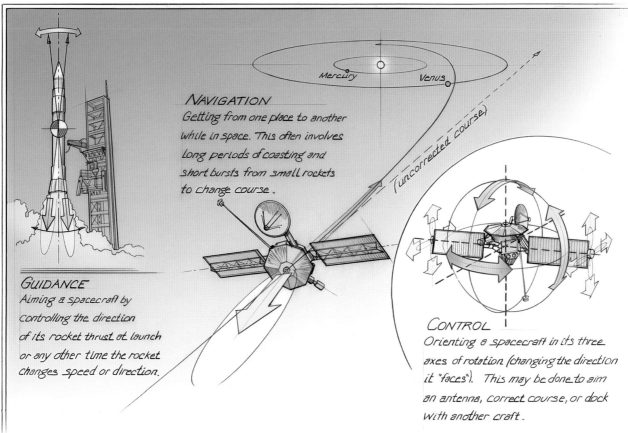

NAVIGATION
Getting from one place to another while in space. This often involves long periods of coasting and short bursts from small rockets to change course.

Mercury Venus

(uncorrected course)

GUIDANCE
Aiming a spacecraft by controlling the direction of its rocket thrust at launch or any other time the rocket changes speed or direction.

CONTROL
Orienting a spacecraft in its three axes of rotation (changing the direction it "faces"). This may be done to aim an antenna, correct course, or dock with another craft.

gyro bearings and other imperfections, and this required an external correction for any long-duration mission. Another drawback was that gravity is also a form of acceleration, and on Earth it is impossible to tell the difference between a force caused by gravity and that caused by the firing of a rocket. That led at least one prominent physicist to proclaim that inertial guidance could never work. That problem was solved ultimately by mapping the earth's gravitational field and subtracting its impact from the measurements taken by the system's accelerometers. For missions to the moon and planets, a similar calculation must be performed based on their gravitational fields.

The Apollo missions to the moon were civilian, not military. In the initial planning stages, there was some concern that the Soviet Union might want to interfere with the American crews. That concern led in part to a selection of an inertial system for Apollo. As the decade progressed, the fear of Soviet interference diminished. By then the

Three words are often used to describe controlling and guiding a spacecraft to its destination: guidance, navigation, and control.

Left to right: Apollo 8 astronauts James A. Lovell Jr., William A. Anders, and Frank Borman.

design of the Apollo navigation system was fixed, and it was too late to modify it to account for the diminished threat from the Soviet Union. The system chosen to navigate to the moon was fundamentally inertial, with periodic sightings of stars to correct for drift. The radiometric techniques developed for deep space missions were modified and used as a backup to the onboard navigation. After lunar missions began in 1968, those roles were reversed. NASA built a set of three twenty-six-meter (85 ft) diameter antennas collocated with the three seventy-meter (230 ft) dishes of the Deep Space network. The NASA network used atomic time and frequency standards based on the element rubidium, much better than the quartz standards in use through the 1950s.

Regardless of how much the ground-based systems had improved in the early 1960s, and even if the threat of Soviet interference was absent, some sort of inertial system was required. At critical stages in the mission, the Apollo crew would have to execute precise rocket burns either behind the moon, where there was no radio contact with Earth, or as they descended to the moon's surface, where the two- or three-second round trip time it took for a signal to travel back and forth made control from Earth impractical.

The rivalry between the Soviet Union and the United States heated up in 1961, when, on April 12, Yuri Gagarin became the first human to orbit Earth. American Alan Shepard's suborbital flight followed in May. In the rush to make new achievements in space, both nations attempted to develop ways to find position while moving through space. Experimentation for early space navigation techniques often focused on enhanced versions of celestial techniques used at sea for centuries. Just as early aircraft navigators drew from their predecessors at sea, so too did early thoughts about navigation in space draw from air and sea pioneers. P. V. H. Weems, who contributed so much to the science of aircraft navigation, took the initiative for human space travel as well, and he argued that the celestial techniques he helped pioneer could be used by space travelers, with a great deal of adaptation. Weems consulted with NASA and developed techniques that used a variation of the familiar sextant to measure the angle between two stars or between a star and the limb of the earth, the moon, or the sun to obtain a celestial version of the "line of position" known to seafarers.

The designers of the capsules for Project Mercury, America's first human space vehicle, did not know how well—or even if—the astronauts could function in space. Would the astronauts become disoriented, pass out, or be unable to hear, see, or swallow in the unknown environment? These were unknown, although in hindsight some of the concerns seem overblown—for example, acrobats on Earth can do all kinds of things upside-down, even if they have never experienced weightlessness. The early design for the Mercury capsule did not even have a window, although one was added at the urging of the Mercury 7 astronauts when they saw the configuration. For John Glenn's historic three-orbit flight of May 1962, the capsule was fitted with an Earth Path Indicator—a small globe attached to a clockwork mechanism that rotated it at the proper speed. Once in orbit, Glenn set a tiny icon representing his capsule over the proper position on the globe, which subsequently told him where he was over the earth. Glenn did not need the device, although it worked perfectly. He had excellent eyesight, and simply by looking down at the earth he could determine his approximate location, while a worldwide network of tracking stations on the ground and on ships at sea provided more precise data. Glenn later remarked that during preparations for the flight in the high deserts of Nevada and California, he could easily see mountain ranges fifty miles distant. From the Mercury capsule, although much farther away from landmarks on Earth, Glenn had only to look through a few miles of dense atmosphere at most. The Earth Path Indicator was carried on the next Mercury flight; then it was removed.

The two-person Gemini flights, which followed Mercury, were likewise tracked by ground stations.

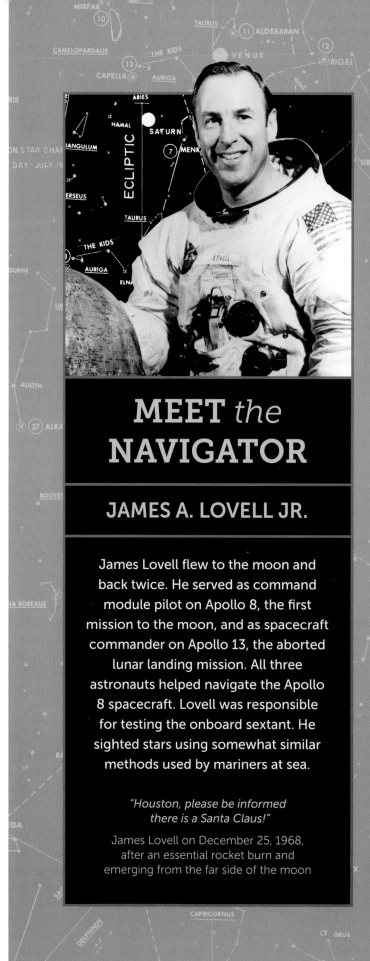

MEET *the* NAVIGATOR

JAMES A. LOVELL JR.

James Lovell flew to the moon and back twice. He served as command module pilot on Apollo 8, the first mission to the moon, and as spacecraft commander on Apollo 13, the aborted lunar landing mission. All three astronauts helped navigate the Apollo 8 spacecraft. Lovell was responsible for testing the onboard sextant. He sighted stars using somewhat similar methods used by mariners at sea.

"Houston, please be informed there is a Santa Claus!"

James Lovell on December 25, 1968, after an essential rocket burn and emerging from the far side of the moon

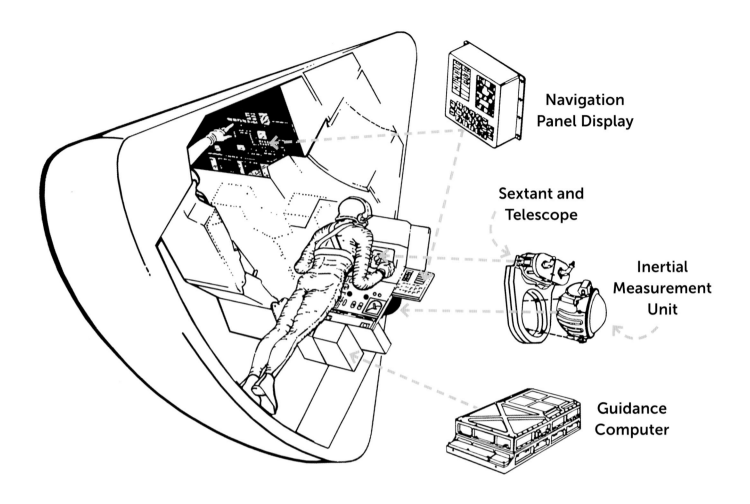

Navigation Panel Display

Sextant and Telescope

Inertial Measurement Unit

Guidance Computer

Using the Apollo Guidance, Navigation, and Control System involved taking readings with a sextant that were automatically fed into the Apollo Guidance Computer—the electronic equivalent of the almanacs and mathematical tables sailors once used.

The major objectives of Gemini were to demonstrate the ability to change one's orbit in space and to rendezvous with other spacecraft. For that purpose, the capsules were fitted with a small digital computer and a radar system. During several early Gemini missions, astronauts conducted experiments to gauge their ability to recognize stars and to use that information to augment their knowledge of the capsule's position in orbit. Gemini XII, the last Gemini flight, carried a sextant which astronaut Buzz Aldrin used to test the feasibility of taking readings on stars as his predecessors did at sea and in the air.

Shortly after Alan Shepard's successful flight in May 1961, President John F. Kennedy challenged the United States to land a man on the moon and return him safely "before this decade is out." The navigation problem for the Apollo missions to the moon was more daunting, as Neil Armstrong suggested. In 1957, the MIT Instrumentation Laboratory did a study for the US Air Force for an unmanned Mars probe, and the lab was able to draw from that for a proposal to NASA. On that basis, the Instrumentation Laboratory received a contract to do some preliminary work on the Apollo guidance and navigation system. In August 1961, NASA Administrator James Webb invited the head of the lab, Charles Stark Draper, to Washington to discuss the proposal. Webb queried Draper about the proposal, and asked him when the system would be ready. "You'll have it when you need it," Draper replied. Webb then asked if the system would work reliably, to which Draper, a skilled pilot who had a reputation for personally testing the flight instruments his laboratory produced, replied in the affirmative, stating further that he wanted to volunteer to fly the first mission. He did not get to do that, but the Instrumentation Laboratory was awarded the contract.

The Apollo guidance and navigation system consisted of an "inertial measurement unit" based on gyroscopes, accelerometers, a general-purpose computer, a scanning telescope, and a sextant. Periodically during the voyage, an astronaut would locate a star with the single-power telescope, then maneuver the spacecraft to a position where the star (or limb of the earth or the moon) was in the sextant's field. He would align the star on the sextant's crosshairs, enter the code for that star into the computer, and mark its position. The onboard computer would compare that position to what it had computed with the inertial system and correct for any error it detected. The astronauts trained for the mission by memorizing the constellations they would see and the numerical codes for a set of the brightest stars.

Of all the parts of this complex system, the onboard computer was the most famous. In its memory was the equivalent of the Nathaniel Bowditch navigation tables carried by nineteenth-century sailors. The computer also controlled the periodic burns of thrusters and rocket engines for the midcourse corrections and for getting into and out of lunar orbit. It also carried out the calculations that translated data from the gyroscopes and accelerometers into position and velocity components of the state vector. Apollo carried two identical computers, the one on the Lunar Module programmed separately to handle the landing on the moon's surface. It was one of the first computers in the world to use the newly invented integrated circuit, developed by Fairchild Semiconductor Corporation in what would later

An Apollo crew used sightings on stars, the moon, and Earth to update navigational data stored in their Apollo Guidance Computer, which calculated the spacecraft's velocity and location. The results were compared with data computed by Earth-based tracking stations.

be dubbed Silicon Valley. According to the legend, when a Saturn V rocket blasted off with its crew of three Apollo astronauts on board, it also carried with it a significant fraction of all the silicon chips in existence in the world. That is not quite true, for similar devices had already been developed for the guidance system for the Minuteman III ballistic missile, but it was not far from the reality. The computational power of the Apollo Guidance Computer is often compared to that of a modern cell phone; in fact, a cell phone has orders of magnitude greater memory capacity and processing power. Human beings trusted their lives to the Apollo computer's ability to carry out vector calculations in real time, however, something that might be difficult to achieve with modern consumer products.

The Apollo computer itself had no backup, but navigation to the moon and back was also accomplished by using Earth-based observations and radio transmissions. The Apollo Lunar Module also carried a special-purpose computer, whose only function was to get the astronauts off the surface of the moon and back to the Command Module in lunar orbit. During the Apollo 13 mission, in which the astronauts lives were jeopardized by a loss of power in the service module, the crew used the Lunar Module as a kind of lifeboat. They relied on visual sightings of Earth through the windows of the Command Module, which had grid lines marked on them, to align themselves for returning to Earth.

For the Apollo 8 mission in 1968, the onboard system was used on the outward journey to confirm positions before entering lunar orbit. This was followed by the crew's dramatic Christmas Eve reading from the book of Genesis, and the later publication of the "Earthrise" photograph, one of the most famous photos ever taken. Later, the onboard system was called into service again to control a careful burn to get the spacecraft out of lunar orbit and back to Earth. As before, this burn had to take place on the far side of the moon, out of communication with Earth. The system worked again. To everyone's relief, the crew made radio contact when they emerged from behind the moon to begin their journey back home.

While the celestial techniques tested during the Apollo 8 mission demonstrated that it was possible to determine position far from Earth, later Apollo missions and other space exploration efforts used techniques based on radio transmissions almost exclusively. The onboard system was not abandoned, however. It was crucial to have a backup, and it provided critical data as the spacecraft was near the moon, where the geometry of the ground tracking made Earth-based navigation less accurate and the time delay was unacceptable.

OPPOSITE: The famous "Earthrise" photograph taken during the Apollo 8 mission in lunar orbit.

ABOVE: Two people work on a Deep Space Network antenna. To concentrate enough power for receiving and sending data, the huge antenna focuses a narrow microwave beam that must be aimed precisely at the spacecraft. To remain fixed on it, the antenna must continually move at the precise rate of Earth's rotation: 0.004 degrees per second.

OPPOSITE: This antenna at Goldstone, California, has become a symbol of space communication. The largest antenna at the site has been in continuous use since 1966, when it tracked Mariner 4 on its mission to fly past Mars.

Missions of space exploration utilize precise frequency standards and radio tracking to determine position and velocity, even when spacecraft are millions of miles away across the solar system. Some of the earliest space missions set the stage for creating radio tracking systems, even before humans landed on the moon. Portable tracking stations were set up at multiple locations to support orbital probes such as Explorer 1 in 1958. Larger permanent stations were developed to support early missions to the moon. Pioneer 4 was launched by NASA to the vicinity of the moon on March 3, 1959. The tiny Pioneer 4 spacecraft had no onboard propulsion; its trajectory was determined at the moment its booster rocket cut off thrust. One of the mission's goals was to sample radiation, if any, from the moon, but the spacecraft did not pass close enough to accomplish that. Its velocity at booster cutoff was about 188 mph (303 kph) too slow. The timing of the cutoff was simply not precise enough. The Pioneer 4 mission was not a failure, however. As it passed by the moon, it detected no serious belts of radiation that could endanger a human crew that might journey that far. That led the famous radio astronomer Bernard Lovell to proclaim that the era of human exploration of deep space was immanent—a bold statement considering that he based it on the flight of a 13-pound (6 kg) spacecraft with no onboard navigation abilities. But Lovell was soon proven right.

As Pioneer 4 traveled to and beyond the moon's orbit, it was tracked by the first of what would eventually become a worldwide network

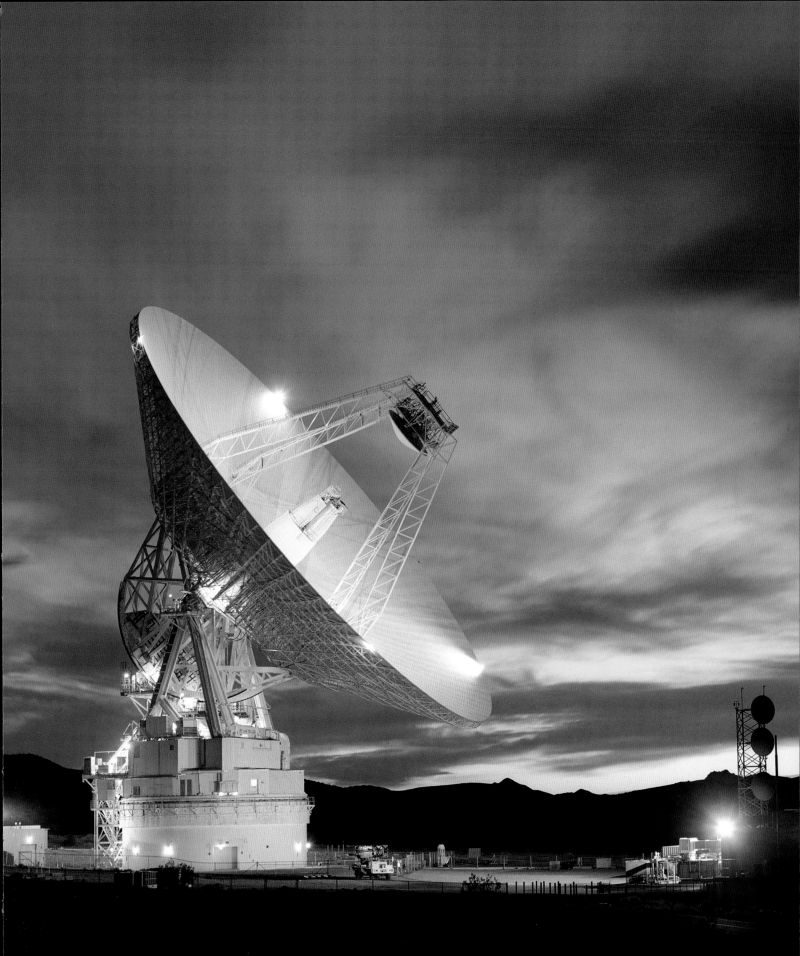

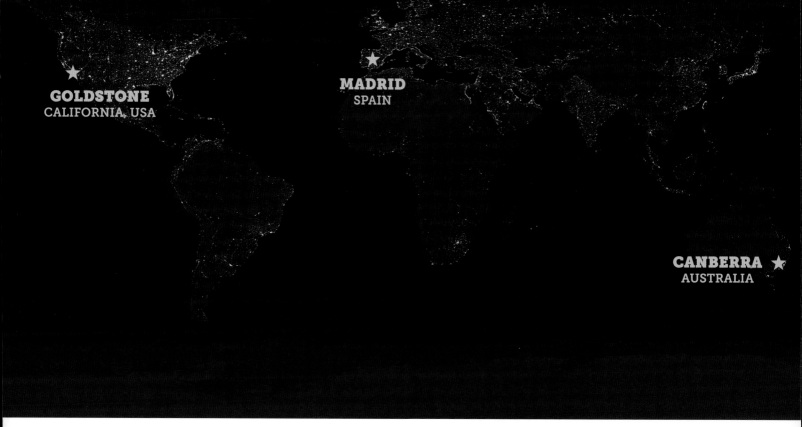

GOLDSTONE
CALIFORNIA, USA

MADRID
SPAIN

CANBERRA
AUSTRALIA

Global map showing the location of the three stations of the Deep Space Network.

of tracking stations. A twenty-six-meter (85 ft) parabolic antenna, located at Goldstone, in the California desert, tracked the spacecraft as it entered an orbit around the sun, becoming an artificial planet. Pioneer 4 remains in solar orbit, although its exact location is not known. A giant radio astronomy dish built by Bernard Lovell at Jodrell Bank, in the United Kingdom, was also pressed into service to track Pioneer 4. Using quartz time and frequency standards, Goldstone was able to track the spacecraft as it passed into solar orbit, until its 180-milliwatt radio ceased transmitting.

The Jet Propulsion Laboratory followed on with the Ranger probes, designed to travel directly to the moon, take photographs, and even eject a seismometer before crash-landing. None of the missions were successful until finally Rangers 7, 8, and 9 returned excellent photographs as they each impacted the moon in 1964 and 1965. Unlike Pioneer 4, the Ranger spacecraft had onboard thrusters that allowed mission controllers to make midcourse corrections as it sped toward the moon. A very slight but carefully controlled thruster firing at an earlier stage of a flight could result in a huge correction at the destination, following the laws of celestial mechanics. For such a technique to work the spacecraft had to be tracked accurately; it had to be aligned perfectly during the thruster burn; and the burns had to be timed carefully.

A global network of radio antennas was required to track missions to other planets. The Jet Propulsion Laboratory, working with international partners, developed stations in Australia and South Africa in 1961 to work with the station at Goldstone, California. Separated by about 120 degrees of longitude each, they could provide continuous tracking of deep space probes as Earth rotates about its axis. Later in the 1960s and 1970s, three enormous seventy-meter (230 ft) antennas were built at stations in California, Spain, and Australia, forming the basis of NASA's present Deep Space Network.

The radio receivers on Earth were fitted with a newly invented circuit, called the "phase-locked loop" (PLL), to track the signal from deep space. Without this circuit, the faint signal would have been lost in the background of radiation from stars and other celestial bodies, especially as the signal's frequency shifted during its travels because of the Doppler effect. The phase-locked loop is integral to the design of nearly all terrestrial radios today, including cell phones, car radios, televisions, and other consumer products.

The large size of the antennas is needed to receive the faint signals from space probes as they travel to the outer regions of the solar system. As massive as they are, the antennas must also be able to point to a precise spot in the sky, and hold that aim as the earth rotates under it at a rate of 0.004 degrees per second. At the heart of deep space navigation is the technique of sending a time signal to the space probe, where it is retransmitted back to Earth. Measuring the time it takes for a one-way trip divided by the speed of light gives the range—how far away it is. In practice, this is not as simple as it sounds. The time it takes to turn the signal around in the probe has to be measured on the ground before launch. One also needs to know the time it takes for a signal to travel from the atomic frequency standards at the site to the antenna. The signal is retransmitted from the deep space probe at a different frequency to avoid interference.

This primary atomic frequency standard, a hydrogen maser, served as a stable frequency source for the Goldstone tracking station.

NAVIGATION
GONE WRONG

U.S.A.

Atlantic Ocean

CAPE CANAVERAL

Gulf of Mexico

Florida

MARINER 1 IS DESTROYED

The first American spacecraft sent to explore another planet, Mariner 1, was launched on July 22, 1962 on a mission to the planet Venus. It never even reached space.

ABOVE: A backup of the Mariner 1 and 2 spacecraft hanging in the National Air and Space Museum.

BELOW: Engineers testing systems before the launch of Mariner 1 in 1962.

WHAT HAPPENED

Unbeknownst to its operators, the launch computer that controlled the Atlas rocket carrying Mariner 1 contained a tiny programming error. A single character had been left out of the guidance equations.

THE CONSEQUENCES

About four minutes into its flight, the Atlas rocket carrying Mariner 1 began behaving erratically. The rocket had to be destroyed, and with it Mariner 1.

LESSONS LEARNED

The disaster revealed a critical need to thoroughly debug software before launch. Mariner 2 was successfully launched in August 1962 and became the first spacecraft to visit another planet. NASA took later corrective actions to engineer software so that small errors did not impact safety. Several Apollo lunar modules safely landed on the moon despite minor software "bugs."

The speed of the signal is affected slightly as it passes through the earth's atmosphere. When the signal comes back, moreover, the antenna is not in the same place relative to the sun as it was when the signal was sent. Depending on the orientation of the earth, the signal may be received by any of the three Deep Space Network tracking stations. JPL navigators are able to compensate for all these factors. One reason is that timekeeping was 100,000 times more precise in the twenty-first century compared to the 1960s. They are thus able to determine the absolute distance of a deep space probe very well.

But more than just range is needed. To measure the craft's velocity—its speed and direction—additional techniques must be used. The most important of those is to measure the change in frequency as the craft moves toward or away from the earth. Einstein's special theory of relativity tells us that the speed of light does not change, but the frequency of the signal increases if the spacecraft is moving toward us and decreases if it is moving away. It is the radio equivalent of the change in pitch of an ambulance siren as it passes by in the street. Radio astronomers use the technique to measure the speed at which galaxies are receding from us by looking at the shift of their light to the red. This is called the Doppler effect, named after Christian Doppler, the Austrian scientist who first described it in 1842. A probe traveling through deep space is therefore tracked by three basic techniques: Doppler measurements, range measurements (both taken at different times from the three DSN stations), and techniques that measure the angle the signal is being received compared to distant radio sources outside the galaxy.

Space exploration requires extensive ground-based infrastructure. The Deep Space Network keeps in contact with NASA missions all over the solar system, but other networks have also been developed. Separate NASA networks of ground stations were used for communication with early crewed NASA flights including Apollo missions to the moon. Beginning in 1959, the Soviet Union also built ground stations for planetary exploration. Three stations remain in use spread over the former Soviet Union. The European Space Agency operates a network of ten stations around the world for communications with European planetary missions. The Chinese Deep Space Network was first developed in 2007 for the Chang'e 1 mission into lunar orbit. It consists of stations in China, with plans for additional stations in other nations. India and Japan both operate stations for deep space communication. Communications for the Hayabusa asteroid mission to the asteroid Ikotawa were maintained using ground stations of NASA's Deep Space Network in addition to Japan's ground station.

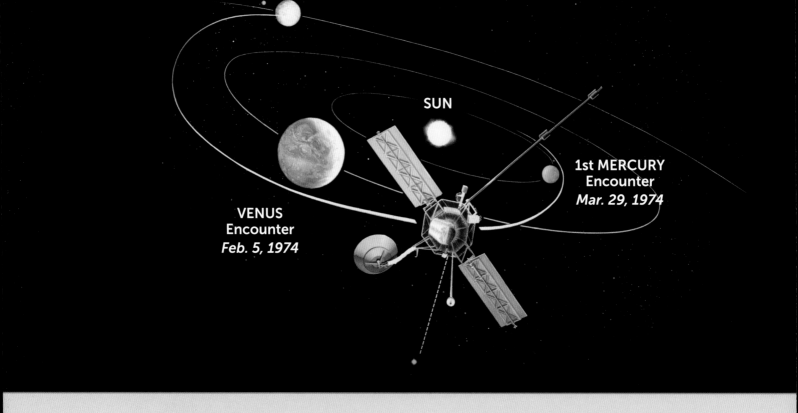

**1st MERCURY
Encounter
*Mar. 29, 1974***

**VENUS
Encounter
*Feb. 5, 1974***

TO OTHER PLANETS *with*
Mariner 10

Improvements in navigation led to a breakthrough in space navigation that has since become the standard for many interplanetary space missions. This was the "gravity assist," a technique of using the gravity of one planet to alter a spacecraft's velocity and help send it on its way to another planet. If a spacecraft is sent on a properly designed trajectory, the velocity of the spacecraft can be greatly altered as it passes by a planet while changing the orbit of the planet by an infinitesimal amount.

Gravity assist techniques, developed in the early 1960s by Michael Minovitch at the Jet Propulsion Laboratory, have enabled

ABOVE: Mariner 10 used the gravity of Venus to propel it to Mercury with a minimal use of fuel. To reach Mercury, Mariner 10 first passed by Venus, threading through a narrow 250-mile (400 km) "window" of space a few thousand kilometers above the surface. That level of accuracy had not been possible with the navigation systems available for the Pioneer 4 mission in 1959.

spacecraft to reach multiple planets without requiring a massive launch vehicle. This was first successfully employed for the Mariner 10 mission, launched in November 1973, which swung by Venus at a predetermined altitude and position, using Venus's gravity to help propel it toward Mercury. The technique required precise space navigation to reach the target at Venus.

While on its journey, Mariner 10 encountered navigation and control problems that could have prevented it from reaching Mercury. The onboard gyroscopes and star tracker often behaved erratically, requiring the NASA mission team to adjust plans for rocket boosts needed to stay on course. On February 5, 1974, Mariner 10 passed near Venus, successfully hitting a target just 250 miles (400 km) wide and taking the first close-up images of that planet. It then used the gravity of Venus to propel it toward the orbit of Mercury. That was the first time that the technique of gravity assist was used in the journey from one planet to another.

Mariner 10 passed within 435 miles (700 km) of Mercury on March 29, 1974, confirming that the planet had no appreciable atmosphere, a cratered moonlike surface, and a weak magnetic field. Mariner then continued on its trajectory in orbit around the sun. In a carefully planned encounter, the spacecraft flew by Mercury again in September 1974, and a third and final time in October 1974. Each time it gathered more data and took more images of the planet's surface. The unprecedented threefold encounter with Mercury was achieved at a low cost of additional propellant and weight of the spacecraft, and it validated the gravity-assist concept used in many subsequent interplanetary missions. ☼

TOP: Mariner 10 spacecraft, which encountered Mercury three times in 1974–75.

BOTTOM: Mariner 10 on the pad before its launch on November 3, 1973.

The identical Voyager 1 and Voyager 2 spacecraft flew by the outer planets and continue their outward paths leaving the solar system.

Since the first use of a gravity-assist trajectory on a planetary mission with Mariner 10, even more diverse targets have been chosen for missions. Planners have devised an ever more complex array of trajectories that allow spacecraft to visit heavenly bodies, even to repurpose an existing spacecraft to do something else, with a sparing use of onboard propellants. The combination of ground-based, onboard inertial, and celestial navigation used for Apollo has likewise evolved. Unmanned spacecraft do not employ a sextant, thus severing the link with centuries-old techniques of navigation. However, they have carried optical trackers to maintain correct orientation. Mariner 2, the first mission to another planet, used a sensor that locked onto Earth while the spacecraft journeyed to Venus. Later spacecraft carried star trackers, which automatically lock on to a star or a known star field and use that data to be sure the craft is oriented properly in space. It was very common for spacecraft on planetary missions through the 1970s to carry trackers aimed at the star Canopus, the second-brightest star visible from earth. Its location in the southern sky makes it constantly visible to spacecraft traveling to other planets in the ecliptic, the plane in which planets revolve around the sun.

Ground-based techniques, with their accompanying time and frequency standards, have improved dramatically. But spacecraft still carry onboard inertial gyroscopes and accelerometers, which must be employed when the craft is accelerating and when the time delays of communications with Earth require them. They also serve as a check against the accuracy of the Earth-based navigation. The

inertial system used on Apollo used mechanical gyroscopes that were carefully hand-assembled and balanced. Current spacecraft use several types of gyroscopes that do away with a lot of that complexity. Some, for example, use a laser beam reflected into a ring shape, with acceleration measured by a shift in the laser's frequency. Others use a rotating beam of light contained in a ring of fiber-optic material. One of the most effective is a gyro that is shaped like a wine glass, which vibrates when energy is applied to it, much as a wine glass hums when rubbed with a wet finger. The phase of the vibration changes as it accelerates, and that data is translated into velocity information.

Advanced timekeeping and navigational methods have made possible extended missions to other worlds. More accurate time standards have enabled navigators to send spacecraft to specific locations and allowed scientists to conduct lengthy and sophisticated explorations. Navigation into the far reaches of the solar system has come a long way from the anxious moments of the Apollo 8 mission in 1968.

The NEAR-Shoemaker mission to the asteroid Eros was not planned to include a landing. But navigation accurate to about a meter (3 ft) enabled controllers to set NEAR gently on the surface in 2001 (shown in this artist's rendering), where it briefly continued to transmit data.

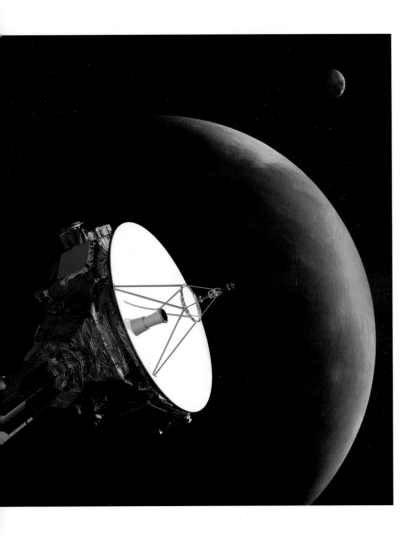

ABOVE: Artist's rendering of New Horizons flying by Pluto in July 2015.

OPPOSITE: Clockwise from upper left: Alberto Cangahuala, Brent Buffington, Troy Goodson, Jim Border, Marina Brozovic, and Tomas Martin-Mur of the Jet Propulsion Laboratory.

Mission planners now not only can reach Mars but can also land within a specific area of interest. Earlier missions, such as the Viking Landers in 1976, were targeted to areas of scientific interest that appeared to be safe for landing. In 2004, NASA's two Mars Exploration Rovers (MER), Spirit and Opportunity, landed on the surface of Mars. Unlike the Viking Landers, which entered orbit around Mars before reaching the surface, the two MER rovers were sent directly from their paths from Earth through the atmosphere of Mars. Mission planners mapped the targeted landing areas as large ellipses. They did not know exactly where within these ellipses the rovers would land, but they arrived on Mars near the center of each. In 2012, the Curiosity rover was aimed at Gale Crater to study the geological history of this area. In particular, scientists were interested in studying a large hill in the crater's center. The possible landing area was much smaller than earlier missions. This was made possible with precise space navigation and improved control as the lander descended through the Martian atmosphere. In August 2012, Curiosity landed right on target within driving distance of Mount Sharp within Gale Crater.

A prominent example of clever trajectory design is the path of the International Sun-Earth Explorer 3 (ISEE-3) spacecraft launched in 1978. Its mission was originally aimed at observing the interaction between the sun and the earth from a vantage point between the two. ISSE-3 was placed into an orbit around a Lagrangian point between the sun and the earth, the first spacecraft to do this. These points are places where the gravitational pull of two bodies is equal. A spacecraft placed at one of these points, or orbiting around it, can remain there without using thrusters or fuel to maintain that position. These points can also be approached and left behind with only moderate amounts of rocket thrusts. In 1982, a new mission for the spacecraft was developed. At that time the Soviet Union, the European Space Agency, and Japan were planning missions to fly by Halley's comet as it approached the sun in 1986. Although the United States did not have a mission to Halley's, the ISEE-3 team was inspired to develop a plan for a modest U.S. comet mission. Renamed the International Cometary Explorer (ICE), a new trajectory was developed for ISEE-

3 to fly by comet Giacobini-Zinner, largely by Robert Farquhar working at the Applied Physics Laboratory of Johns Hopkins University. The path required multiple trips past the earth and the moon to change its velocity to reach the comet. Only small onboard thrusters were required. Leaving its halo orbit in September 1982, the trajectory included loops to pick up velocity from the earth and the moon. It finally flew by Giacobini-Zinner in September 1985, making it the first spacecraft to visit a comet. It also made distant observations of Halley's comet in March 1986. The spacecraft continued in orbit around the sun. It was aimed for an August 2014 flyby of the moon without knowing if it would continue operating. In June 2014, a nonprofit organization working with NASA and other agencies succeeded in regaining contact using the Arecibo Radio Observatory in Puerto Rico. After a twenty-eight-year journey of more than fifteen billion miles (24 billion km) since leaving its halo orbit, ISEE-3/ICE was found to be off course by less than 24,800 miles (40,000 km).

In the 1970s, the two Voyager spacecraft were sent to missions to the outer planets. Voyager 1 arrived at Jupiter in 1979, followed by Voyager 2 in 1980. In 1980 and 1981, the two spacecraft flew by Saturn. NASA mission planners directed Voyager 2 on a trajectory to the planets Uranus and Neptune. Improvements in the antennas and frequency standards used at the Deep Space Network tracking stations made it possible to achieve precise navigation during the continuing mission. At Saturn, Voyager 2 approached within 62,000 miles (100,000 km) of the planet. The Voyager 2 spacecraft flew by the planet Uranus in 1986. Its closest approach was about 50,000 miles (80,000 km), when the planet was about twice as distant from the center of the solar system. Voyager 2's closest approach to Neptune was only 3,100 miles (5,000 km)—and this despite the fact that the Neptune encounter occurred three times farther from Earth than the Saturn encounter.

MEET *the* NAVIGATORS

JET PROPULSION LAB

Navigating in space is a team effort. Most navigation for spacecraft exploring the solar system happens on the ground. NASA's Jet Propulsion Laboratory near Pasadena, California, directs many of those voyages. Five groups of specialists work together to model the ideal mission and then track the spacecraft once it is underway.

- The *Ephemerides Group* calculates the positions of astronomical objects at predicted times.

- *Trajectory designers* plot an efficient path for the spacecraft.

- The *Radiometric Tracking Team* assesses techniques for acquiring and improving the accuracy of radio-based measurements of the spacecraft's velocity, location, and angle relative to Earth.

- *Orbit determination analysts* study radio transmissions and images from cameras to determine the spacecraft's current location.

- *Maneuver designers* plan propulsive maneuvers to keep the spacecraft on the correct flight path.

SPACE NAVIGATION

A TIMELINE OF IMPROVEMENTS

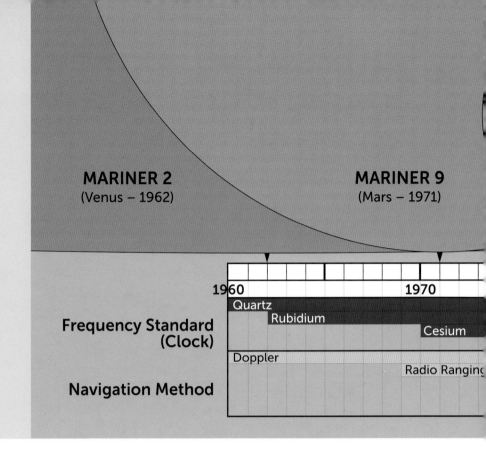

KEY

LESS ACCURATE POSITION → ● MORE ACCURATE POSITION

THE CIRCLES SHOW HOW ACCURATELY
EACH MISSION WAS TARGETED.

MARINER 2
(Venus – 1962)

MARINER 9
(Mars – 1971)

1960   1970

**Frequency Standard
(Clock)**

Quartz
Rubidium
Cesium

Doppler
Radio Ranging

Navigation Method

Navigators on Earth have used radio signals to guide spacecraft to other planets. In this diagram, smaller circles indicate more precise accuracy for finding the spacecraft's position. Note the especially large circle for Mariner 2's uncertainty in 1962.

The NEAR-Shoemaker spacecraft settled onto the surface of the asteroid Eros in 2001, even though that was not part of its initial mission plan. The mission was originally intended to orbit the small asteroid. After that phase of the mission was complete, the trajectory designers and navigators determined that enough fuel remained on board to push the spacecraft toward the surface. It slowly approached the surface, returning a final image showing rocks as small as golf balls. It then settled gently on the surface under the tiny gravitational pull of Eros. The spacecraft was not designed to land, but at least one of its instruments continued to return data two weeks after reaching the surface. Navigation accurate to within a few meters made it all possible.

In 2003, the Japan Aerospace Exploration Agency (JAXA) sent the Hayabusa spacecraft toward Ikotawa, another near-Earth asteroid. Hayabusa (originally named MUSES-C) was intended to approach the asteroid, briefly contact the surface to extract a small sample, and return the sample to Earth. The spacecraft reached Ikotawa on November 19, 2005. A sample collector and a separate surface probe did not work as intended, but Hayabusa did touch the surface. In June 2010, the reentry capsule landed in Australia. The science team found a small number of asteroid particles in the capsule. While some aspects of the mission were not successful, Hayabusa did demonstrate how precise navigation makes it possible to reach new parts of the solar system.

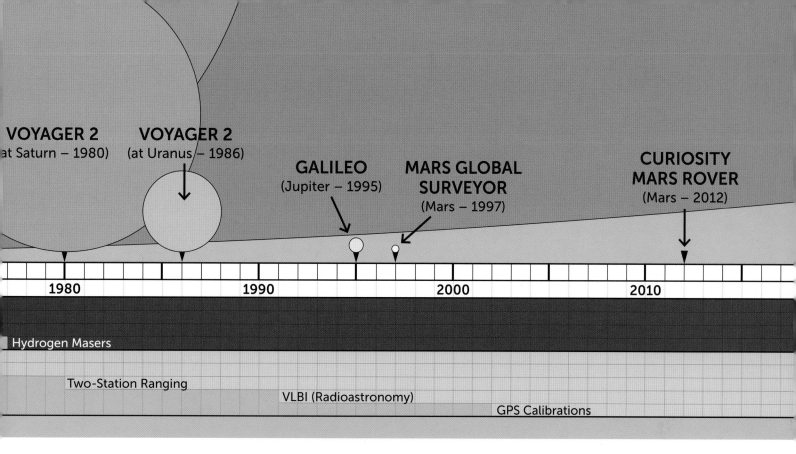

VOYAGER 2
(at Saturn – 1980)

VOYAGER 2
(at Uranus – 1986)

GALILEO
(Jupiter – 1995)

MARS GLOBAL SURVEYOR
(Mars – 1997)

CURIOSITY MARS ROVER
(Mars – 2012)

1980   1990   2000   2010

Hydrogen Masers

Two-Station Ranging

VLBI (Radioastronomy)

GPS Calibrations

NASA's Gravity Recovery and Interior Laboratory (GRAIL) mission was aimed at the moon in 2011 to closely map the lunar gravity field to better understand the structure of the moon's interior. The mission consisted of two spacecraft that orbited the moon in the same path, one closely following the other. The distance between the spacecraft was carefully monitored by the mission team at NASA's Jet Propulsion Laboratory. Using a stable frequency standard on the spacecraft, the offset between the time required for a radio signal to travel between the spacecraft was measured. This allowed the team to determine the distance between the spacecraft so precisely it was possible to observe the varying gravitational pull of the moon below.

Satellite transmissions have also been used for determining positions for human spaceflight in Earth orbit. The Space Shuttle carried star trackers for maintaining orientation. Transmissions from other satellites are now frequently used for this application. GPS receivers were tested on space shuttle flights in 2000, and the International Space Station has used GPS to monitor position and velocity. Future missions to distant goals may require even more precise positioning. Proposals for future space-based systems suggest precise positioning on the moon or Mars might be possible from satellites in orbit around those bodies. In this way, space exploration may take advantage of satellite navigation techniques used every day on Earth.

BRADBURY LANDING

YELLOWKNIFE BAY

ROCKNEST

MT. WILSON

BELL RIVER

PROSPECT MESA

PANORAMA POINT

RONDOUT

COOPERSTOWN

VIOLET VALLEY

MT. CHRISTINE

MT. REMARKABLE

SOL 600

N

METERS

0   250   500   750   1000

EXPLORING MARS *with*
Curiosity

The Mars Science Laboratory was the most ambitious mission to the surface of Mars ever attempted, sending a rover to Mars to drive across the surface conducting geological investigations. Given the name Curiosity, the rover carried multiple cameras for returning images and instruments for observing the structure and composition of rocks. In the first two years of the mission, Curiosity drove 4.3 miles (7 km) on Mars, providing better understanding of the geologic and climate history of the red planet.

ABOVE: The course of the Mars Science Laboratory Curiosity on the surface of Mars. The rover's track is shown from its landing in August 2012, through its six hundredth Martian day ("sol") in April 2014, and beyond.

OPPOSITE: "Self portrait" of Curiosity on Mars taken by a camera on the end of an experiment arm.

TOP: Curiosity descending through the atmosphere of Mars. The image was taken by the HiRISE camera on the Mars Reconnaissance Orbiter as it orbited above.

BOTTOM: Artist's rendering showing Curiosity being lowered by the "Sky Crane" before reaching the surface.

By the time of Curiosity, mission planners could guide spacecraft to more precise landings on Mars than ever before. For the Mars Exploration Rovers in 2004, navigation and time standards were precise enough to narrow the landing site to an ellipse-shaped area 93 by 12.5 miles (150 by 20 km). Improved landing control allowed scientists to target Curiosity closer to interesting geological features than previous missions; the target area within Gale Crater, for example, was about 12.5 miles (20 km) across and was refined as the spacecraft approached Mars.

Missions to the surface of Mars use parachutes to slow decent through the atmosphere. However, the Martian atmosphere is not thick enough for a parachute to slow a lander completely for a safe landing. Many previous missions such as the Viking Landers in the 1970s also used rockets to gently settle on the surface with landing legs. The two Mars Exploration Rovers in 2004 hit the surface surrounded by airbags somewhat similar to the ones in automobiles. In contrast, MSL Curiosity used a "Sky Crane": After releasing the parachute, rockets on the crane would slow the decent and lower the rover on cables. When the rover touched the surface, the sky crane would detach and fly a safe distance away, where it would not interfere with the landing or accidently hit the rover. This complex method made it possible to place a heavy vehicle on the surface, but it had never before been attempted.

After being launched in November 2011, MSL Curiosity was placed into the correct path to reach Mars. The course was checked using radio transmissions received by the Deep Space Network.

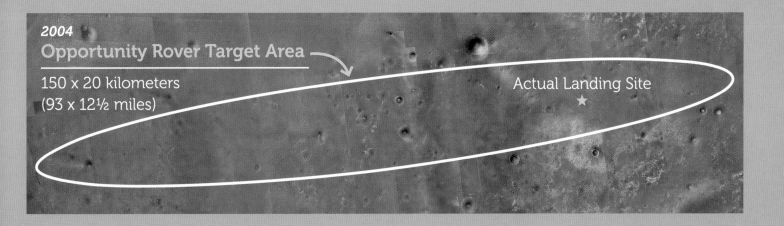

2004
Opportunity Rover Target Area

150 x 20 kilometers
(93 x 12½ miles)

Actual Landing Site

2012
Curiosity Rover Initial Target Area

25 x 20 kilometers wide
(15½ x 12½ miles)

2013
Final Target Area

20 x 7 kilometers wide
(12 x 4 miles)

SCALE
for both areas

0   10   20   km

Landing on Mars was scheduled for August 6, 2012. The landing sequence was completely automated. At that point, there was nothing the mission team could do except wait to hear the result. Would the rover reach the right target? Would the sky crane work? The team nicknamed the nail-biting descent "Seven Minutes of Terror." In the end, on schedule, the signal was received at mission control at the Jet Propulsion Laboratory that Curiosity was safely on Mars. Since landing, Curiosity has returned many significant scientific breakthroughs and continues to explore the planet's surface. ✿

Comparison of landing targets for the Mars Exploration Rover Opportunity in 2004 and Mars Science Laboratory Curiosity in 2013 at the same scale.

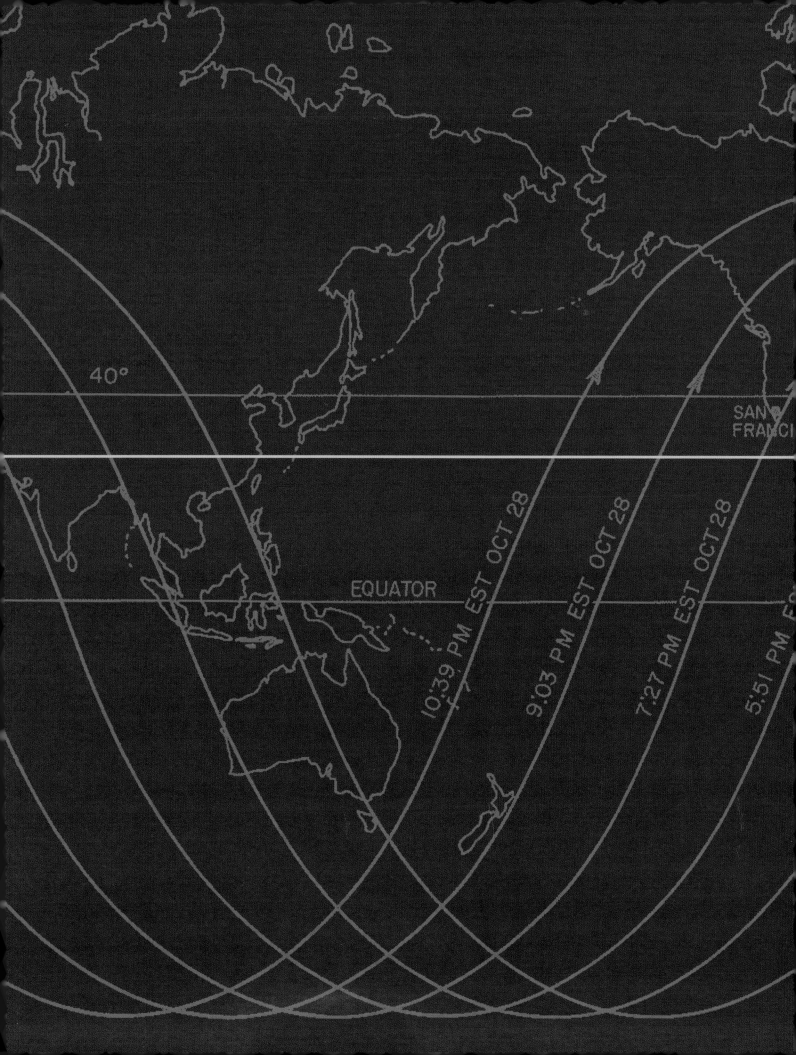

INVENTING
Satellite
NAVIGATION

During the Cold War, the U.S. military sought more reliable global time and navigation systems.

The possibilities of traveling in space inspired plans to navigate from space. Innovators tried different approaches to see whether radio transmissions from orbiting satellites could be used to determine positions on Earth. They found that time from precise clocks on satellites, transmitted by radio signals, could in fact determine location. The military eventually combined elements from several systems to create the Global Positioning System—GPS.

INVENTING *Satellite* NAVIGATION

They were loud and clear, and there was no mistaking the signals coming from space.
William Guier and George Weiffenbach of Johns Hopkins University's Applied Physics Laboratory (APL) had spent the afternoon setting up electronics, including a good receiver and a two-foot piece of wire for an antenna. That day, a Monday, they had come back from the Lab's cafeteria, where the lunchtime chatter had been about the weekend's shocking news of Sputnik. The world had been taken by surprise just a few days before that, when, on October 4, 1957, the Soviet Union

Mathematician William Guier (left) and physicist George Weiffenbach (right) told APL Research Center director Frank T. McClure (center) about using Doppler tracking for Sputnik.

successfully launched the world's first artificial satellite, extending the Cold War from Earth to space. The Soviets were advertising that proof of the satellite was in radio signals that could be heard by anyone with a relatively simple radio receiver.

With a break for dinner and a new high-quality recorder added to their gear, Guier and Weiffenbach at APL detected the signal from Sputnik. They noticed that the radio frequency varied in a particular pattern as it passed overhead. They knew that the small satellite was not sophisticated enough to carry a complicated radio transmitter on board, so they were puzzled by this regular shift in frequency. They soon realized that the variation was due to the Doppler effect: The frequency changed as the satellite approached and receded. Knowing that, they could estimate the satellite's speed and the closest approach of Sputnik to their antenna. Their simple method of tracking Sputnik from a single station in Maryland produced results as good as an elaborate suite of tracking stations built by the U.S. Navy for Project Vanguard, which it pressed into service after Sputnik achieved orbit.

Sputnik's radio signal only lasted a few weeks, but the physicists were able to refine the technique to accurately track the second Soviet satellite and the American satellite Explorer I, launched in January 1958. Their colleague Frank McClure looked at their results and realized that the calculations could be reversed. If one knew the location of a satellite in space, one could fix a position on Earth by measuring the Doppler shift of the satellite's signal. It was the birth of a new idea: Global positioning and navigation from orbiting satellites. ✸

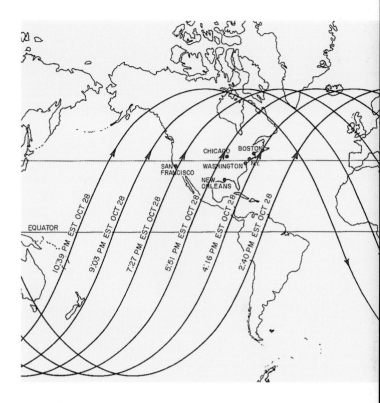

Global map showing the path of the Sputnik satellite.

In the following pages, we will learn how orbiting satellites, including GPS and other systems, were envisioned for determining position on Earth and how these systems were developed to meet diverse needs for time and navigation services.

ABOVE: A backup Transit 5-A satellite from the 1970s. Other versions of Transit carried different antennas and internal components.

OPPOSITE: William Miles (left) and John Dassoulas (right) of the Applied Physics Lab checking the second Transit satellite before launch on April 13, 1960.

By having Sputnik transmit on frequencies that were well known to amateur radio operators, the Soviets in effect got a "free" worldwide tracking network as the 183-pound (83 kg) satellite orbited Earth. But not just amateurs were tracking the satellite. The tracking that took place at the Applied Physics Laboratory of Johns Hopkins University led them to realize that inverting the problem could allow a ground position to be determined based on the known location of an orbiting satellite.

The Applied Physics Laboratory had a long history of understanding and exploiting this effect. During World War II, the lab led the effort to develop one of the war's most effective secret weapons: the proximity fuse, which could explode and disable enemy aircraft without scoring a direct hit. The fuse worked by measuring the Doppler shift of a radio signal as it bounced off the target, which was translated into a range measurement. Among the scientists pressed into service during the war to develop the fuse was physicist James van Allen, who later played a significant role in the scientific exploration of space, including with the first U.S. orbiting satellite Explorer 1. APL scientists were able to accurately track the first two Sputnik satellites from only one location, as well as Explorer I launched in January 1958, by measuring the Doppler shift of their signals as they passed overhead.

In subsequent years, the concept of measuring Doppler shift of a signal from an orbiting satellite to determine position on the earth evolved to meet the needs of the U.S. Navy for navigating vessels at sea. Among the most sensitive assets of the Navy during

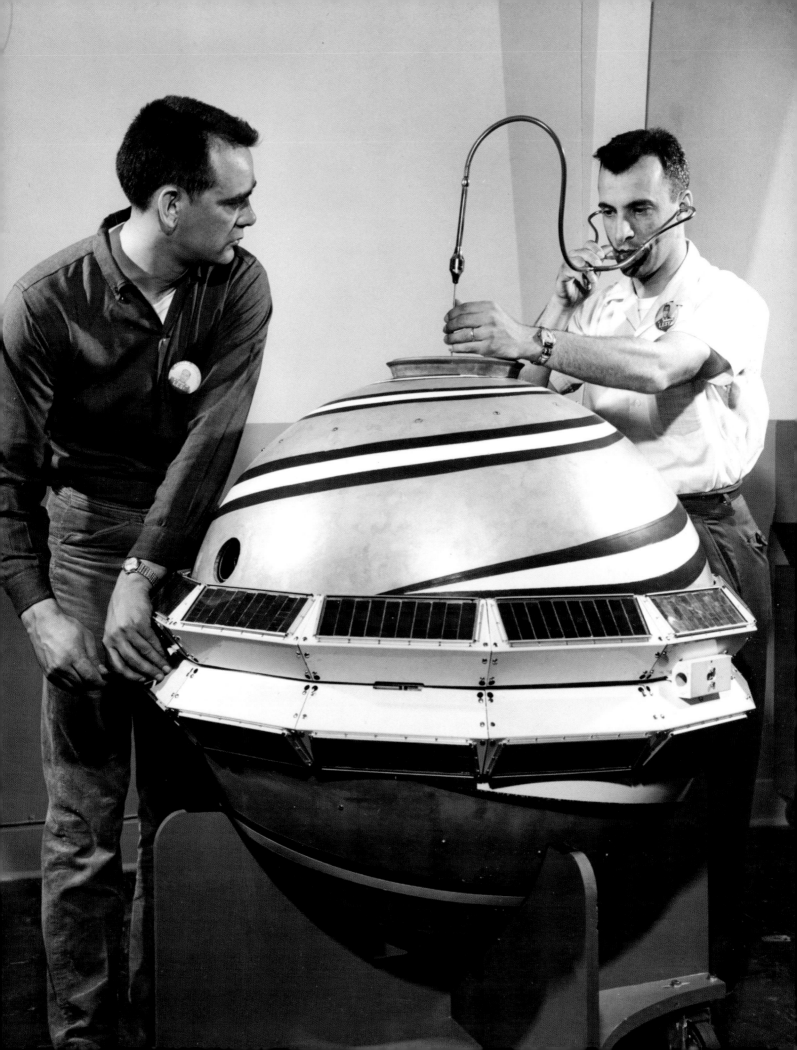

TRANSIT SATELLITE NAVIGATION SYSTEM

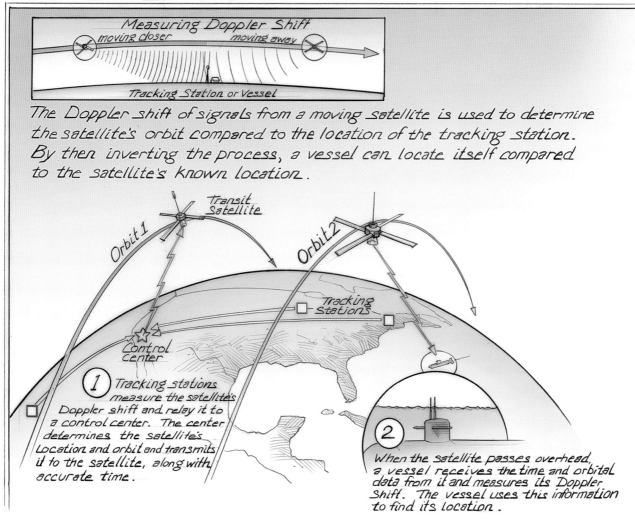

Measuring Doppler Shift

moving closer   moving away

Tracking Station or Vessel

The Doppler shift of signals from a moving satellite is used to determine the satellite's orbit compared to the location of the tracking station. By then inverting the process, a vessel can locate itself compared to the satellite's known location.

Transit Satellite

Orbit 1   Orbit 2

Tracking Stations

Control Center

① Tracking stations measure the satellite's Doppler shift and relay it to a control center. The center determines the satellite's location and orbit and transmits it to the satellite, along with accurate time.

② When the satellite passes overhead, a vessel receives the time and orbital data from it and measures its Doppler shift. The vessel uses this information to find its location.

The Transit system worked by maintaining stable radio frequencies with quartz oscillators and measuring the Doppler shift of signals as the satellites passed overhead.

the Cold War were submarines equipped with ballistic missiles. The viability of these submarines as a nuclear deterrent required that they remain underwater and out of visual or radio contact for long periods. Taking a fix from the stars ran the risk of detection. Under the direction of the Instrumentation Laboratory at the Massachusetts Institute of Technology, an inertial navigation system was developed called the Ship's Inertial Navigation System (SINS). An inertial navigation system uses motion and rotation sensors along with a computer to figure out the position, orientation, and speed of a vehicle without using the stars, sun, moon, or other outside visual references. Consisting of gyroscopes, accelerometers, and a computer, SINS could compute the submarine's position with no reference to the outside world. But as with all inertial systems, the gyros had a tendency to drift over time, and therefore the submarine had to periodically get a fix from an outside source to correct for the error. The Applied Physics Laboratory's plan for navigation by satellite could correct for this drift. With support from the U.S. Advanced Research Project Agency (ARPA), the lab developed a suite of satellites, called Transit. With the launch of the first Transit satellite from Cape Canaveral in September 1959, the era of satellite-based navigation began.

To correct for drift, a submarine did not need to surface, but it would periodically come close enough to the surface to deploy a small antenna, which would receive precise timing and position information from a Transit satellite orbiting about 685 miles (1,100 km) overhead. At the point where the satellite passed closest to the antenna, its frequency would shift, much as a passing ambulance siren changes its pitch as it passes by. By noting the time of that shift, combined with positioning data sent by the satellite, the submarine could locate itself to an accuracy of around 655 feet (200 m). Before a satellite passed over a submarine, its position in space was calculated from a worldwide network of ground tracking stations. These stations in effect reversed the process: Their own location had been surveyed, and they used the Doppler effect to locate the satellite's position in orbit. That information was transmitted to the satellite, which in turn relayed it to the submarine on a subsequent orbit. The accuracy of the system depended on having precise oscillators on the satellites to transmit the signals to the submarines. Signals were transmitted at two frequencies: 150 and 400 MHz, which enabled the system to compensate for delays as signals passed through the ionosphere. The frequency stability was essential. Stable quartz oscillators on the satellites ensured the control of the radio frequency. At sea, a cesium frequency standard provided accurate frequency and time for U.S. Navy vessels using the system.

Navigation systems on U.S. submarines through the 1970s and 1980s included three ways to find position: the ship's inertial

TOP: Ballistic missile submarines like the USS *Alabama*, launched in 1984, used Transit satellites, GPS, LORAN, and inertial systems to navigate.

BOTTOM: Electronics Technician 1st Class David Schlessinger checks a navigational fix provided by GPS aboard USS *Alabama*.

navigation system (SINS), a LORAN-C receiver, and a Transit satellite receiver system for correcting the inertial system. The three worked in tandem to navigate the submarine. The inertial navigation system measured the boat's motion and constantly updated position. Information about position, speed, heading, and attitude was constantly transmitted from the SINS to the missile fire-control system. The boat's exact position was required for launching ballistic missiles. Slung from a gimbal support assembly, the SINS stable platform includes four gyroscopes and three accelerometers. The gyroscopes held the platform level regardless of the submarine's orientation. The MARDAN computer, located in the navigation center, processed the data derived from the gyroscopes and accelerometers inside the SINS inertial guidance units. It calculated the degree of drift from the ship's intended course and recommended corrections. Because it did not rely on radio signals or celestial sightings, SINS allowed the boat to navigate while remaining hidden under the surface. To maintain accuracy, the submarine periodically updated its position using outside navigational radio signals. From the 1960s to the 1990s, Transit satellites and LORAN shore stations provided those signals. The Transit receiver received navigation signals transmitted by the satellites passing overhead. A modified IBM Selectric typewriter connected to a control unit provided input and output for the system computers. The architecture was somewhat similar to the navigation system used by Apollo astronauts. The MIT Instrumentation Laboratory, working with the Sperry Gyroscope Corporation, was the principal developer of both the Apollo system and an early inertial navigation system used on U.S. submarines.

The Transit system was operational by the mid-1960s. It included at least six satellites in polar orbits, providing the most extensive coverage in Arctic regions where U.S. ballistic missile submarines largely operated. The system was accessible worldwide, although users located near the equator could determine position only a few times per day as a Transit satellite passed overhead. Transit service was made

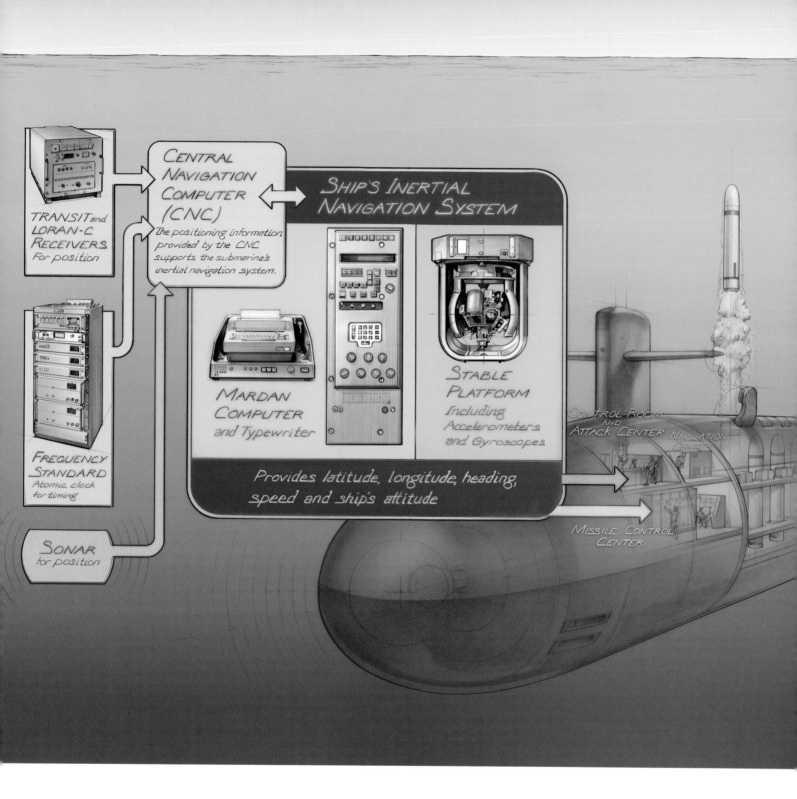

CENTRAL NAVIGATION COMPUTER (CNC)

The positioning information provided by the CNC supports the submarine's inertial navigation system.

TRANSIT and LORAN-C RECEIVERS
For position

FREQUENCY STANDARD
Atomic clock for timing

SONAR
for position

SHIP'S INERTIAL NAVIGATION SYSTEM

MARDAN COMPUTER and Typewriter

STABLE PLATFORM
Including Accelerometers and Gyroscopes

Provides latitude, longitude, heading, speed and ship's attitude

CONTROL ROOM AND ATTACK CENTER NAVIGATION CENTER

MISSILE CONTROL CENTER

available to commercial shipping in 1967 and served both military and civilian users until 1996. After Transit ceased to operate, submarine navigation systems used a GPS receiver for the same function. The availability of GPS eventually replaced both the Transit system and ground-based global positioning systems such as LORAN.

U.S. submarines used multiple sources of information including inertial sensors and radio signals from space and ground-based transmitters.

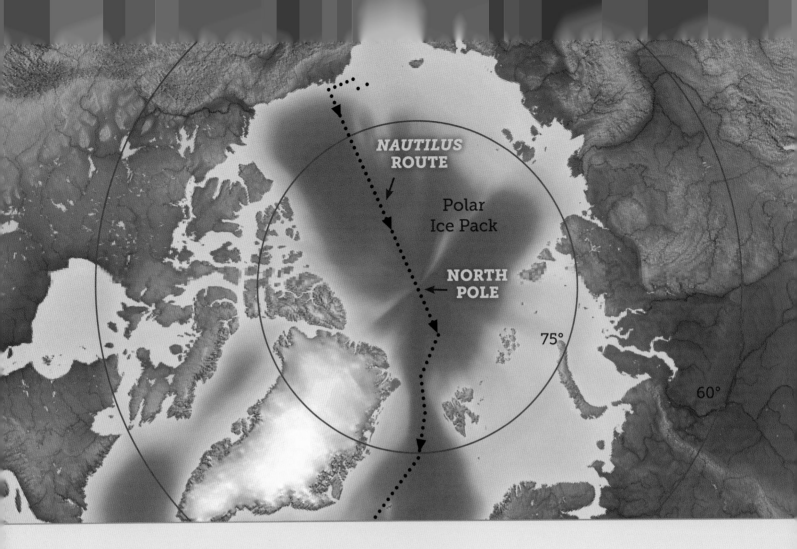

Polar
Ice Pack

*NAUTILUS
ROUTE*

**NORTH
POLE**

75°

60°

TO THE NORTH POLE *with*
NAUTILUS

The orbit of the Soviet satellite Sputnik in 1957 was a
psychological blow to the United States, and the failure of the
U.S. satellite Vanguard not long afterward only made things
worse. One of the responses was to shift attention to another
U.S. satellite, Explorer, which was successfully launched on
January 31, 1958. Another was the journey of *Nautilus*, which
was just as ambitious and had an almost similar effect on world
opinion. *Nautilus*, the world's first nuclear-powered submarine,
journeyed under the Arctic ice pack and passed under the
North Pole on August 3, 1958. The mission was designed to

influence world opinion from the start, showing that the USSR was not the only country capable of high-stakes technological feats. It had a strategic military purpose as well. If an American submarine could navigate in the Arctic Ocean undetected and with impunity, the Soviet Union, with its long Arctic coastline, was clearly vulnerable.

Nautilus had already demonstrated that its nuclear propulsion allowed it to travel for enormous distances at high speeds without surfacing. It was already revolutionizing the notions of submarine operations. For this mission, there were two big unanswered questions. One was to keep *Nautilus* from hitting the ocean floor—a problem all submarines faced—and to keep it from hitting the ice above. To solve that problem, the boat had in effect two sonar systems: one looking down, the other looking up. The second problem was even greater: how to navigate. Magnetic compasses were useless at high latitudes, since the direction they point varies greatly in the Arctic and the Earth's magnetic pole does not coincide with its geographic North Pole. Although a Sperry gyrocompass was installed on the *Nautilus*, such devices were not entirely trustworthy near the North Pole. The solution was to develop an inertial navigation system modified from a system for guidance of the Navaho cruise missile. Built by Autonetics (now part of Boeing), this type of system was used on U.S. submarines such as *Nautilus*. On August 3, 1958, the submarine radioed by Morse code to a naval base in Hawaii the terse message "Nautilus 90 North," indicating that it had arrived at its destination. ✹

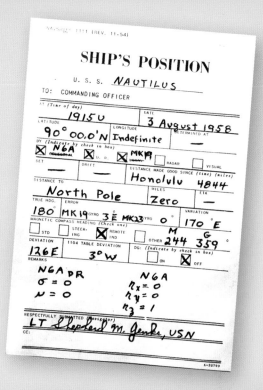

TOP: Navigator's position report to the captain showing USS *Nautilus* at the North Pole.

BOTTOM: The crew in the control room of USS *Nautilus* maintain an exact course while passing under the Arctic ice cap.

TESTING SATELLITE SOLUTIONS

Aerospace Corporation engineer Al Gillogly (left) and Grumman engineer M. Moore test a transmitter for the 621B system at White Sands Missile Range, New Mexico, in 1972.

During the Cold War, U.S. defense planners sought a global navigation system that would be accurate and available at all times while meeting the needs of the several service branches. Transit provided global coverage, but not at all times for all locations. Transit satellites used polar orbits, passing over the North and South Poles. This meant that the system was widely available near the pole, essential for operating in the Arctic Ocean during the Cold War. Closer to the equator, however, several hours could tick by between overpasses of a Transit satellite. This limited the applications of the system around the world. Transit provided accuracy that was adequate for applications such as navigating submarines, but not high enough accuracy for many precise applications such as targeting tactical weapons. An enhanced solution was required for global navigation. Since each had specific navigation needs, the services were not convinced that a single system could serve them all. The U.S. Navy, Air Force, and Army were each exploring the notion of satellite-based navigation and positioning.

From 1964 to 1969, the U.S. Army developed and deployed a satellite-based system called SECOR (Sequential Collation of Range). It was not a general-purpose navigation system, but rather was intended to locate the position of places on the earth to tie them into the worldwide coordinate grid of latitude and longitude. The SECOR system worked by transmitting signals from ground stations to a satellite in orbit. While the satellite was simultaneously visible to multiple ground stations,

TIMATION III A

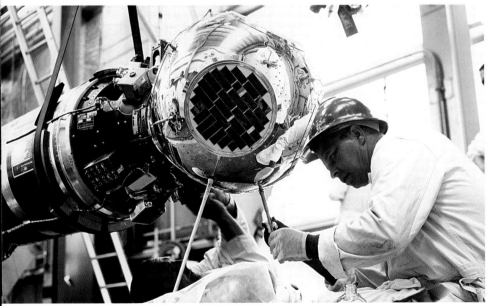

ABOVE: Artist's rendering of Timation 3, a U.S. Navy experimental navigation satellite.

LEFT: SECOR satellite before launch. The U.S. Army successfully launched nine such satellites.

The Navigation Technology Satellite 2 (NTS-2) was launched in 1977 to test new navigation techniques. This engineering model was used at the Naval Research Laboratory (NRL) for testing the satellite before launch.

it would receive signals and then transmit its own signal back to the ground. The distance between the satellite and ground stations was determined by measuring the time required for the signals to arrive. Using that information, the position of a ground station could be accurately determined using "trilateration," determining a position based on measuring the distance to other known positions. SECOR data collected by the Army Map Service in the late 1960s was used to measure the shape of the earth and survey many locations, especially remote islands in the Pacific Ocean.

The Aerospace Corporation, in research funded by the U.S. Air Force, proposed a satellite-based system called "621B" in the early 1960s. The head of the Corporation, Ivan Getting, had worked on a method of guiding ballistic missiles while at his previous position as head of research at the Raytheon Corporation. At that time the Air Force was planning a version of the Minuteman ICBM that would not be housed in hardened silos but would instead be transported on railroad trains to forestall a Soviet first strike on them. That method rendered inertial guidance problematic, since inertial systems depended on knowing precisely the initial location of the missile. Getting proposed flying the ICBMs to their targets by following signals sent from satellites overhead. The concept of a "Mobile Minuteman" was canceled, but Getting took the idea of satellite navigation with him as he moved to the Aerospace Corporation.

Plan 621B was to provide global coverage, using satellites whose position was accurately determined. Like LORAN, 621B receivers would be passive, and therefore the system would serve an unlimited number of users. These features later became essential components of the Global Positioning System. Other features did not, such as the plan to have the 621B satellites in geosynchronous orbits. These orbits had a period of twenty-four hours, matching Earth's rotation, although they were inclined from the equator to appear to move north and south of the equator to a ground observer.

Among the biggest contributions from 621B to what eventually became GPS was the plan for encoding the signals sent from the satellites to the receivers. As with its predecessors LORAN and Transit, the new system was envisioned to serve both civilian and military customers, with the military having access to more detailed and more

NRL's NTS-2 Team. Standing (left to right): Bruce Faraday, Richard Statler, Guy Burke, Roger Easton. Seated (left to right): Al Bartholomew, Bill Huston, Red Woosley, Ron Beard, Woody Ewen, Pete Wilhelm.

secure navigational information than civilians. Drawing on techniques that had been developed at the Jet Propulsion Laboratory and the intelligence community, the Air Force proposed modulating the signals by a sequence of what are called "pseudo-random" numbers—a sequence of digits that appears to be random but in fact are known precisely and matched by both the satellites that transmit them and the receivers that receive them. Civilians would have access to a shorter code than the military, thus serving both user communities without jeopardizing security. The technique also had the very desirable quality of being highly resistant to jamming, and an ability to get the signal through in the presence of background noise, whether intentional or not.

The U.S. Navy had two possible systems in play for future enhancements of satellite navigation. The Applied Physics Lab was in

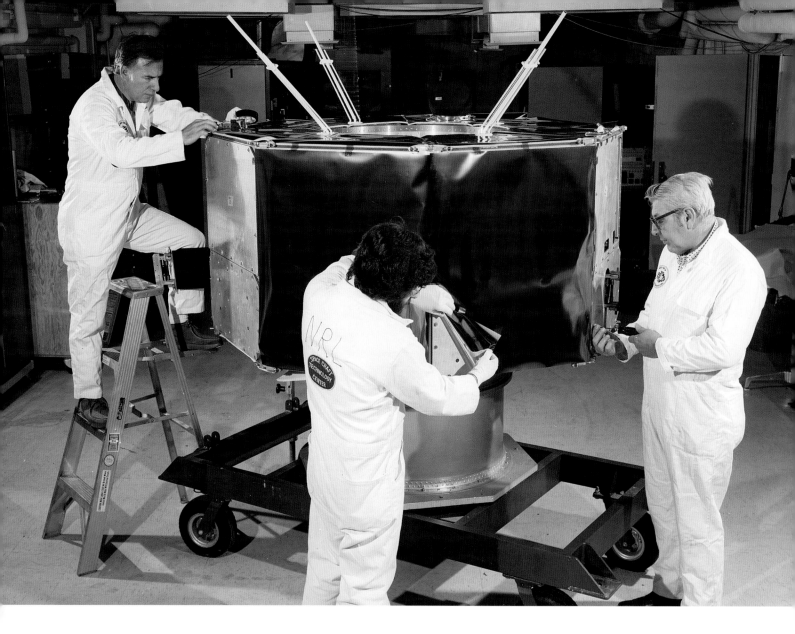

Charlie Buhler (left), Al Jacoby (middle), and Roy Harding (right) of the Naval Research Lab install thermal blankets on the NTS-2 qualification model.

favor of an extension of Transit, which, since its initial deployment, was being steadily improved. New versions of satellites used in the Transit system incorporated different antenna designs and other features. The Naval Research Laboratory (NRL) in Washington, D.C., was developing another experimental system, which they called TIMATION. It was based on placing very precise frequency standards, including atomic clocks, on satellites. By 1956, the first commercial atomic clocks were available, although they were neither cheap nor rugged, nor small. Atomic clocks for space would require new features to enable them to withstand changes in temperature and radiation while maintaining precise time. An entire constellation of satellites equipped with atomic clocks could allow a receiver's position to be calculated by comparing the relative times it took for signals to arrive from several of the satellites overhead. These developments were an extension of the story of the Harrison chronometer, which transformed sea navigation in the nineteenth century, and the quartz oscillator, which had a similar effect on air navigation in the following century. As with the superiority of quartz over the mechanical movements, the key to atomic clock's superiority was its higher period of oscillation—billions of times a second compared to quartz's thousands.

The NRL launched the TIMATION 1 satellite in 1967 and TIMATION 2 in 1969. Both carried precise quartz oscillators. After the NAVSTAR Global Positioning System was created in 1973, the third TIMATION satellite was renamed Navigation Technology Satellite 1 (NTS-1). While developing this satellite, NRL researchers found a small commercial atomic clock marketed by a German firm. They took this product and integrated it into the NTS-1 satellite. NTS-1 performed experiments with these two rubidium atomic clocks—the first atomic clocks carried on satellites. NRL's next satellite, NTS-2, carried two experimental cesium clocks into space in June 1977. These satellites tested a number of other aspects of satellite navigation. NTS-2 transmitted signals matching the design of GPS signals. The clocks on NTS-2 were used to detect the relativistic effects of orbital travel. The key to these experimental satellites was the use of atomic time and frequency standards.

While branches of the U.S. military tested solutions for satellite navigation, other federal agencies provided new satellite services. The U.S. Department of Commerce established a precise time service based on satellite signals in 1974. The National Bureau of Standards provided the time. The electric power industry found the time service useful for synchronizing AC generators to move electricity from one part of the power grid to another. The signals were transmitted by Geostationary Operational Environmental Satellites (GOES) of the National Oceanic and Atmospheric Administration (NOAA) until the end of 2004.

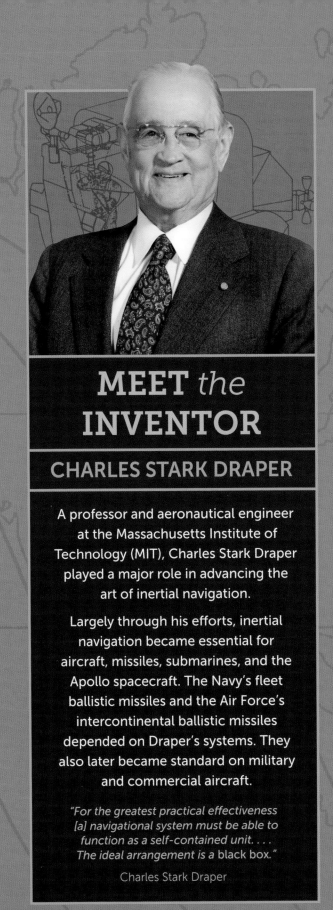

MEET *the* INVENTOR

CHARLES STARK DRAPER

A professor and aeronautical engineer at the Massachusetts Institute of Technology (MIT), Charles Stark Draper played a major role in advancing the art of inertial navigation.

Largely through his efforts, inertial navigation became essential for aircraft, missiles, submarines, and the Apollo spacecraft. The Navy's fleet ballistic missiles and the Air Force's intercontinental ballistic missiles depended on Draper's systems. They also later became standard on military and commercial aircraft.

"For the greatest practical effectiveness [a] navigational system must be able to function as a self-contained unit. . . . The ideal arrangement is a black box."

Charles Stark Draper

GPS: A UNIFIED SYSTEM

The GPS constellation consists of at least twenty-four satellites in six orbital planes.

In 1972, the U.S. Department of Defense decided to combine the competing satellite navigation programs from each of the services under the direction of the Air Force, with Colonel Bradford Parkinson placed in charge of the unification. Parkinson had been trained as a navigator; he also had experience with inertial navigation techniques, having worked at the MIT Instrumentation Laboratory under Charles Stark Draper.

Initially, Parkinson proposed adopting the Air Force's 621B as the new common navigation system, but this was rejected. His superiors at the Pentagon encouraged him to keep working on the problem, and in a meeting held over the Labor Day weekend in September 1973, the basic architecture of GPS was decided—an architecture that has served well to the present day. According to Parkinson, there were around a dozen different configurations being considered. The number of satellites in the constellation, their altitude, their inclination (the angle at which they cross the equator), the codes they transmitted, the locations of the atomic clocks—all these were open to debate. In essence, the system combined the best features of 621B and TIMATION with inputs from other sources. Among the decisions made in 1973 were ones that still form the structure of GPS today: GPS would be a "constellation" of at least twenty-four satellites, atomic frequency standards would be carried on each satellite, signals would be transmitted with pseudo-random coding, and ground equipment would function as passive receivers. Initially called the Defense Navigation Satellite System, it was later renamed NAVSTAR. Today it is most commonly known as the Global Positioning System (GPS).

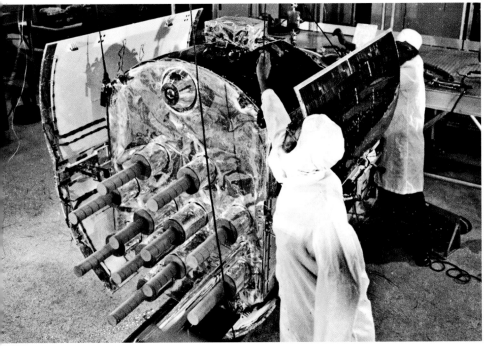

ABOVE: Frank Butterfield (left) of the Aerospace Corporation, Air Force Colonel Bradford Parkinson of the Joint Program Office (center), and Navy Commander Bill Huston discuss GPS in the 1970s.

LEFT: Testing the third prototype GPS satellite before launch, 1978.

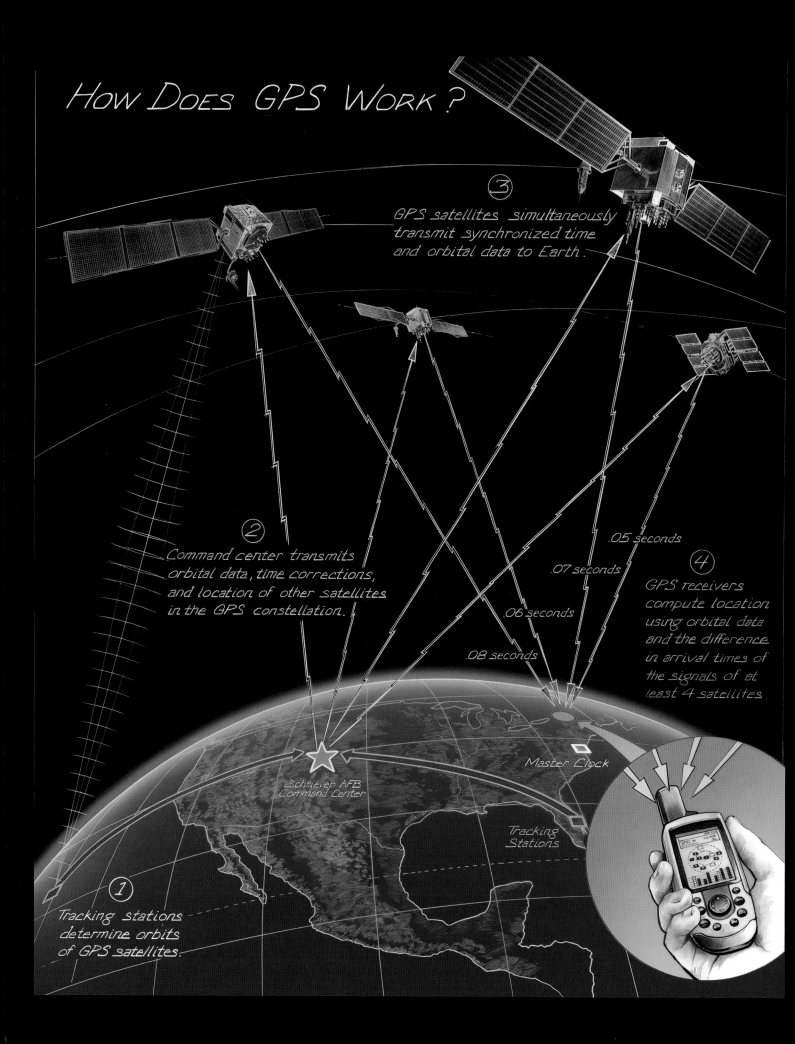

HOW DOES GPS WORK?

③ GPS satellites simultaneously transmit synchronized time and orbital data to Earth.

② Command center transmits orbital data, time corrections, and location of other satellites in the GPS constellation.

.05 seconds

.07 seconds

.06 seconds

.08 seconds

④ GPS receivers compute location using orbital data and the difference in arrival times of the signals of at least 4 satellites.

Master Clock

Schriever AFB Command Center

Tracking Stations

① Tracking stations determine orbits of GPS satellites.

The GPS constellation would consist of two dozen satellites, but it would be viable with as few as eighteen. The satellites would be in six orbital planes, inclined 55 degrees relative to the equator. That would ensure enough satellites would be visible from anywhere in the world, providing worldwide coverage. The satellites would orbit 11,185 miles (18,000 km) above Earth in a twelve-hour period. They were not in geosynchronous orbits or in low orbits where atmospheric drag or irregularities in the earth's gravitational field would complicate their motion. However, the satellites would orbit near the Van Allen radiation belts, so that they had to be hardened against radiation. The satellites would carry atomic clocks on board, synchronized from ground control stations that would track their position and monitor the health and accuracy of the clocks. The satellites would transmit ephemeris data and time with pseudo-random number codes, also known as "Direct Sequence Spread Spectrum." Using these codes, all the satellites could share the same frequencies without interfering with one another. Different codes would make the system usable by both the military and civilians, and the technique was robust against interference or jamming. The receivers would be passive, so they would not need to radiate any signals. Neither do they require an atomic clock on the ground. A receiver's position in three dimensions could be obtained by receiving signals from four satellites. With the fourth signal, the receiver could determine position in three dimensions as well as accurate time.

Although the group came to an agreement about the system's design in 1973, there was no assurance that it would be implemented. The Air Force was reluctant to carry all the costs of a system that the other services would be using. On the civilian side of the federal government, the Federal Aviation Agency was also reluctant to support GPS; it felt that aircraft owners would balk at the requirement that they purchase and install new equipment on aircraft, and there was the inertia that came from having an extensive infrastructure of existing air traffic control systems already in place. With funding for satellites in question, Parkinson's team countered by placing transmitters at a test site at the Army's Yuma Proving Ground in Arizona. The transmitters were on the ground but behaved as if they were in space, so the team called them "pseudolites." The demonstration worked, and testing at Yuma continued in the late 1970s. By getting the Army involved in the testing, GPS received support from a branch of the military that was a potential customer for many receivers.

TOP: First-generation rubidium frequency standard, or atomic clock, built for the first GPS satellites.

BOTTOM: Cesium frequency standard built for GPS satellites. Atomic clocks like this one underwent extended miniaturization and testing for use in space.

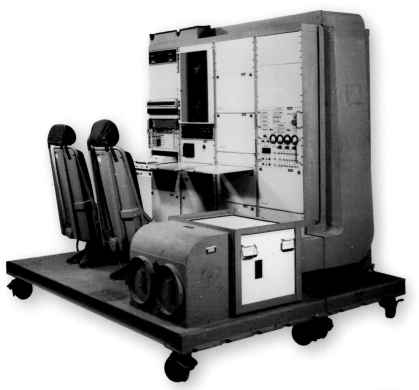

This instrument from 1977 weighed more than 270 pounds (120 kg) and was the first military GPS five-channel receiver built by the company now known as Rockwell Collins.

While funding for the project was in jeopardy, support came from an unexpected quarter. The Department of Energy (the successor to the Atomic Energy Commission) looked at the proposed constellation of satellites and noted its worldwide, continuous coverage. It arranged to place on each satellite sensors that could detect nuclear explosions, knowing that nations wishing to join the nuclear "club" were likely to conduct tests in remote regions of the globe, even over the open ocean. The satellites would thus play a significant role in enforcing the Nuclear Non-Proliferation Treaty that was signed in 1968. The addition complicated the design of the satellites, but it also gave NAVSTAR/GPS a source of funds outside the Pentagon channels. The Joint Program Office was given a final go-ahead to build the system in August 1979.

GPS required the development, testing, and refinement of satellites, receivers, atomic clocks, and other components. Rockwell International (now a division of Boeing) was contracted to build GPS satellites beginning in 1974. By 1986, eighteen had been launched into orbit, making the system usable for many applications. The full suite of twenty-four satellites needed for global coverage was in orbit by early 1995. Beginning in the 1990s, Lockheed Martin built new generations of GPS satellites. More than thirty GPS satellites were operational after 2010. An instrument the size of a tiny car was the first military GPS five-channel receiver built by the company now known as Rockwell Collins in 1977. It was one of several programs launched to study the feasibility and operational utility of GPS. The receiver weighed more than 270 pounds (120 kg) and was mounted on an Air Force flight test pallet.

As GPS began to take form, a number of unforeseen developments and events shaped its trajectory. The initial concept of having a well-controlled dual access for civil and military customers remained a goal, but the Joint Program Office, and later the Air Force, soon found that technical and political factors upset the best planning. Continued funding for the multi-decade project was uncertain, major launch difficulties would arise, and political decisions would ultimately overwhelm the initial idea of having a positioning system solely for aircraft, soldiers, and ships.

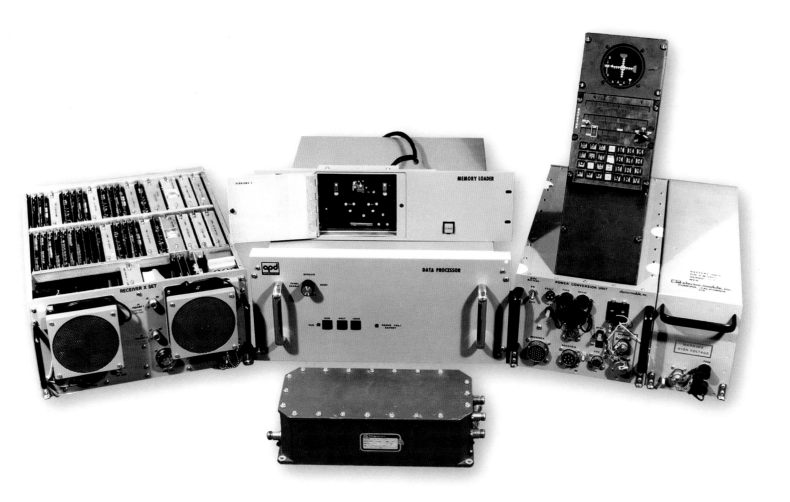

On September 1, 1983, a Korean Airlines Boeing 747, en route from Anchorage, Alaska, to Seoul, South Korea, strayed over restricted Soviet territory and was shot down (see page 165). The tragedy inflamed the already hostile relations between the United States and the Soviet Union, and those tensions prevented the reasons for the tragedy's cause from being made public for years. Among the responses from the Reagan administration was that the Global Positioning System, then under construction, would be made freely available for civilian use to prevent such tragedies from occurring in the future. This pronouncement was part of a coordinated diplomatic and military response to the event, emphasizing the openness of American society in stark contrast to the Soviet response, which alternated between denial, misinformation, and contradictory statements.

Although President Reagan did not know all of the details surrounding the tragedy, his statement implied that GPS was

Magnavox built these experimental test receivers in 1974–75 to demonstrate the feasibility of the GPS system.

superior to the inertial navigation system the aircraft was carrying. That impression influenced the public perception of GPS as the "next, new thing," although inertial navigation was, and remains, a very capable technology. A lack of attention by operators or crew is a problem that could equally apply to any system. The popular press is full of stories of drivers who turn down a closed road because their GPS system "told them to." More recently, civilian and military ships have run aground in spite of having working satellite navigation systems aboard. The designers of these systems have taken steps to prevent similar disasters, but the problem of designing a failure-resistant human interface has not gone away.

Throughout the initial deployment of GPS, funding was by no means assured. The system designers even developed a contingency plan that allowed the service to achieve "initial operational capability" with a smaller constellation of eighteen satellites, which was achieved by 1984. The designers hoped to gain support by introducing the lower-cost Course Acquisition (C/A) code right away. Defense customers held off supporting GPS until they could see the results of the more accurate codes, but a surprising thing happened: The civil code was much more accurate than initially intended, giving accuracies in the 65–100 foot (20–30 m) range. Later refinements could give accuracies of around twenty feet (6 m) for the C/A code alone. This helped win support, but it also upset the plan to deny civilians higher precision.

Manpack GPS receiver in the field.

The C/A code had two functions. One was to provide coarse position data for civil users. The other was to allow the military to quickly acquire a fix on the satellites overhead, after which they could get more precise positioning from the longer P code. In addition, the satellites deliberately degraded the C/A code so that civil users could not get a position closer than 150 feet (45 m). They called this feature "Selective Availability." In this way, the U.S. military could ensure that the system would find widespread commercial and civil use but would not impinge on its ability to use GPS for military operations. Selective availability was permanently turned off in May 2000. Both military and civilian GPS users can obtain higher accuracy by using a second unit at a fixed nearby location—a method called Differential GPS. In this way, positions can be determined with an accuracy of less than half an inch (1 cm). For military users, additional encrypted signals can provide high accuracy.

GPS requires precise clocks to provide astounding positional accuracy. Each GPS satellite contains atomic clocks to maintain the correct frequencies to transmit signals for time and position. Using rubidium and cesium, these clocks underwent extended miniaturization and testing to become useful in space. Keeping track of nanoseconds, or billionths of a second, is essential. The atomic clocks in GPS satellites require taking into account Albert Einstein's understanding of time, space, and relativity. Because GPS satellites experience less gravity and move at high velocity, their clocks operate at a different rate than those on Earth. A difference of 38 millionths of a second per day must be accounted for in GPS operations. GPS time is maintained by a suite of atomic clocks, closely matching the time distributed by the U.S. Naval Observatory from Washington, D.C., the official source of time for the U.S. Department of Defense.

All GPS satellites are monitored constantly and adjusted as needed. The GPS Operations Center at Schriever Air Force Base in Colorado Springs, Colorado, controls the constellation of satellites that provides navigation data to military and civilian users worldwide.

GPS has transformed U.S. military operations. Since becoming operational, GPS became an indispensible military asset and transformed space into a platform for war. Public awareness of GPS grew during the 1990–91 Persian Gulf War, which showcased its effectiveness to synchronize operations, provide navigation information, pinpoint targets, and locate personnel. GPS now is the core navigation system for U.S. military aircraft, vessels, vehicles, and personnel. It has changed the nature of weapons targeting, command and control, guidance of unmanned systems, and supply delivery on the battlefield.

Munitions can be designed with smaller and more precise explosive power. The U.S. military designed the GBU-39 Small Diameter Bomb, a GPS-guided, 250-pound (113 kg) glide bomb to reduce unintended damage to structures and injuries to people near a target. Accuracy substitutes for a larger explosive warhead, which reduces weight and allows it to be carried on more types of aircraft, including drones.

TOP: The handheld Precision Lightweight GPS Receiver (PLGR), popularly known as the "Plugger," was similar to civilian receivers of the time but used higher-precision GPS signals.

BOTTOM: The Defense Advanced GPS Receiver (DAGR), widely called the "Dagger," integrated map graphics with two channels of GPS signals coded specifically for the military.

Navigation devices used by personnel on the ground have become more portable over decades. The PSN-8 Manpack GPS Receiver was one of the first portable GPS receivers for combat troops. It weighed about seventeen pounds (8 kg). About 1,400 were manufactured from 1988 to 1993 and were used by coalition ground troops in Operation Desert Storm in 1991. GPS allowed quick and precise navigation in the almost featureless desert and provided a tactical advantage. The handheld Precision Lightweight GPS Receiver (PLGR), popularly known as the "Plugger," replaced the Manpack in 1993. These units were similar to civilian receivers but used higher-precision GPS signals coded specifically for the military. Beginning in 2004, Rockwell Collins made the smaller Defense Advanced GPS Receiver (DAGR, pronounced "dagger"), which integrated a map graphic with two channels of GPS signals coded specifically for the military; predecessor receivers showed only words and numbers.

Satellite navigation is now an essential part of nearly all U.S. military operations, including transportation, surveillance and troop movements. Aircraft dropping supplies by parachute have to fly at dangerously low altitudes and can miss the intended target. The Joint Precision Airdrop System (JPADS) addresses this challenge by including a GPS guidance unit and parafoil to steer cargo dropped from higher altitudes to a preprogrammed landing zone. The Honeywell RQ-16 T-Hawk Micro Air Vehicle, an autonomous air vehicle using GPS and inertial navigation, has proved its worth for observation missions in hazardous situations without exposing its operator to risk. RQ-16s provided the first detailed interior imagery of damaged nuclear reactors in Japan in the 2011 tsunami and have flown with police SWAT teams and military bomb disposal units. Another GPS application is the Blue Force Tracker, a networked system that integrates GPS positioning with real-time map and intelligence data on an electronic display. Commanders can use it to issue orders and reduce the risk of friendly fire. This type of intergration of satellite positioning and digital map data mirrors what took place with civilian applications, part of a process that transformed GPS from a military application to a utility used all over the world.

TOP: The Joint Precision Air Drop System (JPADS) uses GPS and three-dimensional terrain mapping to steer a parachute to deliver supplies accurately.

BOTTOM: The Blue Force Tracker is a networked system that integrates GPS positioning with real-time map and intelligence data on an electronic display.

NAVIGATION GONE WRONG

SOVIET UNION · Alaska · CRASH SITE · Pacific Ocean

SOVIETS SHOOT DOWN AN AIRLINER

While flying from Anchorage, Alaska, to Seoul, South Korea, on September 1, 1983, a Korean Air Lines jumbo jetliner strayed into Soviet airspace. The error proved tragic.

SOVIET UNION · Actual Path · CRASH SITE · Intended Path · S. KOREA · JAPAN

ABOVE: The intended and actual flight paths of KAL-007.

BELOW: Seen in regular service, KAL-007 was shot down by Soviet interceptors on September 1, 1983.

WHAT HAPPENED

Mostly out of range of land-based radio beacons and air traffic radar stations, the crew of KAL Flight 007 had to depend on inertial navigation. But flying without an assigned navigator, the pilot and copilot failed to notice that the plane's autopilot was not following the waypoints programmed into the inertial navigation system.

THE CONSEQUENCES

The Boeing 747 strayed more than 110 miles (180 km) off course and into Soviet airspace. It was seen as a potential threat, and fighter planes were ordered to shoot it down. All 269 people on board perished. The incident greatly increased East-West tensions. President Ronald Reagan used the incident to draw a contrast with the secretive Soviet Union by emphasizing that GPS was to be freely available to civilian users around the world.

LESSONS LEARNED

The tragedy highlighted a continuing issue with overreliance on automated navigation systems. The flight crew trusted a specific system so much that they ignored other indications of error. The use of GPS in recent years has helped reduce navigational errors, but accidents due to complacency still occur.

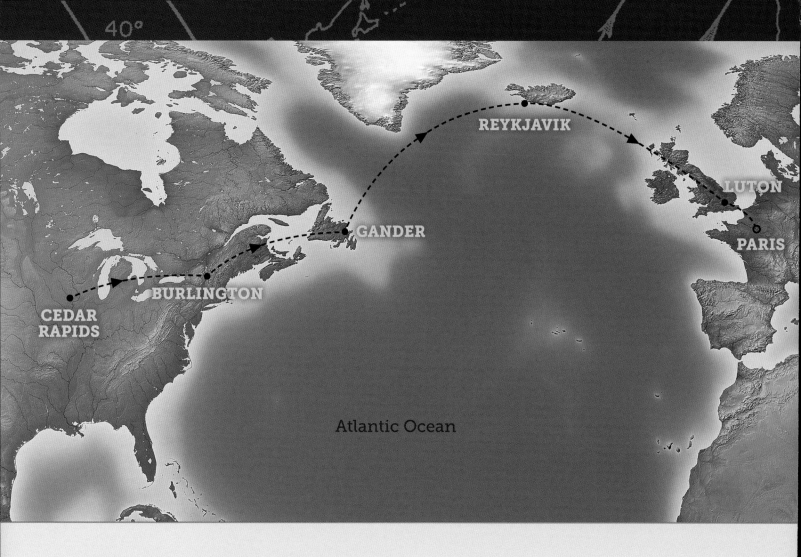

40°

REYKJAVIK

LUTON

GANDER

PARIS

BURLINGTON

CEDAR
RAPIDS

Atlantic Ocean

USING SATELLITES TO FLY *with*
NAVSTAR

In 1983, there were just enough satellites operational to demonstrate the feasibility of the system. When President Reagan announced that GPS would be made available for civilian use, the basic architecture of the system had been determined, and satellites were being launched at a steady rate. Some of the details of its implementation had yet to be worked out. Among those was the question of whether civilians, and especially customers from other nations, would somehow be charged a fee to use the system. Nevertheless, civilian use of NAVSTAR, as it was called then, was already

Route of the 1983 flight across the Atlantic using GPS guidance.

underway. In July of that year, Rockwell International staged a dramatic flight by a Sabreliner business jet, flying from Cedar Rapids, Iowa, home of the division of Rockwell where aircraft electronics were developed, to Le Bourget Airport in Paris, the field where Charles Lindbergh landed in 1927. At the time, only five GPS satellites were functioning well enough to broadcast suitable GPS signals. The Sabreliner had to land several times between Cedar Rapids and Paris, not just to refuel but also to wait for enough satellites to come into view to get an accurate fix. A minimum of three satellites was required to be simultaneously visible to determine at two-dimensional position. GPS satellites have a twelve-hour period—they move relatively slowly across the sky. With a full constellation of at least twenty-four satellites in orbit, one can usually be assured that enough will be in view anywhere in the world at any time to fix a position in three dimensions. But that was not the case in 1983, when only seven GPS satellites had been placed into orbit. Because of the twelve-hour orbits of the GPS satellites, the flight had to wait for times when enough satellites were visible. But using GPS—and GPS alone—it navigated to Le Bourget and taxied to within twenty-five feet (7.5 m) of a presurveyed stopping point. The flight was publicized in the trade literature and in a widely circulated videotape, *NAVSTAR Crosses the Atlantic*. It was a demonstration that made it clear GPS could be useful for civilian as well as military customers. These new navigation capabilities using GPS satellites would be marketed in the United States and around the world. ✿

TOP: Crew of the flight, clockwise from upper left: David Selzer, Charles Hall, Loren DeGroot, David Van Dusseldorp, Alex Rankin, Randy Weyer, Benjamin Elson.

BOTTOM: Guided by GPS, the aircraft landed at Le Bourget Airport and taxied to the intended parking spot, visible as the white mark on the ground under the right wing.

ABOVE: Two regulators, made by Sigmund Riefler of Munich, Germany, in a clock vault at the U.S. Naval Observatory, about 1905.

OPPOSITE: Advertisement for the Synchronome Company's free-pendulum clock, promoted as "The Perfect Clock," from the *Horological Journal*, March 1928.

Time must be measured carefully for navigation and finding position, and reliable clocks are essential. A perfect clock always keeps time to the second. But the second, the most basic subdivision of time, is an ideal standard, and no clock yet built can keep time perfectly. For a clock to measure the passage of time reliably, an important factor is the stability of its rate. Good clocks tick very consistently over long periods. Individual clocks used for navigation may tick at slightly different rates, so they may gain or lose time. As long as a clock ticks at a consistent rate that has been measured and recorded, it can be used with celestial sightings to determine position.

Over the seven centuries since the mechanical clock was first invented, a timekeeper's accuracy has been defined by its rate, an expression of how close it can get to keeping time to the ideal second, and its stability, how long it maintains the rate. The earliest clocks had such enormous errors that their dials often bore only one hand, for telling time to the closest hour. Clocks could count seconds only at the end of the seventeenth century, with the invention of the pendulum and the anchor escapement. Even John Harrison's extraordinary sea clock H-4 had an error—on a voyage to Jamaica in 1761, it lost five seconds in six weeks, and on another to Barbados three years later, it gained thirty-eight seconds in seven weeks.

As the twentieth century began, astronomical observatories installed the best mechanical clocks ever made, by Sigmund Riefler in Munich and by the Synchronome Company in London. Despite the

THE PERFECT CLOCK

ASTRONOMERS have now stated that the RATE of the "SYNCHRONOME" FREE PENDULUM at

GREENWICH OBSERVATORY

but for the very small growth of the Invar Rod which was known and forecasted, has been INVARIABLE. Over a period of nearly TWELVE MONTHS while it was under the closest observation,

NO CHANGE OF RATE COULD BE DETECTED.

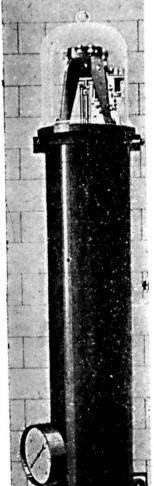

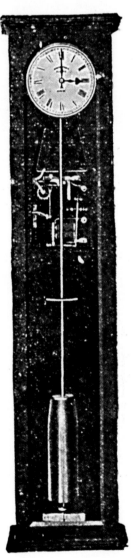

THE SYNCHRONOME FREE PENDULUM

was designed by Mr. W. H. SHORTT, M.Inst.C.E., in combination with the Synchronome System, the invention of Mr. F. HOPE-JONES, M.I.E.E., F.R.A.S.

PROFESSOR W. de SITTER of Leyden, discussing in "NATURE" of Jan. 21st, 1928, this entirely new conception of the possibilities of clocks, asks—

> *"Can these wonderful clocks be of use as a control upon the uniformity of astronomical time like the motion of the moon, the sun, and the planets? Can the handiwork of man compete with the heavenly bodies?"*

All who are interested in this astonishing achievement, and who wish to know more of the SYNCHRONOME SYSTEM, particularly its applications to commercial purposes in the supply of UNIFORM AND ACCURATE TIME for Industrial Establishments and Institutions, should apply to:

THE SYNCHRONOME Co., Ltd.,

32 & 34, CLERKENWELL ROAD, LONDON, E.C.1.

Tel : No. CLERKENWELL 1517.

MENTION THE "HOROLOGICAL JOURNAL."

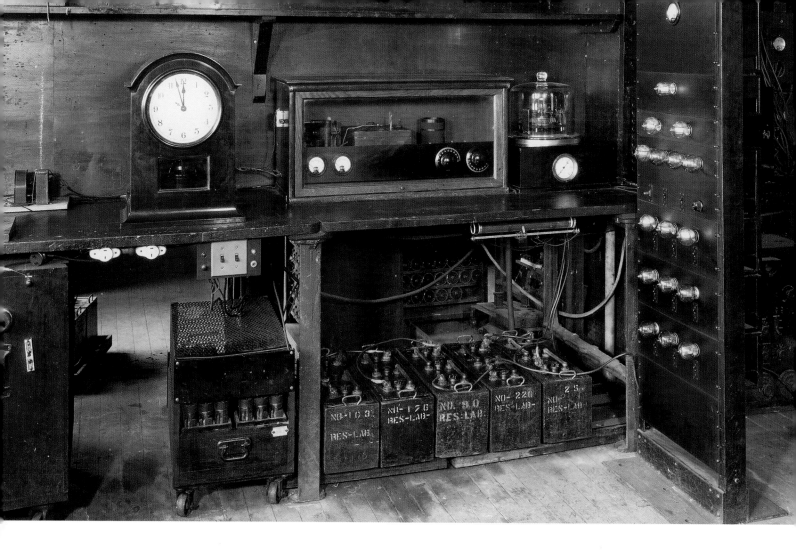

The first quartz clock at Bell Laboratories, 1927.

advertisement shown here, they too were imperfect, although their errors were only seconds over the course of a year. Today's best clock, a laboratory instrument based on the natural "beats" of an atom rather than a mechanical machine, is expected to neither gain nor lose one second over about three hundred million years. Who needs this kind of accuracy? And how do we know how long a second is?

The earliest definition of the second came from an averaging of Earth's daily rotation: 1/86,400th of twenty-four hours. The Synchronome clocks in the 1920s, however, began to confirm what scientists had long suspected: Earth does not keep uniform time. It speeds up and slows as it orbits the sun, we now know, and it wobbles on its axis as it spins. A day varies in length by tiny fractions of a second. Such deviations were not measurable before astronomers could compare their observations with the best clocks. A search for a better time standard got underway.

In the same decade, timekeeping headed unexpectedly in a different direction. In 1927, Warren Marrison, a Canadian telecommunications engineer at Bell Telephone Laboratories, developed a clock based on counting the vibrations of a quartz crystal. This invention emerged from work on ways to monitor and control precise electromagnetic frequencies that carry telephone and radio signals. Installed in some observatories and laboratories in the 1930s and 1940s, quartz clocks proved more accurate than any existing mechanical timekeeper, with an error of about a second in three years.

The shift from measurement of time based on moving mechanical parts to a measurement that harnesses the fundamental properties of matter and energy accelerated with new electronic technologies during World War II, when the military applications of radar, sonar, and LORAN raised the possibilities of what could be done with finely controlled radio frequencies. In the process, astronomers yielded their centuries-long lead in stimulating timekeeping improvements to physicists.

Aiming to develop an even more stable standard, physicists began to extract the "beats" of electromagnetic radiation from atoms. The original idea for atomic clocks lies in I. I. Rabi's work on magnetic resonance in the 1930s. Because of Rabi's work, it was clear that, since all atoms of a given chemical element are identical, a reproducible and uniform frequency reference could result. Quartz frequencies, in contrast, varied from one piece of crystal to another, depending on size and shape. Harold Lyons and colleagues at the U.S. National Bureau of Standards undertook the construction of the first atomic clock in 1948. In 1956, an American commercial atomic clock, the Atomichron, went on the market. Based on the atom of the shiny metal cesium, the earliest version of the Atomichron stood seven feet (2.1 m) high, weighed 500 pounds (227 kg), and cost $50,000. Cesium standards proliferated when Hewlett Packard began to produce a clock the size of a suitcase in 1964.

By international agreement in 1967, the fundamental unit of time is the second, defined as how long it takes the cesium 133 atom to vibrate more than nine billion times—9,192,631,770, to be exact—when subjected to electromagnetic waves. Atomic clocks count these tiny fragments of a second. Today's best atomic clocks, created and operated at national laboratories such as the National Institute of Standards and Technology in the United States, can stay accurate to within one second over tens of millions of years.

Atomic clocks serve what one specialist in the field has called "a hierarchy of users," with a very small number of researchers at the top

The first atomic clock with inventor Harold Lyons (right) and Edward Condon, director of National Bureau of Standards, 1949.

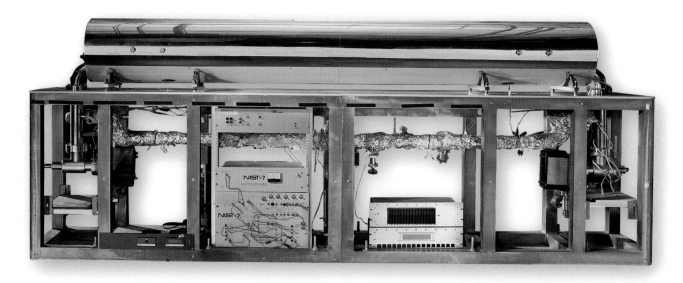

In the 1990s, this instrument, known as NIST-7, was the most accurate clock in the country and helped keep the GPS clocks synchronized. It determined the length of a second of time for the U.S. government.

and a broad base of less demanding commercial customers below. The best clocks have always been in the service of science and navigation, where measurements of time and space were critical. Scientists dealing with deep space—astrophysicists measuring radiation from distant pulsars and NASA's navigators of space vehicles have the most exacting requirements. Successful interplanetary navigation, just like sailing the oceans, depends on knowing the position of the spacecraft. The better the time measurement, the better the location can be determined. Navigating in space uses time to plot the location of the spacecraft relative to an astronomical coordinate system, just as finding latitude and longitude with a chronometer was essential for the mariner. Just as the nautical almanac located the relative position of heavenly bodies, computerized ephemerides—calculated with the aid of radar, imaging technologies, and radio signals—predict the dynamics of the solar system.

Slightly less demanding but more numerous than deep-space navigators are those using atomic clocks for defense, including communications systems and the Global Positioning System, which requires precise clocks to provide positional accuracy. Miniature cesium and rubidium atomic clocks in GPS satellites keep time to within three nanoseconds—three-billionths of a second. GPS satellites are monitored and controlled at the GPS Operations Center at Schriever Air Force Base in Colorado Springs, Colorado. Also on site is the alternate master clock operated by the U.S. Naval Observatory, which provides a time reference for all the clocks in the system.

The success of GPS has transformed the availability of time. Once, the bottom of the hierarchy of atomic clock users was occupied by hundreds of radio and television broadcast stations, electric light and power systems, and computer networks. Most have shifted to synchronizing their operations to GPS.

ABOVE: The GPS Operations Center at Schriever Air Force Base controls GPS satellites. Senior Airman Nayibe Ramos serves as a satellite system operator for the 2nd Space Operations Squadron.

LEFT: The U.S. Naval Observatory Alternate Master Clock at Schriever Air Force Base.

LONDON
OTTAWA
GENEVA
SAN FRANCISCO
BOULDER
WASHINGTON
TOKYO
MOJAVE
HAWAII

TRAVELING *with*
MR. CLOCK

If you flew internationally on Pan Am or TWA in the 1960s, you might have encountered Mr. Clock. Beginning in that decade, a select group of portable atomic timekeepers became frequent flyers on commercial airlines. Continuing a tradition that started with transporting marine chronometers from place to place to compare time, these modern clock trips transferred the most precise time available between observatories and national laboratories worldwide. Each timekeeper was ticketed as "Mr. Cesium Clock" or "Mr. P. Clock" (P for portable), strapped into a passenger seat, and escorted by two handlers.

ABOVE: Portable atomic clocks flew these routes in 1964–65 to compare time at different laboratories.

The first flying atomic clocks for a 1959 experiment were so large they traveled in cargo planes. But in 1964, Hewlett Packard released the HP5060A, a suitcase-sized cesium beam clock, and demonstrated its portability on three separate worldwide "flying clock experiments." The U.S. Naval Observatory began a time transfer service in early 1966 that synchronized clocks worldwide to within a within one-millionth of a second. Comparing clocks at a distance from each other has always been an interesting technical necessity. Even in the age of radio comparisons, transporting clocks remained necessary among precision time users because of delays in transmissions. Flying clocks remained in service until the 1980s, when Global Positioning System receivers replaced them.

The most famous flying clocks tested Einstein's theories of space and time, known as special relativity and general relativity. In October 1971, physicists Joseph Hafele of Washington University and Richard Keating of the Naval Observatory took cesium atomic clocks on jet flights around the world and compared the moving clocks with those on the ground at the Observatory. As predicted by special relativity, the clocks lost time flying east (moving in the direction of the earth's rotation) but gained time flying west (moving against the earth's rotation). In addition, they observed the impact of general relativity, which caused the flying clocks to run slightly faster because of the weaker gravitational pull at high altitude. ✸

TOP: Ticket receipt for a "Mr. Cesium Clock" from Washington, D.C., to Spain and Italy.

BOTTOM: Patrick Lloyd (left) and Don Percival (right) strapping in "Mr. Clock" for his flight.

TRAVELING *with* MR. CLOCK   **175**

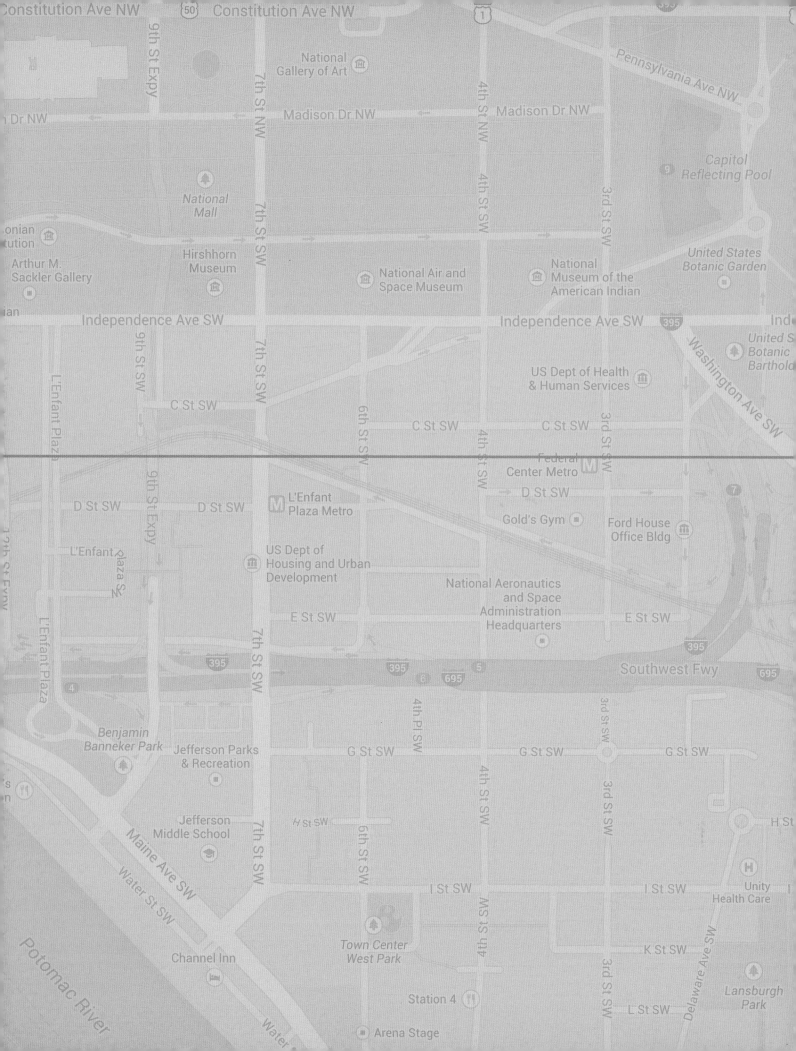

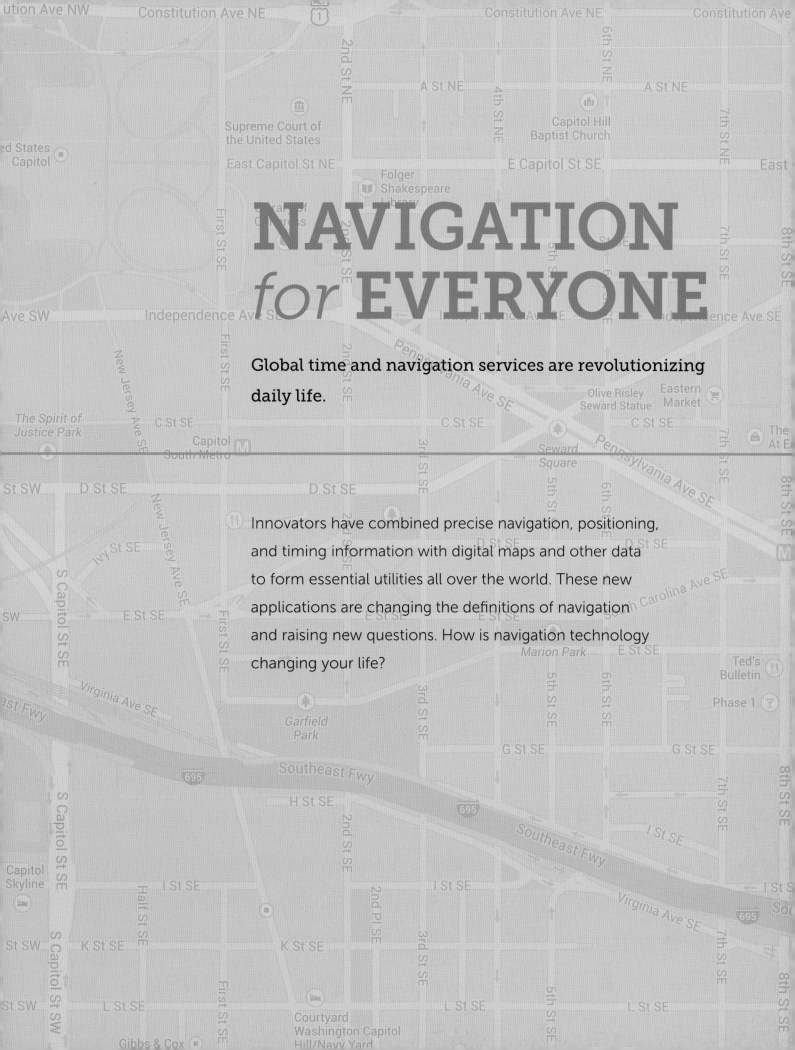

NAVIGATION *for* EVERYONE

Global time and navigation services are revolutionizing daily life.

Innovators have combined precise navigation, positioning, and timing information with digital maps and other data to form essential utilities all over the world. These new applications are changing the definitions of navigation and raising new questions. How is navigation technology changing your life?

NAVIGATION *for* EVERYONE

There is a hidden story connecting everything from farms, factories, and homes. A farmer driving a combine harvester over soybean fields may not seem, at first glance, a good example of the connections between time and navigation. The way farmers use agricultural equipment may seem little changed from many decades ago. But take a closer look. Inside the cab, assisting the farmer, is advanced satellite navigation technology. Farmers today use satellite navigation systems to know exactly where to apply the right amount of fertilizer and keep track of their crop yields. In just a generation, agriculture

Roy Bardole, a corn and soybean farmer in Rippey, Iowa, driving farm equipment equipped with satellite navigation gear.

has been profoundly altered by the availability of technology previously available only to professional navigators. Satellite positioning allows farmers to precisely plant, fertilize, and harvest crops within different parts of their fields.

The story does not end with the farmer in the field. After harvest, crops need to be transported. Tracking technology can play an important role in food safety, making sure that food can be traced back to its origin to find potential problems. As industrial products are moved to and from factories, time and navigation technology is essential for the commercial and transportation links every step of the way. GPS devices keep track of trains to move them along and avoid collisions. On trucks, GPS tracking enables drivers and planners to determine the most efficient routes. Within retail establishments, tracking technology enables managers to monitor goods on store shelves and replenish supplies when needed. Shoppers can be told about different products. In automobiles or on public transportation, individuals use personal navigation technology to obtain directions and traffic information while getting to their homes.

Time and navigation technology is everywhere today. Just as in the past, it is still used by specialists and on advanced military vehicles. Today, however, most people performing global navigation are simply living their normal lives. Economic, transportation, and social networks connect with time and navigation technology in surprising ways.

The promises of these technologies are vast, as are the questions they raise. What privacy concerns exist? Can we become too dependent on global systems? People will continue to utilize new advances and explore the future as we live in a globally connected society. ☀

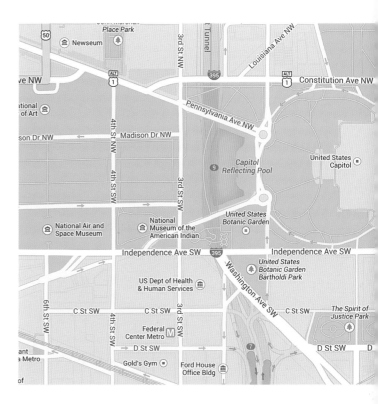

Image from Google Maps from 2012 showing central Washington, D.C.

In the following pages, we will read about how time and navigation technology has revolutionized society through examples that show how global navigation expanded from the realm of specialists to become a utility that touches the lives of people all over the world.

In the 1980s, specialized survey teams used instruments such as this Texas Instruments TI-4100 NAVSTAR Navigator GPS Receiver for surveying Earth's precise shape.

The accessibility of precise positioning methods revolutionized the way the earth is studied and mapped. Manufacturers of GPS receivers for military users—Texas Instruments, Rockwell Collins, Magnavox, and Interstate Electronics—were the first to offer them to civilians. Scientists and surveyors were eager to use satellite navigation signals for research and precise mapping. Made by Texas Instruments beginning in 1981, the TI-4100 was one of the first commercial GPS receivers designed for professional surveyors. TI-4100 units were used by organizations such as the National Geodetic Survey, the U.S. Geological Survey, the Naval Surface Weapons Center, and the research organization University NAVSTAR Consortium (now UNAVCO) to accurately determine position. With its antenna and data recorder, the total weight exceeded 65 pounds (30 kg), not including the large batteries required to provide power. These units were transported to many remote locations to collect satellite data. With later processing very accurate positions could be determined.

Many of these early GPS units were deployed to accurately measure the shape of the earth. An accurate model of the precise shape of the earth, or "geoid," is essential because Earth is not a perfect sphere. The planet's irregular topography and mass distribution need to be taken into account for global mapping and navigation. Highly detailed descriptions of the earth's shape were required to match the high precision of new surveying tools.

Engineers and surveyors found ways to improve GPS accuracy using Differential GPS (DGPS). This method utilizes a GPS receiver

Smithsonian geologist Ted Maxwell used the Transit system in the Egyptian desert in 1987. The system's compass is the black device on the roof in front of the luggage rack. The receiver was mounted inside the vehicle.

at a carefully surveyed ground station. Known as a base station, this receiver would record data from orbiting GPS satellites. Slight errors resulting from uncertainty in timing and the distance to each satellite can be detected. That information can be sent to other nearby GPS receivers. Often DGPS devices were intended to be used in tandem to provide positional accuracy better than three feet (1 m) using differential corrections. Others provided accuracy of centimeters and allowed surveyors to take readings quicker than with traditional surveying tools.

Data from the base station could be saved for later processing. Surveyors could take readings in the field and apply corrections later at an office, where they had access to powerful computers and other specialized equipment. Another DGPS variant was to send data in real-time through radio links, which could broadcast this information to mobile GPS devices over a wide area.

As technology advanced, GPS receivers became smaller and easier to use and included more features. Most early units provided simple map

GEODETIC SURVEYING

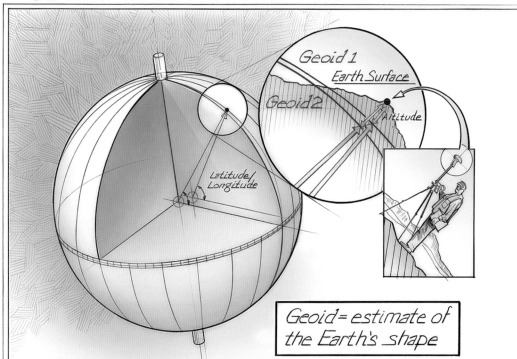

Geoid 1

Earth Surface

Geoid 2

Altitude

Latitude/
Longitude

Geoid = estimate of
the Earth's shape

Geodetic surveys provide data based on the shape of the planet and common reference systems for geographic coordinates. Precision navigation would not function properly without these global references. Accurate mapping and navigation must take into account the irregular shape of the Earth.

Knowledge of Earth's precise shape is necessary to create consistent mapping references.

data, while later devices incorporated information and communication links. GPS devices produced during the 1990s by Trimble, Ashtech, and other manufacturers were often intended for specific applications such as land surveying. Along with listing a user's latitude and longitude, some GPS receivers could provide timing as accurate as an atomic clock for sequencing scenes during film and video production.

Using traditional techniques, surveyors used chains, rods, and simple optical tools to determine the relative location of ground points. The tools included a theodolite, an angle-measuring instrument with a small telescope. A magnetic compass could be used to measure the direction of ground lines. The arrival of satellite position did not always provide better accuracy at first, but it revolutionized the way many types of surveys were performed. During the 1990s and 2000s, GPS survey gear was marketed to professional surveyors as an augmentation or replacement for traditional surveying tools. Satellite positioning, integrated with technologies such as laser rangefinders, allows surveyors today to use specialized GPS equipment to accurately map infrastructure and survey large sites. GPS is often used to map construction sites, property lines, and the location of telephone poles, sewer lines, fire hydrants, and the like. Forestry, mineral exploration, and wildlife habitat management professionals use GPS to define precise positions of important assets and to identify changes. During data collection, GPS points can be assigned codes to identify them as roads, streams, or other objects. These data can then be compared and analyzed in computer programs called Geographic Information Systems (GIS). The use of GPS became widespread in fields that require geospatial information for managing assets over large areas.

GPS has allowed scientists to perform new types of geographic analyses. Geologists use GPS to determine the precise shape of surface features, measure expansion of volcanoes, and detect movement along fault lines. GPS positioning with differential corrections became so precise that movement of tectonic plates could be tracked to the millimeter. Scientists have installed networks of GPS devices at permanent locations, enabling them to observe the changes in volcanoes before they erupt and slight variations in plate movement before and after earthquakes. Ecologists can use GPS to map differences in a forest canopy. While satellite image data is widely used to observe forest cover over small and large areas, information on standing trees must be collected on the ground. During this process, GPS is used to record the locations of standing trees for comparison to overhead views. Biologists can track animals using devices that transmit GPS data. Species can also be tracked using radio transmitters, but using satellite data enables data to be collected from a remote location. Tracking devices enabled with satellite positioning became small enough to be placed on migratory birds and even smaller animals. Many individual animals can be tracked from a field location or laboratory, illustrating migration patterns and habitat ranges. This information can be used to help form conservation plans for endangered species.

The global geoid is shown here with colors and exaggerated heights from multiple points of view.

This Prototype Emergency Vehicle Location System was the basis of a federal experimental emergency response system from 1995. Tested in Colorado, the system relied on GPS data, cellular telephone connections, and map databases.

As use of GPS expanded, eventually nonmilitary users far outnumbered military users and new commercial markets grew for positioning technology. Applications for GPS were developed to meet the wider demands, and civilians gained access to higher accuracy. The management of the GPS program incorporated shared oversight between the U.S. Department of Defense and civilian federal government agencies such as the U.S. Department of Transportation. Although there were some discussions in the 1970s of charging civil customers a fee for using GPS, that was rejected as impractical. GPS remains free worldwide, funded by the U.S. government.

In 1991, during the Persian Gulf War, the U.S. military found the partially completed GPS system to be very useful, given the treeless, featureless deserts of Kuwait and Iraq and the lack of reliable maps or other navigation aids in the area. The military had a shortage of GPS receivers, and it responded by purchasing civilian units domestically and shipping them to the theater of war. The Air Force turned off Selective Availability, which limited the accuracy of GPS positions for nonmilitary users, and suddenly everyone's GPS receivers, not just the military's, gave better readings. Selective Availability was permanently set to zero in 2000, a decision supported by President Bill Clinton. That not only helped convince military skeptics of the advantages of GPS over existing military navigation systems, but it also spurred even more civilian activity. Along with the response after the downing of

The earliest "breadboard" used to test circuitry and components at Magellan Systems Corporation in 1986.

KAL 007 by the Reagan administration, the actions of two presidents, combined with unforeseen, rapid advances in microelectronics and computer technology, pushed GPS into consumer, recreational, and social markets.

By the 1980s, engineers affiliated with several civilian government agencies and companies were developing ways to circumvent Selective Availability, especially techniques using differential GPS (DGPS). Methods for distributing DGPS corrections expanded through the 1990s. The U.S. Coast Guard transmitted corrections to provide precise positioning for ships navigating near ports. Differential corrections became commercially available through communications satellites in geostationary orbit, which broadcast this information to GPS receivers over a wide area. Differential corrections could also be shared over radio links, sent either from local base station transmitters, though communication satellites, or via mobile devices such as cellular modems.

During the late 1980s, several companies began developing GPS receivers for a broader civilian and commercial market, focused on recreational users and emergency responders. Although not open to the most accurate signals, these early GPS devices provided map coordinates from anywhere on the globe. The Magellan Systems Corporation produced some of the earliest handheld GPS units for civilian use. In 1986, its engineers began experimenting with electronic prototypes of a navigation unit. Magellan went on to develop a handheld, battery-powered GPS receiver for the civilian market in 1988 for use while hiking, boating, and other recreational purposes.

A surveyor in Gilchrist County, Florida, holds a Magellan GPS receiver in about 1990.

Efforts to combine GPS positioning with communication links moved forward in the 1990s. The U.S. federal government prototyped an emergency vehicle location system in 1995 and tested it in Colorado and Washington. The Washington equipment depended on DGPS, while the Colorado test system relied on GPS data, cellular telephone connections, and map databases. GPS devices connected to mobile phones in automobiles were told to transmit location to a central location when requested. The successful test proved that a user's location could be sent if help were needed. Commercial services—Ford's Rescu and General Motors OnStar—superseded the test system. In the late 1990s, Magellan released the first turn-by-turn navigation system for civilian drivers. The display screen allowed the user to see a map and follow directions. A large computer received GPS data from an antenna and sent it to a dashboard-mounted display.

Transportation networks came to depend more widely on positioning technology. Integrated with real-time data sources on traffic and travel distances, more efficient routes could be calculated and driven. Modern navigation technology found its way onto more ships crossing the oceans. Individual containers on ships began to be tracked as they moved off ships and onto trucks. In the 1990s, navigation technology helped manufacturing businesses to adopt the business strategy known as "just-in-time logistics." To maintain high efficiency, the right quantity of goods must arrive at shipping centers at the right time. Too few and production of new goods will falter. Too many would waste time and resources storing and retrieving the goods. At other processing and manufacturing centers, more positioning technology came into play. The whereabouts of delivery vehicles and construction equipment could be determined at all times. Vehicles such as bulldozers could be positioned with pinpoint accuracy during construction projects.

Personal GPS devices gradually grew smaller, more portable, and more user-friendly. Through the 1990s, the U.S. market for GPS devices grew to billions of dollars, and multiple manufacturers produced diverse units to meet the demand. Garmin, TomTom, Magellan, and other companies produced GPS receivers for automobile navigation, hiking, and recreational use. Many GPS receivers recorded positions and provided simple graphical presentations of map data. Around the year 2000, demand exploded as new devices, more accurate signals, and new sources of map data gradually became available.

NAVIGATION
GONE WRONG

NANTUCKET
U.S.A. ⊗
Atlantic Ocean
BERMUDA

CRUISE LINER RUNS AGROUND

Despite having the latest GPS navigation gear, the cruise ship *Royal Majesty* runs aground approaching Boston.

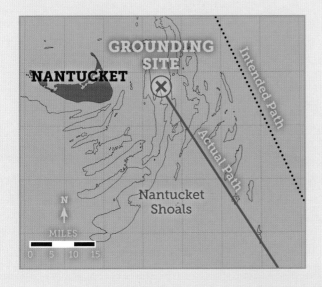

ABOVE: The intended and actual paths of the *Royal Majesty*.

BELOW: The *Royal Majesty* after running aground on Rose and Crown Shoal near Nantucket Island.

WHAT HAPPENED

Late in the night of June 10, 1995, the cruise ship *Royal Majesty* was carrying more than 1,500 people on its way to Boston from Bermuda. All seemed well with the GPS navigation system on the bridge. In fact, the antenna had accidently come unattached from the GPS receiver. In the absence of satellite data, the system continued to estimate position based on the compass heading and speed. This did not account for wind and sea drift, so it was giving inaccurate positions.

THE CONSEQUENCES

Off course by about fifteen miles (24 km), the *Royal Majesty* ran aground on shoals east of Nantucket Island, Massachusetts. The next day, five tugboats were required to free the vessel. There were no deaths or injuries, but damage to the ship and lost revenue amounted to approximately $7 million.

LESSONS LEARNED

A central factor in the accident was overreliance on automated navigation features. The only indication that the GPS data were not being received was a tiny readout on the GPS display that was easily missed. As a result of its investigation of this accident, the U.S. National Transportation Safety Board recommended steps to improve how positions are confirmed during navigation.

TIME AND NAVIGATION IN EVERYDAY LIFE

In March 2006, Jeremy Rose of the U.S. Army Corps of Engineers recording images and GPS location of damage in New Orleans, about six months after Hurricane Katrina.

At the beginning of the twenty-first century, the world is connected as never before by webs of transportation links made possible by global navigation tools. Centuries ago, thousands of ships crossed the seas. With connections partially enabled by global navigation tools, the number of ships became hundreds of thousands. Land transportation routes on highways and rails are serviced by positioning technology to enhance their ability to handle large amounts of traffic. Directions provided by global navigation services and digital maps enable individual travel and efficient transportation connections.

Many people use the new time and navigation utilities as part of their jobs: delivering packages, growing crops, constructing new buildings. Others deal with more mundane tasks: meeting family members, catching a train, finding a parking spot, keeping tabs on the whereabouts of others. Armed with mobile devices connected to global time and navigation systems, people lead their lives in a way impossible even in the very recent past.

From maintaining infrastructure, transporting goods, delivering services, or just meeting friends, people today often use navigation technology just as sophisticated as that used by pilots and soldiers. These new technologies and applications are changing definitions of navigation and raising new questions about how people find their way in modern society.

ABOVE: A visitor to Washington, D.C., checks his GPS-equipped tablet computer to get directions.

LEFT: Fruit for sale at a market in Umm Qasr, Iraq, in April 2010. Global navigation plays a role in the transportation of goods to large and small markets alike.

ABOVE LEFT: The Magellan Corporation developed the Magellan NAV 1000 GPS Receiver for the civilian market in 1988.

ABOVE RIGHT: The Seiko Epson Digital Assistant from 1997 was one of the earliest devices to incorporate a wide range of communication and navigation features, including electronic map tools, a mobile phone, a digital camera, data links, a touch-sensitive screen, and GPS navigation.

OPPOSITE: Artist's rendering of a GPS satellite, part of a new group, or "block," of GPS satellites developed by Lockheed Martin beginning in 2008. More than 11 feet (3.4 m) tall, they were designed to provide enhanced capabilities for both military and civilian users.

Systems like GPS and easy-to-use devices make it easier for a wide range of people to access global navigation tools. For the first time, people can navigate and see maps of almost anywhere on Earth, all with devices in the palm of their hand.

GPS devices of the late 1980s contained enough processing power to track multiple GPS satellites and display simple positions, listing latitude, longitude, and altitude. The altitude was always much less accurate than the horizontal position, a shortcoming caused by the geometry of the GPS satellite orbits. Along with the Selective Availability of the GPS timing signal, this caused GPS-measured altitudes to vary greatly—indeed, a high hill might well be displayed as lying below sea level. Latitude and longitude coordinates were valuable information to navigators on ships or professionals. For most people, however, latitude, longitude, and altitude were largely meaningless numbers. It was only when integrated with digital map data that these numbers became truly useful.

Some devices in the late 1990s began to incorporate a wide range of communication and navigation features integrated into one unit, including electronic map tools, mobile phone, digital cameras, data links, touch-sensitive screens, and GPS navigation. Devices made by companies such as Magellan and Garmin, with names such as eXplorist and eTrex, provided location information in small packages.

With enhancements and new types of corrections, GPS continued to develop better accuracy. In the 1990s, for example, the U.S. Department of Transportation and the Federal Aviation Administration developed the Wide Area Augmentation System (WAAS). It was available beginning in 2003 for general use in North America. It provided positioning information good enough for vertical guidance during approaches to

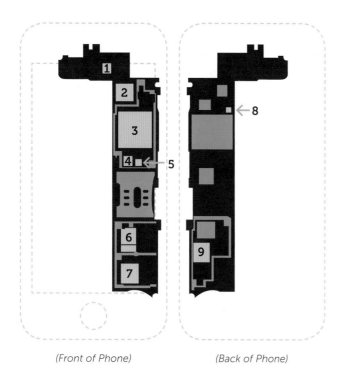

(Front of Phone)   *(Back of Phone)*

1	GPS receiver
2	Digital network receiver
3	Main Processor
4	Three-axis gyroscope
5	Three-axis accelerometer
6	Signal transceiver
7	Signal processor
8	Magnetic compass
9	Memory

ABOVE: A mobile phone in common use in 2012 integrated capabilities found separately in previous navigation tools.

OPPOSITE: Enhanced accuracy with satellite navigation is accessible through systems such as the aviation-oriented Wide Area Augmentation System (WAAS). These systems provide higher accuracy using GPS in conjunction with corrections transmitted by other satellites.

major airports. WAAS also provided higher accuracy for handheld devices, as long as they were within the North American service area. Other services such as OmniSTAR offered higher accuracy by transmitting differential GPS corrections from communications satellites.

Digital map data revolutionized how satellite positioning technology was used by most people. In the 2000s, companies such as Navteq and Google acquired and developed cartographic data that could be distributed through web clients on computers and mobile GPS devices. Eventually these data sets were widely accessed from map applications on mobile phones, and Navteq became part of the mobile phone company Nokia by 2008. After 2010, it became more common for mobile phones to include navigation features. Mobile phones in common use by 2012 integrated capabilities previously found in separate devices, such as communications links and map displays.

The story of how the world became accessible at anyone's fingertips is a story of miniaturization and integration with multiple forms of information. A close look at any common smart phone shows how hardware, software, and mapping data have become integrated in mobile devices. Today's mobile phones have receivers for acquiring multiple types of radio signals, including signals from GPS and other satellite systems, ground-based cellular towers, and digital network connections such as Wi-Fi. They also incorporate inertial sensors to detect movement and orientation. These include gyroscopes and accelerometers to enable the device to record how it moves. Other sensors are packed into the phone, such as a magnetic compass for measuring orientation with Earth's magnetic field. The average phone is a fully integrated mobile positioning and navigation system, with capabilities similar to a submarine navigation system—though instead of occupying an entire room, the mobile phone rests in the palm of one's hand.

While the portable devices changed, the orbiting satellites also continued to evolve. The first GPS satellites transmitted signals for nonmilitary users, but with degraded accuracy. Satellites launched in the 1990s and 2000s contained improved atomic clocks. In 2008, Lockheed Martin began developing a third group, or "block," of GPS satellites. More than eleven feet (3.4 m) tall, the Block III GPS satellites were designed to provide enhanced capabilities for both military and civilian GPS users. For the first time, GPS satellites were planned to transmit signals intended expressly for use by nonmilitary users.

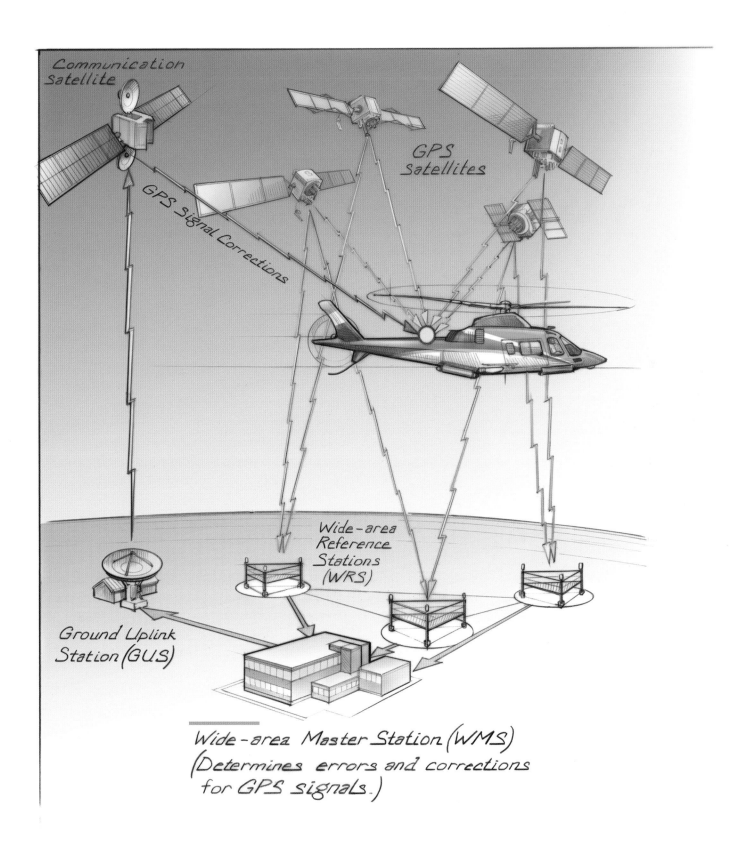

Communication
satellite

GPS
satellites

GPS Signal Corrections

Wide-area
Reference
Stations
(WRS)

Ground Uplink
Station (GUS)

Wide-area Master Station (WMS)
(Determines errors and corrections
for GPS signals.)

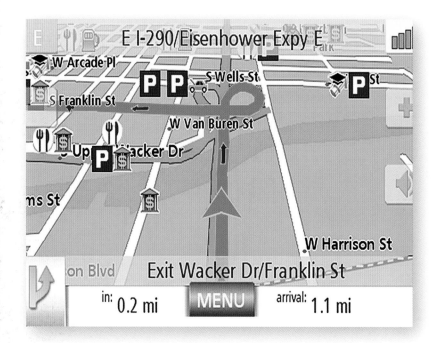

ABOVE: Driving directions from a common GPS navigation device in about 2010.

OPPOSITE: Representation of a ship's navigator taking a lunar distance observation from 1879.

Today almost anyone can be a navigator. Instead of trying to cross the ocean or climb the highest mountain, the modern navigator is more likely to be walking down the street, ordering a taxi, or checking a map to reach appointments, all with a small portable device. People engaging in these activities are performing a type of global navigation, perhaps without even knowing it.

Navigators of the past who used tools such as sextants and chronometers and required specialized equipment and training accessible to a select few. Navigating at sea involved skillful use of those tools, many complex steps, and learning from another experienced navigator. Correctly operating a sextant required careful sighting of the sun or stars and the horizon. The elevation in fractions of degrees would be read from the scale on the sextant and the time of each observation would be noted. After on-deck observations of stars or the sun, a navigator would go below to calculate the ship's position. He would have consulted an almanac for star tables, plotted on a chart, and then finally reported position to his shipmates and in the ship's log. Most of this skilled work could only be learned aboard a working ship. Through most of the twentieth century, understanding how to navigate an aircraft still required weeks of training. Air navigators used smaller chronometers and sextants. Navigating spacecraft to other planets was possible only with advanced technology and teams of talented engineers.

Driver receiving navigation help from a GPS and map display in the dashboard.

The arrival of global satellite navigation forever changed the way land transportation networks form and operate. Fleets of thousands of trucks can be monitored and tracked to their destinations. Fuel and time are saved by accessing digital map tools. Trains can be followed and directed to the correct tracks. Goods from factories and warehouses can be guided to their destinations by ship, truck, railroad, or aircraft. Tracking provides near real-time location data on shipments across entire fleets of vehicles.

The accessibility of global navigation technology has transformed global commerce and connections. By 2012, the total size of global market for satellite navigation tools had grown to $180 billion. Among the largest growth fields for satellite positioning technology was agriculture. For example, between 1998 and 2009 the proportion of U.S. durum wheat cultivation aided by satellite navigation increased from 3 percent to 74 percent. The ways that people and goods moved around the world were altered. Improvements in air transportation were developed to smooth traffic. In 2010, UPS trucks reduced driving by 1.8 million miles (2.9 million km) using routing technology, and in that same year autonomous vehicles, which partially depended on GPS to navigate, drove 140,000 miles (225,000 km) to test their capabilities in traffic. Nevada became the first state to approve autonomous cars on public roads in 2011.

Perhaps the most visible changes occurred in the ways individual people found their way around. In 2011, one survey found that 28 percent of adults in the United States and Europe used personal navigation devices. A wide range of specialized applications were developed to serve this growing community of navigators, from providing driving directions to helping locate friends and family. In 2009, there were 96 million users of these types of mobile applications, providing what was often known as "location-based services." By 2012, there were 526 million users of approximately seven thousand different spatially aware mobile applications.

The types of devices used to navigate changed radically during this shift, as people moved away from paper maps and even stand-alone GPS devices. Replacing these were mobile smartphones that included GPS capabilities. In just one year, between 2005 and 2006, U.S. sales of handheld GPS devices declined by 26 percent. By 2011, only one-quarter of drivers in the United Kingdom reported using paper maps, according to one survey. Beginning in 2007, annual U.S. expenditures for mobile phones exceed those for landline phones.

As the importance of global time and navigation services continued to rise, national governments invested significant resources to ensure their continued availability. Much of this spending historically began during the Cold War to support military navigation requirements, including the U.S. Navy's Transit system and then GPS beginning in the 1970s. Today GPS is operated in coordination with several parts of the U.S. government, which through 2010 spent more than $1 billion annually for the system. Since 2012, Russia has planned a budget of more than $400 million annually to support its GLONASS satellite navigation system. The total spending for development of Europe's Galileo satellite navigation system reached $4.7 billion by 2010.

While many benefits have arisen from the availability of global navigation for everyone, many people raise questions about issues of privacy and control in the modern world. New ways for people to digitally interact with mobile devices seem to crop up daily. These include apps that share map locations with other phone users. Some people love these new ways of interacting, but not everyone does. The whereabouts of individuals is potentially valuable information for advertisers and communications providers. Controversy erupted in 2011 when details emerged of Apple's use of phone users' location information. Many people also question government actions. Since 2010 some U.S. courts have approved police use of GPS tracking devices without warrants. Privacy activists have raised awareness of systems that could be used by companies and governments to locate mobile phone users worldwide.

Although satellite position technology has enabled many new applications, the arrival of GPS is not the end of the story for navigation. Many challenges remain for the engineers of today and the future. For instance, satellite navigation services usually do not work indoors, and they often do not function well if buildings or trees obscure the sky. New solutions for making global navigation even more robust and useful continue to be developed by combining satellite data, inertial sensors, small precise frequency standards, and other radio signals from digital networks.

Students using GPS as part of an environmental education class in Cuyahoga Valley National Park in Ohio.

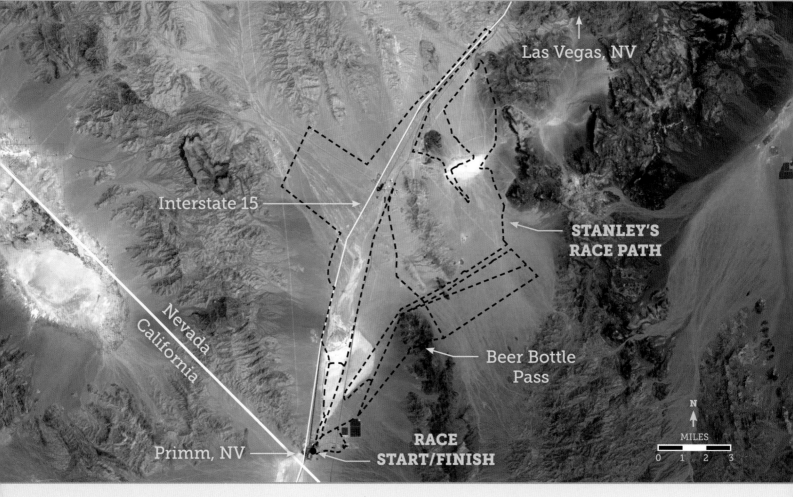

Las Vegas, NV

Interstate 15

STANLEY'S
RACE PATH

Nevada
California

Beer Bottle
Pass

N

MILES
0   1   2   3

Primm, NV

RACE
START/FINISH

DRIVING *with*
STANLEY

Stanley, a modified Volkswagen Touareg, is a robot vehicle that can navigate for itself, without a human in the driver's seat or at remote controls. In a brief but spectacular racing career, Stanley beat twenty-two other robot vehicles for the $2 million prize in the Defense Advanced Research Projects Agency (DARPA) Grand Challenge, held in October 2005. In the DARPA robot race the year before, no contestant drove further than eight miles. The 2005 robot finalists represented a giant technical step forward, by completing a demanding 132-mile (212 km) desert course near Las Vegas, Nevada.

ABOVE: Map of the course for the DARPA Grand Challenge in the Mojave Desert in 2005.

DARPA held robot races in 2004, 2005, and 2007 to stimulate invention for a future fleet of driverless military vehicles. Funded by the U.S. Congress to meet its own mandate that one-third of the military's ground vehicles be driverless by 2015, millions of dollars in prizes went to innovative winners. The challenge for the competitors was unprecedented: to build machines that replicate the parts of human intelligence we call on when we drive.

With software in onboard computers, Stanley decided how to navigate mapped terrain and unmapped obstacles in real time. Three antennas work with GPS receivers to provide data on position, pitch, and heading. Until two hours before the start of the 2005 race, the exact course was top secret. The route was expressed as more than three thousand coordinates of latitude and longitude on computer files. The vehicle also integrated stored memory of past experiences and new information about the road ahead gathered from rooftop laser sensors, video cameras, and radar.

Behind Stanley's driverless accomplishment was the work of nearly a hundred people at Stanford University, Volkswagen's Electronics Research Laboratory, and MDV-Mohr Davidow Ventures.

The development of mobile robots controlled by onboard computers is a fast-growing field that will influence the way we drive. Engineers are developing new technologies for electronic driving aids and driverless cars that can share roads and highways with different types of vehicles, holding the promise of enhacing safety and increasing road capacity. ✸

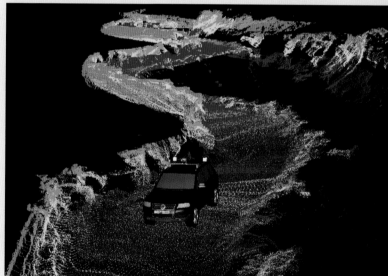

TOP: Stanley, a robot vehicle, and the Stanford Racing Team, the vehicle's creators, at the finish line of the DARPA Grand Challenge.

BOTTOM: Along with GPS, Stanley used a video camera and laser sensors to "see" the terrain.

DRIVING *with* STANLEY   **199**

An experimental self-driving vehicle being developed by Google in 2014. Developers suggest such a car could operate like a robot taxi.

Global navigation systems have revolutionized many aspects of life, creating a whole new world for people living in the early twenty-first century. Innovators have combined precise navigation, positioning, and timing information with digital maps and other data to form essential utilities all over the world. Many people have become experts in using satellite navigation for specific jobs. Others may be using the technology without being aware of the connections between their lives and complex global systems. Examples of many technological advances and daily experiences described below illustrate the impact of time and navigation.

Satellite navigation systems may one day shape how you drive. Researchers are beginning to craft a future where drivers with electronically enhanced cars, buses, and trucks will navigate automated highways. Transportation planners envision a highly efficient road system and are taking steps to foster the technologies to make it happen. Advances in navigation can enhance highway safety, a pressing need when more than thirty thousand people die every year on U.S. highways. The development of self-driving cars like Stanley, winner of the second DARPA Grand Challenge event in 2005 (see page 198) contributed to advances in autonomous vehicles. By 2014, self-driving cars developed at Google had traveled 700,000 miles (1.1 million km), and GM was forecasting a Cadillac with autonomous features for 2017. Nissan, Volkswagen, Toyota, Daimler and other automakers had versions of self-driving vehicles in development. Cars might eventually become completely autonomous, with the ability to rove the streets of an urban area and arriving on demand. Changes have been incremental, with

many vehicles in the early 2010s incorporating automatic features such as adaptive cruise control, blind spot monitoring, and self-parking.

A revolution in air traffic control promises safer and more efficient air travel. In 2003, U.S. aviation agencies joined those of other nations in a program to modernize management of global air traffic and improve air safety. Based on satellite positioning, the Next Generation Air Traffic System, or NextGen, is planned to replace the existing network of ground-based navigation beacons and radar, both of which have limitations in range and accuracy. Ground-based Very High Frequency Omni Range (VOR) stations have provided the primary navigation system in the United States since the 1950s. Aircraft navigated station to station in inefficient zigzag routes. Equipment introduced in the early 2000s replaces or supplements radar with aircraft transmitters that report position and other data to ground antennas. This information

ADS-B (Automatic Dependent Surveillance-Broadcast)

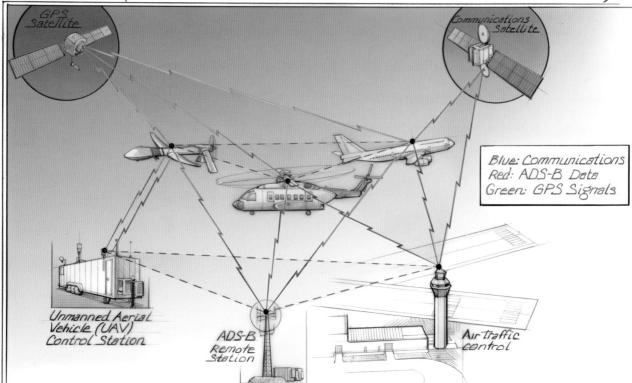

GPS Satellite

Communications Satellite

Blue: Communications
Red: ADS-B Data
Green: GPS Signals

Unmanned Aerial Vehicle (UAV) Control Station

ADS-B Remote Station

Air Traffic Control

ADS-B is the core technology of next-generation systems of air navigation and air traffic control. It uses satellite-based navigation and positioning information broadcast between aircraft and ground stations. ADS-B provides better coverage and accuracy than previous networks of ground-based radio beacons and radar stations.

In 2003, the United States began modernizing its system of navigation and air traffic control centered on ground-based beacons and radar. The new program depends on data links that share satellite positioning data, a system known as Automatic Dependent Surveillance-Broadcast (ADS-B).

can be distributed anywhere, including to other aircraft. The new air traffic systems also improve communications. New technology like the Universal Access Transceiver (UAT) allows the sharing of more than audio signals over radio. Weather depictions, air traffic information, and other critical data can now be shared between aircraft and controllers. Having a system of navigation, control, and communications built around the accuracy of GPS has many advantages, but it also brings new questions: Because GPS is subject to interference, what technologies can serve as a backup? Does a centralized system reduce the freedom enjoyed by private pilots? How much do we want to limit human involvement in making safety of flight decisions?

Other researchers are at work to meet the challenge of indoor navigation. Because satellite positioning systems depend on low-strength signals that must travel in straight lines to a device on the ground, the signals cannot penetrate buildings or walls. Finding a solution for indoor navigation is especially important for emergency responders. New navigation systems combining radio signals with inertial navigation are now in testing. Cell phone companies, retailers, and other organizations are also exploring the possibilities of indoor navigation technology.

John F. Sullivan, deputy chief of the Worcester, Massachusetts, fire department, has seen the problems of indoor navigation more than most people. "When firefighters enter a burning structure, they can quickly lose visibility and their ability to maintain orientation," he says. One incident in particular stands out. "In 1999 we responded to a fire in a vacant warehouse," he recalls. "Two of our colleagues became lost while searching through the smoke-filled structure for two homeless people reportedly inside. We sent in several teams of firefighters to try to locate them and lead them to safety. Before they could get out, the structure collapsed, killing the lost team and four of their would-be rescuers." Better positioning, navigation, and timing technology is essential to addressing these problems. "We are getting close to a reliable and affordable solution that uses technologies such as inertial navigation and others to provide real-time positional data of our firefighters," Sullivan adds. "Knowing where your teams are at all times can be critical when things go wrong." Working with engineers, firefighters have tested possible solutions. Worcester Polytechnic Institute, for example, developed a prototype navigation unit to relay the location and health status of emergency response personnel to incident commanders. It uses radio signals and inertial navigation for positioning inside smoke-filled buildings and other environments where GPS signals are unavailable.

Better positioning has also revolutionized farming. New navigation solutions have evolved into "precision agriculture," a process of combining precise positioning, geospatial data, and information about soil or plant requirements. The ability to map fields, plant and harvest crops, treat pests, and manage farm operations with real-time position information has revolutionized how food is grown. Satellite navigation helps farmers maintain high crop yields, reduce costs, and lessen environmental impact.

Satellite positioning does not usually work indoors, where firefighters face low visibility in smoke-filled buildings in which accurate navigation can mean the difference between life and death.

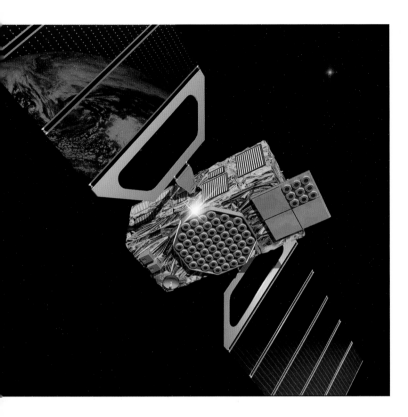

Artist's rendering of a Galileo satellite, part of a system under development by a consortium of European nations as a civilian-operated global navigation system.

Roy Bardole, a corn and soybean farmer in Rippey, Iowa, uses satellite technology to navigate his land, collect data and maneuver implements. "As field equipment has gotten larger, it's become nearly impossible to drive it accurately," he said. "We either skipped or lapped rows, both of which cost us money." With GPS equipment, a Bardole can set a work area perimeter, instruct tractors and implements to steer automatically on either a straight or contoured path, and log data about the work accomplished. "All of our tractors, and the combine and sprayer,", he points out, "are capable of hands-off steering—letting GPS guide the vehicle—to make us more efficient. It sometimes allows us to operate when we simply couldn't otherwise."

Global navigation technologies in handheld devices have done more than create new businesses; they have changed our way of life. Meeting friends, shopping, or getting across town have become different experiences as more people use digital map data and satellite positioning. Mobile phones with integrated navigation capabilities have created new ways for people to find their way around. Plans can change on the fly. Voice communication combined with text and data links, mapping databases, and Internet access has made navigation a social experience. Eva González, a student living in Washington, D.C., uses a smartphone to navigate through each day. "For many years I used a mobile phone to keep in touch with family and friends," she says. "It worked well, but I always wanted something more—a source of information and a better way to get from point to point. So I got a new phone with features like navigation, mapping, and Internet connectivity." How does she use the phone to navigate? "I have a really bad sense of direction, so it's easy for me to get lost," she says. "But my phone always knows where I am. In big cities, where I walk everywhere, it helps me get around easily." Among the most important features of the phone is its ability to connect with others. "It allows me to share time with my family and friends, even though many of them are in other countries. I can see their faces and even their locations. It makes me feel like we are together even when they are far away." But the technology that allows her and others to share position has unintended consequences. "Once I was studying for exams in a coffee shop when I got a message from my mother asking why I was shopping when I was supposed to be studying! We were using an application that tracked our locations, and a clothing store happened to be right next door!"

NATIONS OPERATING OR PLANNING SATELLITE NAVIGATION SYSTEMS

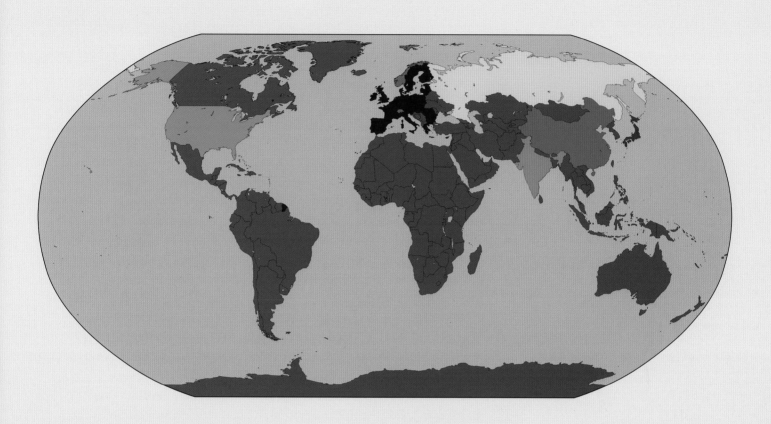

GPS
Operated by the U.S. Department of Defense and coordinated with the U.S. Department of Transportation and other civilian government agencies.

GLONASS
Initially developed by the Soviet Union during the Cold War and now operated as a global system by Russia's Federal Space Agency.

Galileo
Under development as a civilian-operated global system by a consortium of European nations. Operations are coordinated by an agency under the auspices of the European Commission.

Beidou
The Beidou Navigation Satellite System (BDS) was planned and developed by the government of China. Global coverage with about 35 satellites was planned for 2020.

IRNSS
The Indian Space Research Organisation (ISRO) began developing the Indian Regional Navigational Satellite System (IRNSS) in 2006 to provide positioning services around India.

QZSS
The Japanese government planned to develop the Quasi-Zenith Satellite System (QZSS) to provide data links and positioning services for Japan.

The Global Positioning System, operated by the U.S. Department of Defense and coordinated with the U.S. Department of Transportation and other civilian government agencies, is not the only satellite navigation system. As with Europe's maritime empires in the 17th century, nations with global ambitions seek to have independent global navigation capabilities. In the 1990s and 2000s, many nations began developing or improving their own systems. With the advent of other systems, the term Global Navigation Satellite Systems (GNSS) has been used to describe the different systems, while "GPS" refers to the U.S. system.

The earliest of the other global systems is GLONASS, developed by the Soviet Union during the Cold War and today operated by Russia. This system uses a constellation of satellites somewhat similar to GPS. A consortium of European nations is developing Galileo, a civilian-operated global system. Operations are coordinated by an agency under the auspices of the European Commission. The government of China is building the Beidou Navigation Satellite System (BDS), and plans global coverage with about thirty-five satellites by 2020. At least two other regional systems are planned. The Indian Space Research Organisation (ISRO) began developing the Indian Regional Navigational Satellite System (IRNSS) in 2006 to provide positioning services around India. The Japanese government is developing the Quasi-Zenith Satellite System (QZSS) to provide data links and positioning services for Japan. Although the systems were developed separately, multiple constellations of satellites can improve positioning, navigation, and timing for everyone. International coordination depends on cooperation among the system operators on both technical and diplomatic levels.

Satellites provide essential navigation services, but they operate under constraints and threats. Radio interference from both natural and human sources could present serious problems for the system's myriad users. Sources of potential problems for satellite systems include solar interference, unintentional radio interference, intentional jamming, and even acts of war. Solar storms occasionally interrupt clear reception of signals from space. Satellite systems designers must plan for these disruptions and be aware of how solar activity varies with the eleven-year sunspot cycle. GPS and other satellite positioning systems were designed to use quiet parts of the radio spectrum. However, these channels face the danger of being overwhelmed by communications signals from other nearby frequencies. Engineers must test the possibility of interference from multiple systems. Acts of war could endanger global navigation systems. The increasing reliance on navigation satellites for military and commercial activities makes

OPPOSITE: Clockwise from top left: Multiple factors must be considered to maintain global navigation services. These images show a GPS jamming device, a handheld GPS receiver with no signal, an F-15 launching a missile at a satellite target, the GPS operations center, and an image of solar activity that can interfere with satellite transmissions.

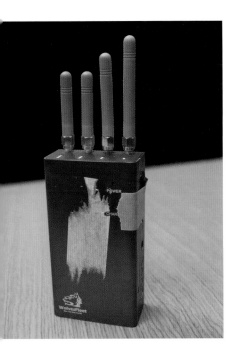

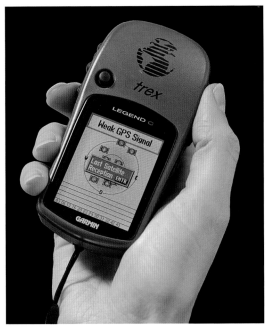

them a tempting target. While it is difficult to disable the satellites themselves, these and other GPS components must be protected from interference or attack. The successful operation of a satellite navigation system requires around-the-clock monitoring of the satellites' health and the periodic replacement of older satellites. The process is labor-intensive and expensive and requires multiple backups to ensure continuous operation. Because of their relatively low power, GPS signals can also be intentionally jammed with small devices. Although their use is illegal in the United States, portable GPS jammers are traded clandestinely and used by those who wish not to be tracked or otherwise located by GPS. These devices cause nearby navigation systems to malfunction, potentially threatening public safety. Engineers and scientists continue to develop solutions to ensure the continued operation of global navigation services.

Solutions to make navigation systems more robust have been in development throughout the entire history of satellite navigation. With the final shutdown of the LORAN-C system in 2010, only satellite systems provide widely available global positioning and navigation. Other systems could provide backup for times when satellite signals are blocked or too weak to be used. Plans for new ground-based backup systems have been proposed to complement GNSS signals from space.

Many new advances may originate from Micro-Electro-Mechanical System (MEMS), which includes structures such as sensors and actuators so small that a microscope is required to make them visible.

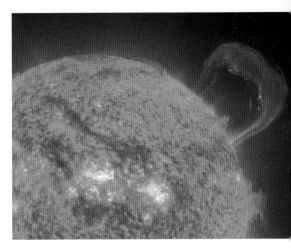

An experimental device to provide fully integrated positioning and navigation, the Time and Inertial Measurement Unit (T-IMU) was developed at the MicroSystems Laboratory at the University of California, Irvine, as part of a DARPA project. The T-IMU is a microscale navigation system that can measure position with high precision, even if GPS is not available.

The ability to manufacture MEMS makes it possible to embed new tools within portable devices. For personal navigation, time and inertial measurement can be combined with satellite systems. They integrate information from inertial sensors and external radio signals. The inertial part of these systems includes gyroscopes and accelerometers that detect movement. Gyroscopes have a vibrating mass that reacts when it is rotated or moved. Accelerometers detect movement using a small microscopic weight that shifts slightly every time the unit changes its movement. The gyroscopes and accelerometers on some experimental devices in 2014 were more than 300,000 times more sensitive than similar components in common mobile phones and gaming consoles. Often developed to advance navigation for platforms such as aircraft and missiles, these advances in inertial positioning may lead to future applications integrated into handheld devices. Laboratories funded by the U.S. Defense Advanced Research Projects Agency (DARPA) such as the MicroSystems Laboratory at the University of California, Irvine, device makers such as Honeywell, and other institutions are exploring these connections.

Fully integrated positioning systems also require a precise time reference for the inertial sensors. The time reference also provides a backup to allow continued precision operations if GPS is temporarily unavailable. MEMS time references in development can keep time over short periods with precision similar to some atomic clocks. The stability decreases if used for longer periods so they cannot completely replace time distributed from GPS or atomic frequency standards, but they could be used for short periods when out of range of those data sources. Other new developments will provide precise time in small packages. Research labs such as the National Institute of Standards and Technology and Sandia National Laboratories, along with commercial companies such as Microsemi (formerly Symmetricom), have developed "chip-scale" atomic frequency standards that could be small enough to be included in mobile devices. These may allow future applications of determining position using radio sources such as cellular signals or wireless network signals. Stable miniaturized timing references, when integrated with radio signals used by mobile phones and other digital devices, could potentially lead to new tools for indoor

navigation or provide navigation assistance when satellite systems are not available.

Navigation has always involved multiple forms of information and specialized tools. More than just map coordinates are required. Methods of positioning, navigation, and timing, or "PNT," are interconnected technologies that provide essential services. *Positioning* refers to determining location; *navigation* means finding the way from one place to another; and *timing* refers to how electronic signals are used to give a common synchronized time. All three are used together with map data and other information such as weather or traffic data in modern navigation systems.

Combining many types of information is especially important with modern navigation that incorporates satellite signals, internal

Sandia National Laboratories researcher Darwin Serkland measures the wavelength of a tiny laser for chip-scale atomic clocks.

A robot developed by Team SHAFT, later acquired by Google, is shown here clearing debris while competing in the DARPA Robotic Challenge in 2013.

sensors, and ground-based communication links. Digital technology provides vast quantities of layered information for people all over the globe. Combining digital maps with real-time information and electronic databases has revolutionized how we navigate and view our environment. Layers of map data with different themes provide powerful insights, whether for planning real estate developments or for soldiers on the battlefield. Government agencies distribute dynamic maps used by the public, and companies provide updated information on factors such as traffic flow that can be accessed from mobile devices.

The long history of government funding to encourage new navigation and positioning technology, including the longitude prizes offered in Europe centuries ago, continues today. Just as with the competition coordinated by DARPA that lead to the self-driving car Stanley, DARPA has coordinated a Robotic Challenge to encourage the development of robotic devices. Positioning technology is also potentially useful for mobile robotic devices, which could be used for emergency response when areas are too dangerous for humans.

The compilation of global map databases requires mapping over large areas and collecting vast amounts of data. Companies such as Google have deployed fleets of vehicles equipped with cameras and other sensors to make maps that can be accessed by users worldwide. These digital maps provide many popular services, but wide-scale mapping can also be controversial. Numerous times since 2010, authorities in Europe have questioned Google's mapping of wireless routers and collection of images showing homes.

While global maps are used for navigation over large distances, advancing technology and the integration of multiple forms of data can also lead to new ways of navigating in small areas. Methods for mapping the magnetic fields present in all structures have been developed by IndoorAtlas and other companies. These data can be stored for later access, to allow future visitors to determine their location within the building to within about three meters. Radio sources such as wireless networks can also be used to determine position within a structure. This type of information can be used by retailers to target advertising or guide shoppers to specific products. Since 2010, multiple companies have developed mobile apps that give

A range of paper maps used less frequently in the modern era of satellite navigation. How many of these items do you still use?

visitors to retail establishments, hotels, and museums information on their location and surroundings while indoors. While this can provide useful information, many consumers dislike the perceived infringement on their privacy. By 2014, several other mobile apps had been developed to block this type of positioning and tracking.

As the previous examples show, location-based applications have changed not only the way we find our way, but also many other daily routines. No longer just a military navigation system, GPS has become an essential utility. This has been made possible by generations of technological advances. But the changes wrought by precise positioning and timing services are far from completed. Engineers continue to work on addressing new challenges. Navigation solutions in development promise even more changes in the future.

WHERE ARE WE HEADED?

For centuries, the connection between time and place has been an enduring part of finding our way. The technological innovations described in this book have fundamentally altered the way people move about and live their lives. As those technologies continue to evolve, global navigation services will play an increasingly large role in many aspects of daily life. Opportunities for future innovation abound. Challenges and questions also arise.

Revolutions in positioning, navigation, and timing have provided countless benefits and empowered people all over the world. The simple accessibility of global navigation tools makes it possible for almost anyone to be his or her own navigator. This provides real flexibility and opens new possibilities for ordinary people. Global navigation for everyone makes it possible to imagine a future where most people can get the information they need and get almost anywhere they wish to go. The navigation services that many people take for granted can offer a sense of individual freedom.

As the same time, people all over the world are more dependent than ever on complex global systems. Modern navigation is more centralized than in the past. Navigators in ships centuries ago, with the right tools and experience, could independently determine position. Although they depended on others for chronometers, mathematical tables, and maritime charts, navigators made their way without connection to a larger network. Today's navigation is very different. People performing navigation today need to be constantly connected to global systems, including satellite positioning services and data links. These important systems operate every day without most people being aware of how they function or how dependent much of modern society is on their continued operation.

New navigation technology offers significant benefits and raises questions for the future. How will technology change in the future? What kind of new navigation tools will become available? Who will benefit from, and pay for, changes in technology? What would happen if global time and navigation services stopped working? Other questions arise about the impact of global time and navigation in society. Are we losing skills by relying on navigation devices? Can we become too dependent on the technology? What identity and privacy issues exist in a connected world? How will people navigate in the future? As solutions for global time and navigation continue to develop, more questions will arise about how we find our way from here to there. The answers await us.

A drawing from the 1970s predicting that by 2076 small airborne vehicles would provide comfortable travel at 120 miles per hour (193 kph).

FURTHER READING

Akerman, James R., ed. *Cartographies of Travel and Navigation.* Chicago: University of Chicago Press, 2006.

Baidukov, George. *Over the North Pole.* Translated by Jessica Smith. New York: Harcourt, Brace and Company, 1938.

Bartky, Ian. *One Time Fits All: The Campaigns for Global Uniformity.* Stanford, CA: Stanford University Press, 2007.

Bennett, J. A. *The Divided Circle: A History of Instruments for Astronomy, Navigation and Surveying.* Oxford: Phaidon, 1987.

Blair, Charles F. *Red Ball in the Sky.* London: Jarrolds, 1969.

Blanchard, Walter, ed. *Air Navigation: From Balloons to Concorde.* Sussex, England: Woodfield, 2005.

Conant, Jennet. *Tuxedo Park: A Wall Street Tycoon and the Secret Palace of Science That Changed the Course of World War II.* New York: Simon & Schuster, 2002.

Crosby, Harry H. *A Wing and a Prayer.* New York: HarperCollins, 1993.

Dick, Steven. *Sky and Ocean Joined: The U.S. Naval Observatory, 1830–2000.* Cambridge, MA: Cambridge University Press, 2002.

Dunn, Richard, and Rebekah Higgitt. *Finding Longitude: How Clocks and Stars Helped Solve the Longitude Problem.* London: National Maritime Museum/Collins, 2014.

Easton, Richard D. and Eric F. Frazier. *GPS Declassified: From Smart Bombs to Smartphones.* Lincoln, NE: Potomac Books, 2013.

Ellis, F. H., and E. M. Ellis. *Atlantic Air Conquest.* Toronto: Ryerson Press, 1963.

Guerlac, Henry E. *The History of Modern Physics, 1800–1950: Radar in World War II.* Boston: American Institute of Physics, 1987.

Harbold, Norris B. *The Log of Air Navigation.* San Antonio, TX: Naylor, 1970.

Heinmuller, John P. V. *Man's Fight to Fly.* New York: Aero Print Company, 1945.

Hughes, Arthur J. *History of Air Navigation.* London: George Allen & Unwin, 1946.

Ifland, Peter. *Taking the Stars: Celestial Navigation from Argonauts to Astronauts.* Malabar, FL: Krieger, 1998.

Jespersen, James, and Jane Fitz-Randolph. *From Sundials to Atomic Clocks: Understanding Time and Frequency.* Revised edition. New York: Dover Publications, 2011.

Launius, Roger D., and Andrew K. Johnston. *Smithsonian Atlas of Space Exploration.* New York: HarperCollins, 2009.

Mackenzie, Donald. *Inventing Accuracy: A Historical Sociology of Nuclear Missile Guidance.* Cambridge, MA: MIT Press, 1993.

McCrossen, Alexis. *Marking Modern Times.* Chicago: University of Chicago Press, 2013.

Messimer, Dwight R. *No Margin for Error: The U.S. Navy's Transpacific Flight of 1925.* Annapolis, MD: Naval Institute Press, 1981.

Parkinson, Bradford W. and James J. Spilker, Jr., eds., *Global Positioning System: Theory and Applications*, 2 vols., Washington, DC: American institute of Aeronautics and Astronautics, 1996.

Philbrick, Nathaniel. *Sea of Glory: America's Voyage of Discovery, the U.S. Exploring Expedition, 1838–1842.* New York: Viking, 2003.

Post, Wiley, and Harold Gatty. *Around the World in Eight Days.* Garden City, NY: Doubleday, 1931.

Richardson, F. C. *Man Is Not Lost.* Shrewsbury, England: Airlife Publishing, 1997.

Rogers, Francis M. Precision. *Astrolabe: Portuguese Navigators and Transoceanic Aviation.* Lisbon: Academia Internacional da Cultura Portuguesa, 1971.

Roland, Alex, W. Jeffrey Bolster, and Alexander Keyssar. *The Way of the Ship: America's Maritime History Reenvisioned, 1600–2000.* Hoboken, NJ: John Wiley & Sons, 2007.

Saward, Dudley. *The Bomber's Eye.* London: Cassell, 1959.

Smith, Richard K. *First Across! The U.S. Navy's Transatlantic Flight of 1919.* Annapolis, MD: Naval Institute Press, 1973.

Sobel, Dava, and William J. H. Andrewes. *The Illustrated Longitude.* New York: Walker & Company, 2003.

Stephens, Carlene E. *On Time.* Boston: Bulfinch Press, 2002.

Sturtevant, Rick. "NAVSTAR, the Global Positioning System: A Sampling of its Military, Civil, and Commercial Impact." In *Societal Impact of Spaceflight in Context*, edited by Steven Dick and Roger Launius, 331–352. Washington, DC: GPO, 2007.

Taylor, E. G. R. *The Haven-Finding Art: A History of Navigation from Odysseus to Captain Cook.* London: Hollis & Carter, 1971.

Viola, Herman J., and Carolyn Margolis. *Magnificent Voyagers: The U.S. Exploring Expedition, 1838–1842.* Washington, DC: Smithsonian Institution Press, 1985.

Weems, P. V. H. *Air Navigation.* New York: McGraw-Hill, 1931.

Williams, J. E. D. *From Sails to Satellites: Origin and Development of Navigational Science.* Oxford: Oxford University Press, 1992.

Wright, Monte Duane. *Most Probable Position: A History of Aerial Navigation to 1941.* Lawrence, KS: University Press of Kansas, 1972.

ILLUSTRATION CREDITS

FRONT MATTER

2–3: NASM (TMS A20060700000cp02); **4–5:** Courtesy of the SIL, Washington, D.C.; **5:** In order from top to bottom: LOC, Geography and Map Division, NASM (9A05290), NASM (2011-02863), NASM, NASM.

TIME AND PLACE CONNECTION

6: Image by Ashley Hornish, NASM; **7:** National Maritime Museum, Greenwich, UK; **8:** NASM (2014-01751); **9:** Illustration by Bruce Morser, NASM (9A11815); **10:** Illustration by Bruce Morser, NASM (9A11834).

NAVIGATING AT SEA

12–13, 14, 15: Courtesy of the SIL, Washington, D.C.; **16:** From *Journal of the China Branch of the Royal Asiatic Society for the Year*, 1885; **17:** De Agostini Picture Library/Getty Images; **18:** Göttingen State and University Library, from the book *The Viking Ship Discovered at Gokstad in Norway Described by N. Nicolaysen* by Nicolay Nicolaysen, 1882; **19:** A: SIL, from the book *Voyage to the Pacific*, by John Webber, 1784, Atlas, Plate 61, B: Courtesy of Kaimana Barcarse; **20:** Photo by Jaclyn Nash, NMAH (JN2012-1283); **21:** By Permission of the Folger Shakespeare Library; **22:** A: Courtesy of the Huntington Library, San Marino, California, B: From the book, *History of the Nordic Peoples (from 1555)* by Olaus Magnus, image provided by Lars Henriksson; **23:** Bruce Morser, NASM (9A11809); **24:** Bruce Morser, NASM (9A11808);

25: A: SIL, from the book *A new Systeme of the Mathematicks*, by Sir Jonas Moore, B: SIL, from the book *Adriani Metii … De genuino usu utriusque globi tractatvs. / Adjecta est sciatericorum, & artis navigandi ratio novis instrumentis, & inventionibus illustrata*, by Adriaan Adriaansz Metius; **26:** Made with Natural Earth, courtesy of Tom Patterson; **27:** A: Photo by Jaclyn Nash, NMAH (JN2012-1287), B: Photos by Richard Strauss, NMAH (RWS2014-02660, RWS2014-02661); **28:** LOC, Geography and Map Division; **29:** Ludolf Backhuysen, *Ships in Distress off a Rocky Coast*, Ailsa Mellon Bruce Fund, Image courtesy of the NGA, Washington, D.C.; **30:** A: Courtesy of the SIL, Washington, D.C., B: Photo by Jaclyn Nash, NMAH (JN2012-1334); **31:** A: Courtesy of the SIL, Washington, D.C., B: Photo by Jaclyn Nash, NMAH (JN2012-1337); **32:** AR: Courtesy of Dieter Rein, AL: NASM, B: National Maritime Museum, Greenwich, London; **33:** Courtesy of the LOC; **34:** Science Museum/Science & Society Picture Library; **35:** A: Courtesy of Becky Bacheller, B: Courtesy of the SIL, Washington, D.C.; **36:** Photo by Jaclyn Nash, NMAH (JN2012-1310); **37:** Courtesy of the SIL, Washington, D.C.; **38:** Cover of *The Nautical Almanac and Astronomical Ephemeris, for the year 1767*, provided by the Google Ebook Program; **39:** Photo by Jaclyn Nash, NMAH (JN2013-1403); **40:** Photo by Mark Avino, NASM (2013-00569); **41:** SIL, *The New American Practical Navigator*, by Nathaniel Bowditch; **42:** Illustration by Ashley Hornish, NASM; **43:** A: Harvard Art Museums/Fogg Museum, Harvard University Portrait Collection, B: Division of Work & Industry, NMAH; **44:** The Bancroft Library, University of California, Berkeley; **46:** Courtesy of the SIL, Washington, D.C.; **47:** Courtesy of the SIL, Washington, D.C.; **48:** National Oceanic and Atmospheric Administration/Department of Commerce; **49:** A: Photo by Eric Long, NASM (2013-00788), B: Photo by Eric Long, NASM (2013-00785); **50:** Photo by Rick Vargas, NMAH (SI 91-2029); **51:** Manuscripts and Archives Division, The New York Public Library, Astor, Lenox and Tilden Foundations; **52:** Courtesy of NARA; **53:** Image courtesy of the U.S. Naval Observatory Library.

NAVIGATING IN THE AIR

54–55: U.S. Air Force, NASM; **56:** NARA (NARA RG 342-FH 3A20906-58980AC); **57:** U.S. Air Force, NASM; **58:** NASM; **59:** NASM; **60:** Made with Natural Earth, courtesy of Tom Patterson; **61:** *NC-4* by Ted Wilbur, Gift of Stuart M. Speiser, NASM; **62:** A: Photo by Harold Dorwin, NMAH (DOR2014-2305),

ILLUSTRATION CREDITS

B: U.S. Naval History Photograph; **63:** A: NASM (91-7085), B: NASM (89-16712); **64:** NASM (USAF-3741AC); **65:** A: NASM (9A11692), L: NASM (00046281); **66:** TR: Courtesy of Dieter Rein, A: NASM, BL: NARA, B: NASM (2003-37199); **68:** NASM; **69:** Photo by Hugh Talman, NMAH (ET2012-13495); **70:** Made with Natural Earth, courtesy of Tom Patterson; **71:** NASM (2010-00001); **72:** A: Photo by Eric Long, NASM (2013-00225), B: Photo by Eric Long, NASM (2013-00135); **73:** Made with Natural Earth, courtesy of Tom Patterson; **74:** Illustration by Bruce Morser, NASM (9A11811); **75:** A: NASM (2013-02693), B: Photo by Mark Avino, NASM (2014-02467); **76:** A: NASM (00167019), B: NASM; **77:** A: NASM (00179937), B: NASM (2013-02693); **78:** Illustration by Bruce Morser, NASM (9A11827); **79:** NASM; **80:** A: NASM (77-508), B: NARA (NARA RG 342-FH 3B-11143-14238-AC); **81:** A: NASM, B: NASM; **82:** TR: Courtesy of Dieter Rein, A: NASM, BL: Courtesy of Purdue University Libraries, Karnes Archives and Special Collections, B: NASM (71-1060); **83:** A: Photo by Eric Long, NASM (2013-00142), B: NASM (74-10901); **84:** Made with Natural Earth, courtesy of Tom Patterson; **85:** NASM (88-6822); **86:** A: Photo by Eric Long, NASM (2014-01654), B: Photo by Eric Long, NASM (2012-02186); **87:** A: NASM, B: NASM; **88:** Photo by Eric Long, NASM (2013-00527); **89:** A: Courtesy of the MIT Museum, B: NASM (TMS A20060700000cp02); **90:** Illustration by Bruce Morser, NASM (9A11813); **91:** A: NASM (TMS A20060700000cp02), L: Courtesy of NARA (NARA 80-G 211852); **92:** © Gil Cohen/Knightsbridge Press 1994, All rights reserved; **93:** NASM, Rebecca Crosby Hutchinson; **94:** Photo by Eric Long, NASM (2012-02134); **95:** NASM (9A08289); **96−97:** Courtesy of the Royal Air Force Museum; **98:** Photo by Eric Long, NASM (2014-00635); **99:** NASM (88-14858); **100:** A: Photo by Eric Long, NASM (2013-00439), B: U.S. Air Force photo by Tech. Sgt. Michael Haggerty; **101:** Illustration by Bruce Morser, NASM (9A11839); **102:** Made with Natural Earth, courtesy of Tom Patterson; **103:** A: Photo by Dane Penland, NASM (2012-02107), B: NASM (9A06505).

NAVIGATING IN SPACE

104−5: NASM (2011-02863); **106:** NASM (6A29540); **107:** NASM (2011-02863); **108:** Photo by Eric Long, NASM (2012-02157); **109:** A: Courtesy of NASA Marshall Space Flight Center, L: Courtesy NASA/JPL-Caltech; **110:** A: Courtesy NASA/JPL-Caltech, R: Courtesy NASA/JPL-Caltech;

111: T: Photo by Eric Long, NASM (2005-22904), B: Photo by Jaclyn Nash, NMAH (JN2012-1326); **112:** A: Courtesy of NASA, B: Courtesy of NASA; **113:** Illustration by Bruce Morser, NASM (9A11812); **114:** Courtesy of NASA; **115:** A: NASM (00167624), B: NASM (2011-02865); **116:** Image provided courtesy of The Charles Stark Draper Laboratory, Inc.; **117:** Courtesy of NASA; **119:** Courtesy of NASA; **120:** Courtesy of NASA/JPL-Caltech; **121:** Courtesy of NASA/JPL-Caltech; **122:** Data courtesy Marc Imhoff of NASA GSFC and Christopher Elvidge of NOAA NGDC. Image by Craig Mayhew and Robert Simmon, NASA GSFC; **123:** Image by Ashley Hornish, NASM; **124:** TR: NASM, A: Photo by Eric Long, NASM (2005-22904), B: NASM (7B20498); **126:** NASM (9A06789); **127:** A: Photo by Dane Penland, NASM (80-4979), B: Courtesy of Jet Propulsion Laboratory; **128:** Photo by Eric Long, NASM (2005-22901); **129:** Courtesy of Johns Hopkins University Applied Physics Laboratory; **130:** Courtesy of NASA/Johns Hopkins University Applied Physics Laboratory/ Southwest Research Institute; **131:** Courtesy NASA/JPL-Caltech; **132−33:** Illustration by Ashley Hornish, NASM; **134:** NASM; **135:** Courtesy of NASA/JPL-Caltech/Malin Space Science Systems; **136:** A: Courtesy of NASA/JPL-Caltech/ University of Arizona, B: Courtesy of NASA/JPL-Caltech; **137:** A: Courtesy of NASA/JPL/MSSS, B: Courtesy of NASA/ JPL-Caltech.

INVENTING SATELLITE NAVIGATION

138−39: United States Naval Research Laboratory; **140:** Courtesy of Johns Hopkins University Applied Physics Laboratory; **141:** United States Naval Research Laboratory; **142:** Photo by Mark Avino, NASM (2014-03199); **143:** Courtesy of Johns Hopkins University Applied Physics Laboratory; **144:** Illustration by Bruce Morser, NASM (9A11824); **145:** A: Courtesy of U.S. Navy/General Dynamics Electric Boat, B: Official U.S. Navy Photograph #DN-ST-89-08475, by PH1 Mussi, from the Department of Defense Still Media Collection, courtesy of dodmedia.osd.mil. & submitted by Bill Gonyo; **146:** Photo by Eric Long, NASM (2013-00299); **147:** Illustration by Bruce Morser, NASM (9A11833); **148:** Made with Natural Earth, courtesy of Tom Patterson; **149:** A: U.S. Naval History and Heritage Command, B: U.S. Navy Photo—Submarine Force Museum; **150:** Reprinted with permission of The Aerospace Corporation;

151: A: NASM (7B31753), L: NASA; 152: Photo by Mark Avino, NASM (2012-02356-R); 153: United States Naval Research Laboratory; 154: United States Naval Research Laboratory; 155: A: NASM (75-16329), B: Image provided courtesy of The Charles Stark Draper Laboratory, Inc.; 156: NASM (9A03222); 157: A: Reprinted with permission of The Aerospace Corporation, L: Reprinted with permission of The Aerospace Corporation; 158: Illustration by Bruce Morser, NASM (9A11830); 159: A: Photo by Dane Penland, NASM (2013-00431), B: Photo by Dane Penland, NASM (2013-00433); 160: Image © Rockwell Collins, Inc.; 161: In Memory of Vito Calbi; 162: Image © Rockwell Collins, Inc.; 163: A: Photo by Jaclyn Nash, NMAH (JN2012-1330), B: Photo by Jaclyn Nash, NMAH (JN2012-1322); 164: A: U.S. Air Force photo by Senior Airman Tyler Placie, B: Courtesy of Northrop Grumman Corporation; 165: TR: Courtesy of Dieter Rein, A: NASM, B: Harro Ranter, Aviation Safety Network; 166: Made with Natural Earth, courtesy of Tom Patterson; 167: A: Image © Rockwell Collins, Inc., B: Image © Rockwell Collins, Inc.; 168: United States Naval Observatory; 169: SIL; 170: Courtesy of the AT&T Archives and History Center; 171: Courtesy of the National Institute for Standards and Technology; 172: Photo by Eric Long, NASM (2013-00223); 173: A: U.S. Air Force photo by Airman 1st Class Mike Meares, L: U.S. Air Force photo by Donald S. Branum; 174: Made with Natural Earth, courtesy of Tom Patterson; 175: A: Photo by Harold Dorwin, NMAH (DOR2014-2318), B: United States Naval Observatory.

NAVIGATION FOR EVERYONE
176–77: Courtesy of Google Inc.; 178: Photo by Dane Penland, NASM (2012-02364); 179: Courtesy of Google Inc.; 180: Photo by Eric Long, NASM (2013-00529); 181: NASM; 182: Illustration by Bruce Morser, NASM (9A11810); 183: Courtesy of the National Geospatial-Intelligence Agency; 184: Photo by Jaclyn Nash, NMAH (JN2012-1325); 185: Photo by Jaclyn Nash, NMAH (JN2012-1324); 186: Magellan Systems Corporation GPS Records, Archives Center, NMAH; 187: TR: Courtesy of Dieter Rein, A: Courtesy of Dieter Rein, B: National Transportation Safety Board; 188: Courtesy of the Federal Emergency Management Agency, photo by Marvin Nauman/FEMA photo; 189: A: Photo by Mark Avino, NASM (2014-03196), L: United States Army, photo by

Spc. Christopher Wellner; 190: AL: Photo by Jaclyn Nash, NMAH (JN2012-1318), AR: Photo by Dane Penland, NASM (2012-02122); 191: United States Government, National Coordination Office for Space-Based Positioning, Navigation, and Timing; 192: Illustration by Ashley Hornish, NASM; 193: Illustration by Bruce Morser, NASM (9A11828); 194: Magellan GPS; 195: National Maritime Museum, Greenwich, UK; 196: Photo by Mark Avino, NASM (2014-03195); 197: Image Courtesy of the National Park Service, Ted Toth; 198: NASM/ United States Geological Survey; 199: A: Courtesy of the Defense Advanced Research Projects Agency (DARPA), B: Courtesy of Stanford University, Stanley Project; 200: Courtesy of Google Inc.; 201: Photo courtesy of United Airlines; 202: Illustration by Bruce Morser, NASM (9A11806); 203: U.S. Air National Guard photo by Senior Airman Christopher S. Muncy, 106th Rescue Wing; 204: Courtesy of European Space Agency (ESA); 205: NASM; 207: TL: Federal Communications Commission, Enforcement Bureau, TC: Photo by Mark Avino, NASM (2014-03308). TR: United States Air Force, photo by Paul E. Reynolds, C: United States Air Force, photo by Staff Sgt. Don Branum, B: NASA/SDO and the AIA, EVE, and HMI science teams; 208: University of California—Irvine; 209: Photo by Randy Motoya, Sandia National Laboratories; 210: Courtesy of the Defense Advanced Research Projects Agency (DARPA); 211: Image by Ashley Hornish, NASM; 213: NASM (9A02305).

INDEX

Pages in *italic* denote photographs and illustrations.
Names for specific craft appear under *aircraft; space exploration.*

117; star charts and star logs, *16*, 19, *69*, 75, *107*; star tracker, 103, 127, 128, 133; training simulator, 93

Central Navigation Computer, *147*

cesium, *132*, 145, 155, *159*, 163, 171, 172, 174–75

China, *16*, 18–19, *26*, 26–27, 125, 205, *205*, 206

chronometer, marine, 31, 34–35, 39, 42, 44, 48, 155, 194. *See also* clocks, sea clock

circumnavigation, 46, *48*

Civil War, 45

clocks, 168–73; atomic (*see* atomic clocks); Earth as the oldest, 8; eight-day, 72; master clocks, *6*, 158, 163, 172, *173*; micro-electrico-mechanical, 208; pendulum, 29–31, 33, 168, *169*; pocket watch, *50*; quartz, 8, 89, *132*, *170*, 170–71; regulator, *168*; sandglass, 22, *23*, 33; sea clock, 9, 28–31, 33–35, 39, *40*, 42, 168; second-setting watch, *69*, 75, *75*; spring-regulated, 29, 42; sundial, *8*; weight-driven, 34, 42

codes: Course Acquisition code, 162; Morse code, *78*, 82, 94, 149; P code, 162; pseudo-random numbers, 153, 156, 159

Cold War, 98, 101, 113, 114, 141, 144, 148–49, 150. *See also* Korean Air Lines; missiles

comets, 130–31

commercial broadcast radio, 79, 172

compasses: aperiodic, 86; astrocompass, 93, 103, *103*; directional gyro, 86, 93; earth inductor, 72, *72*; magnetic, 19–22, 62, 149, 192, *192*; radio, 64, *64*, 67, 87

computers: Apollo Guidance Computer, *107*, 116–18, 146; in autonomous vehicles, 199; Central Navigation Computer, *147*; chip-scale atomic frequency standards, 208,

209; Fairchild-Maxson Mark I Line of Position, *83*; K-system electromechanical, 98, *98*, 99; manual flight, 77; MARDAN, 146, *147*; in mobile phone, *192*; Ship's Inertial Navigation System, 144–45, *147*; solid-state microprocessors, 100; wind-plotting, 62

Connor, Harry, 79, 83

Cook, Capt. James, *19*, 31, 38

Cooke, Maj. Gilbert, 67

Coutinho, Gago, *65*, 67

Crosby, Maj. Harold, *92*, *93*, 93–94

cross staff, 20, *21*, 25

D

Dalton, Philip, 77

dead reckoning, 11, 22, *23*, 43, 62, 70, *72*, 79, 92

Decca, 90, 100

Deep Space Network, 114, 120–23, 125, 130, 136

Defense Advanced GPS Receiver (DAGR), *163*, 164

Defense Advanced Research Projects Agency (ARPA; DARPA), 145, 198–200, 208, *208*, 210, *210*

Defense Navigation Satellite System, 156. *See also* Global Positioning System

differential GPS, 163, 180–81, 185, 186, 192

direction finding, ground-based for aircraft, 66, 80, 82

Distance Measuring Equipment, 100

dividers, navigational, 20, *20*, *21*

dividing engine, *39*

Doppler effect, 98, 103, 123, 125, *132*, 141, 142, *144*, 145

Draper, Charles Stark, 112, 117, 155, *155*, 156

drift, 107, 114, 187

drift indicator/sight, 62, 64, 67, 72, 86, *86*, *87*, 93

drones, 164, *202*

E

Earhart, Amelia, 77, 82, *82*

Earth: circumnavigation, 46, *48*, 79, 81–87; as the first clock, 8; rotation, *10*, 11, 28, *28*, 36, *120*, 123, 170; shape, 180, *182*, *183*; tracking of, 115, 118, 128

Earth Path Indicator, 115

Easton, Roger, 153

Einstein, Albert, 125, 163, 175

Ellsworth, Lincoln, 75, 76

emergency response, *184*, 186, *188*, 203, *203*, 210

Equator, *9*, *10*

escapement, 33, 35, 168

Europe, early, 20–27. *See also specific countries*

European Commission, 205, 206

European Space Agency, 125, 130

Explorer 1, 120, 141, 142, 148

F

Federal Aviation Agency, 159, 190

fire fighting, 203, *203*

Flight KAL 007, 161–62, 165, *165*, 185

Flying Cloud (clipper ship), 43, *44*, 45

"flying the beam," 78, *78*

formation, flying in, 94

France: Lindbergh's transoceanic flight to, 59, 67, 69, 70–73, 167; and longitude, 28, 34; NAVSTAR transoceanic flight, *166*, 167, *167*; Navy, 35, 43; and the prime meridian, 52; and radio time signals, 53; sea clock research, 29, 33–34; during WWII, 94

frequency-based time measurement. *See also* atomic clocks; cesium; quartz crystal oscillator; rubidium: air travel, 55, 58–59; chip-scale, 208, *209*; GPS, 11, 59, *90*, 141, 145, *158*; space travel, 11, *111*, 114, 120, 125

Frisius, Gemma, 28, 39

future capabilities, 200–213

INDEX

INDEX

Ranger 7 lunar probe, 111, *112*, 122; Ranger 8 lunar probe, 122; Ranger 9 lunar probe, 122; Saturn V launching rocket, 118; Space Shuttle, 133; Viking Landers, 130, 136; Voyager 1, *128*, 131; Voyager 2, *128*, 131, *133*

Spain, 18, 22, 25–29, 50, *122*

Sputnik, 140–41, *141*, 148

Stanley (autonomous vehicle), 198–200

Star Altitude Curves (Weems), *69*, 75, 77, 86

star catalog/almanac, 36, 194

submarines, 112, 142, 144–49

Sumner, Thomas, *42*, 42–43

Sun, 11, 25, 130–31, 206, *207*

surveyors, use of GPS, 182–83, *186*

T

tables, reference, 25, 36, 38, *38*, 41, *41*, 45, 75, 194

telegraph, 43, 51, 53

telescope, 29, *106*, 117, 1178

Thurlow, Thomas, 77, 83

TIMATION satellite system, *151*, 154–55, 156

time: accurate, 6, 44, 155, 168, 172, 208; connection with place, 6–11; correlation with longitude, *28*, 28–29, 44, 50, 51, 53; day length, 170; and the earth's rotation, *10*, 11, 28, *28*, 35; Greenwich mean, 52; impacts of relativity, 125, 163, 175; local, *24*, 28, 36, 38, 42, 43; measurement of, 168, 171 (*see also* clocks); nanosecond, 163; and navigation in everyday life, 186, 188–90, 192, *196*, 196–97, *197*; second, 170, 171, *172*; services which provide, 155; synchronization challenges, 50–53, 89, 163; synchronized, *158*, 159, 163, *172*, 175, 208

time delay, of radio signals, 114, 123, 128, 133, 145

time signals, 43, 51, 53, *53*, 58–59, 75, 114, 155

time zones, *50*, *51*, 52–53

traffic monitoring, use of GPS, 179, 186, 188, *189*, 196, 209, 210

transmitters. *See* receivers and transmitters

transportation, use of GPS, 179, 186, 188, *189*, 196, 200, 209, 210

two-station ranging, *133*

U

Universal Access Transceiver (UAT), 202

Uranus, 131, *133*

U.S. Air Force: Aerospace Corp. funding, 152; Alternate Master Clock, *173*; chief of staff, 79; GPS Operations Center, *158*, 163, 172, *173*, 206, *207*; Republic jets, *99*, 103; satellite navigation unified under, 156, 159

U.S. Army, *109*, 150, *151*, 152, 159

U.S. Army Air Corps, 79, *80*, 83

U.S. Army Air Forces, *56*, 56–57, *57*, 77, 88, 92, 93–94

U.S. Army Corps of Engineers, *188*

U.S. Coast Guard, 40, 185

U.S. Department of Commerce, 155

U.S. Department of Defense, 156, 163, 184, 206

U.S. Department of Energy, 160

U.S. Department of Transportation, 184, 190, 206

U.S. Exploring Expedition, *14*, 14–15, *15*, 42, 44, 46–49

U.S. Navy. *See also* U.S. Exploring Expedition: Depot of Charts and Instruments, 43–44, 45, 48; fleet, 35, 40; Naval Academy, 45, 75; Naval Observatory, *6*, 44, 48, 53, 81, 163, 172, 175; Naval Research Laboratory, 68–69, 94, *152*, *153*, 154, *154*; Naval Surface Weapons Center, 180; *PN-9-1* crash, 66, *66*, 67, 69, 72; time signals by, 53, *53*, 75; use of chronometers, 35, 42; during WWII, 88, 93

USS *Alabama* (submarine), *145*, *146*, *147*

USS *Nautilus* (submarine), *148*, 148–49, *149*

USS *Peacock* (sloop-of-war), *14*, 14–15, *15*, 49

V

Van Allen, James, *109*, 142

van Ceulen, Johannes, 30, *31*

Vanguard Project, 141, 148

Venus, 124, *124*, *126*, 126–27, 128, *132–33*

Very High Frequency Omni Range (VOR), 100, *101*, 201

Vikings, 18, *18*

W

War of 1812, *40*, 42

Weems, Lt. Comm. Philip Van Horn, *68*, *76*, 77; air navigation innovations and instruction, 66, *68*, *69*, 75, 75–77; and Blair, 102, 103; and Gatty, 79, 81, 86, *86*; and Lindbergh, *69*, 76, *76*, 79; multicrew simulator by, 93; publications by, *69*, 75, 76, 77, 81, 86; space navigation, 114–15

Weems System of Navigation, 75, 76, *76*, 79, 83, 86, *86*

Weiffenbach, George, *140*, 140–41

Wide Area Augmentation System (WAAS), 190, 192, *193*

Wilkes, Lt. Charles, 42, 44, 46, 48, *48*, 49, 51

wireless networks, 192, 208, 210

World War I, 53, 64, 68

World War II, 88–97; aircraft carriers, 94, *94*; bombers, *56*, 56–57, *57*, 81, 89–94; electronic-based navigation, 59, 88–97; role of Weems, 76, 93

Y

YE-ZB system, 94, *95*

Z

Zheng He (Cheng Ho), Admiral, *16*, 19

This book may be purchased for educational, business, or sales promotional use. For information, please write: Special Markets Department, Smithsonian Books, P. O. Box 37012, MRC 513, Washington, DC 20013

Published by Smithsonian Books
Director: Carolyn Gleason
Production Editor: Christina Wiginton

Edited by Gregory McNamee
Designed by Ashley Hornish
Image Research by Thomas Paone

Library of Congress Cataloging-in-Publication Control Number: 2014027164

Manufactured in China

19 18 17 16 15 1 2 3 4 5

Visit the *Time and Navigation* website: timeandnavigation.si.edu